JOYCE'S BOY

The LIFE *and*
TIMES *of*
ALAN E. HALL

Joyce Hansen Hall

---

*My mother was the ultimate benefactor. She gave
me the power to pursue my wildest dreams.*
— Alan E. Hall

Hundreds of thousands of people associate the name Alan E. Hall with leadership, entrepreneurship, philanthropy, service, and education. He's received grand honors in front of applauding audiences. His signature has authorized thousands of university degrees. He gives fifty public speeches a year and has written hundreds of articles on business for *Forbes* and Utah newspapers. He has appeared in the media spotlight as an expert of his trade. Thousands have raised their hands in stake conferences to support his church leadership. But one of his proudest titles is being known as his mother's boy.

This biography presents the events, stories, and lessons that have shaped one of Northern Utah's most inspiring and influential leaders.

Joyce's Boy: The Life and Times of Alan E. Hall
By Crystalee Beck
Edited by Jeanne Nowak Hall and Elayne Wells Harmer
Editing assistance by Naomi Clegg and JaNae Francis

ISBN: 978-1-7320263-0-8

Printed and bound in the United States of America
First printing: May 2019
Paperback first printing: September 2019

Cover art and design by Design Type Service
Interior design and typesetting by Design Type Service

Dedication

*Dedicated to Randall Melvin Hall.
I doubled my life on his behalf.*

— Alan Eugene Hall

*Dedicated to my first boy, Bryson Jay Beck.
I love watching you grow.*

— Crystalee Webb Beck

i

Preface

——⊸o⊂✦⊃o⊶——

"Life's great happiness is to be
convinced we are loved."
— Victor Hugo, *Les Misérables*

We all start life as precious, pure little people. It's during our growing up years we sometimes forget our innate worth and tremendous potential for good. From his entrance into this world, Alan's mother, Joyce, loved him so deeply and dearly, he never forgot.

You'll soon read how being born "Joyce's boy" set Alan Eugene Hall on a powerful path to later create a far-reaching legacy as a family man, accomplished entrepreneur, church leader, community trailblazer, and influential philanthropist.

This book is about the man behind the titles. You'll find his public successes are reflections of the abounding love he feels at home from—and for—family and God. You'll see the span of his life as a child, teenager, newlywed, daddy, and grandfather.

You'll also see his achievements have come at a high price. It is fitting to find Alan's name in the phrase "B**ALAN**CE C**HALL**ENGES." He's endured painful losses, bounced back from expensive failures, and survived many life-threatening moments. Every time he's faced a refiner's fire, Alan has come through with cheerful determination for his next big endeavor. If you read closely, you'll see into the very heart of his "why," the divine motivation behind everything he does.

This book required countless editorial decisions. Alan's life weaves simultaneous threads of family, work, church, and community, so the first half covers a chronological order of events, while the second half focuses on meaningful personal themes. The bulk of this biography came from Alan's recollections in personal interviews, made clearer with Jeannie's sharp memory and eagle editing eye. To add color and context, I've also included research from third-party sources. I have done my best to be accurate with dates, names, and historical details.

I've never felt so honored to be part of a project, or so intimidated. Writing something worthy of Alan's story, that portrays him as both the larger-than-life figure he is *and* a three-dimensional human with faults and flaws, has often felt beyond my capacity as a writer. It's stretched and humbled me, and I can't thank him enough for entrusting me with glimpses into his soul.

Writing Alan's life story has changed my own story in many happy ways. I'll never be the same. He's taught me to unapologetically create my life with love and purpose. To embrace being myself. To go after my wildest dreams, launch my own businesses, and empower other mom entrepreneurs to do the same. This book has forever influenced how I think, live, and give. I hope it does the same for you.

Joyce, you can sure be proud of your boy.

Crystalee Webb Beck
May 2019
Ogden, Utah

Contents

1

Parents and Early Years

The world breathed a sigh of relief when World War I ended in 1918. Millions had died. When Germany signed an armistice, finally the living could go on.

As in every other community across America, it was a time of new beginnings for Ogden, Utah, a railroad town in the heart of the Wasatch Mountains, thirty-eight miles north of Salt Lake City, Utah. "As soon as the country was released from war activities, Ogden went forward with a bound," read the 1920 issue of R. L. Polk & Company's Ogden City Directory. With a population of 37,910, local residents voted approval on bonds for schools, paving, sewers, and parks, kicking off the "largest fund for civic improvements ... ever at the disposal of the city."[1]

The Halls and Hansens, after the Great War

Howard and Florence Tracy Hall were young parents in Ogden. They named the first of their five sons Howard Tracy Hall. He was known as "Tracy." They welcomed their second son, Eugene Melvin Hall, on December 31, 1920. As was customary at the time, Florence gave birth to him at home. Born on New Year's Eve, his birthday every year coincides with fireworks and parties across the world. "Gene," as he

has been known, met many peers with his name throughout his life—
Eugene was in the top twenty-five "most popular boy names" during the
1920s. The Halls had three more sons: Wendell, Donald, and Delbert.

Their family and church service were pillars in the Halls' lives. Both
Howard and Florence were members of The Church of Jesus Christ of
Latter-day Saints. Florence was a third-generation member and her
husband, Howard, was a convert to the religion.

Many other couples in Ogden were also starting their families. Equilla
Ferdinand Hansen and his wife, Estella Nelson Hansen, welcomed their
first child, Wendell, in 1919. Two years later on September 29, 1921,
they celebrated the arrival of a healthy baby girl. They named her Joyce.

With a secure job as a conductor for the Union Pacific Railroad,
Equilla was able to buy a comfortable home in a middle-class
neighborhood. Estella worked as a nurse and spent her life serving her
family and others. Their children grew up knowing their Danish roots
and spending time with the many relatives who lived close by.

Howard and Florence Hall, on the other hand, struggled financially
to meet the needs of five growing sons. Howard had worked on the
railroad for many years, but after his conversion to The Church of Jesus
Christ of Latter-day Saints and his temple marriage to Florence, he felt
strongly that he needed to leave his job because it required working on
Sundays. After serving six months in World War I, the war ended and
Howard went back to working with his dad in the transfer business.
Florence helped with the bills as much as she could by ironing clothes
and sometimes cleaning in a downtown hotel. For several years, the
young family enjoyed life on a farm they purchased in the small town of
Marriott, Utah. Neighbors and friends bought their extra produce and
Howard sold milk to the dairy where he worked. Although they lost the
farm after eight years and returned to the city, they raised five noble,
hard-working, educated sons.

The Great Depression and a new high school

The ripple effect of the 1929 economic crash spread its influence
into Ogden, where families stretched their dollars to survive the Great
Depression. Eugene was nine years old and Joyce was eight at the time,

too young to realize their childhood was part of an economic crisis that would be talked about for generations to come. There were silver linings to the Great Depression. For example, Joyce, Eugene, and their peers were beneficiaries of President Franklin Delano Roosevelt's "New Deal" project, which partly funded construction of the state-of-the-art Ogden High School in 1937.

Both Gene and Joyce graduated from the city's prized educational facility. Built on Weber County's east bench in a yet-to-be-developed field, Ogden High School was elaborately designed in a fashionable Art Deco style. "They took great pride in their school," Alan says of his parents. "They loved it. For them, it was a thing of great beauty. It had a gym, cafeteria, auditorium—it was one of the finest buildings in northern Utah."

The $1.2 million price tag of the educational facility was a point of contention among local taxpayers. Many people were struggling to get by with $50 or less a month at the time and criticized the "million dollar" high school. Others were proud of such an impressive icon in their neighborhood. "In architectural beauty, Ogden's new school is unsurpassed in all the West," reported the October/November 1937 *Utah Educational Review*. "The auditorium, which will seat over 2,000 pupils, is commodious and beautiful in every detail. The auditorium will also fill a community need where musicals, lectures, and plays can be held at frequent intervals."[2]

Eugene and Joyce, tying the knot

As an older teenager, Joyce noticed Eugene singing in the Ogden 18th Ward boys' choir. She proclaimed to her friends, "That's the boy I'm going to marry one day." Following graduation and after a few dates, Eugene brought Joyce home to meet his parents. It didn't go well with his mother—Florence didn't think Joyce was good enough for her son. Gene and Joyce, being twenty-one and twenty years old respectively, decided to marry regardless of others' opinions.

---

[*] Machinist's mates operate, maintain, and repair ship propulsion machinery and other equipment on board a ship.

They were married on March 18, 1942, in the Salt Lake Temple and were companions until Joyce passed away on September 22, 2003.

World War II separated many newlyweds, and Eugene and Joyce Hall were no exception. Just six months after they married, Gene enlisted in the U.S. Navy and traveled by bus to Naval Training Center San Diego, leaving Joyce behind. She contributed to the war effort too by loading bullets into machine gun belts at the Ogden Ordnance Depot, the only Army ammunition plant west of the Mississippi. By December 1942, "the arsenal employed almost 6,000 people, the majority of them women, since most men were in military service."[3]

After Gene completed basic training as a machinist's mate* and was assigned to the USS *Sacramento* (PG-19), Joyce moved to San Diego. They rented a small apartment and Joyce soon found two jobs, clerking at a five-and-dime and at Chenkin's Children's Store. Working gave her something to keep her mind off the war while Gene worked on the ship; he was only granted R&R every two weeks. In time, Joyce noticed her dresses getting tighter—an unmistakable sign she was expecting a baby.

During her pregnancy, Joyce moved back to Ogden to help care for her mother, Estella, who had cancer. She died on Joyce's birthday, September 29, 1944. Three months pregnant and heartbroken by the loss of her mother, Joyce also worried constantly about her husband and her older brother, Wendell.

Following a battle in the Pacific, Wendell was captured by the Japanese. Along with tens of thousands of Filipino and U.S. Army soldiers, he was forced to make the 60-mile trek, later known as the Bataan Death March. Although beaten and abused, Wendell survived the march and was taken to a prison camp in Manchuria, China.

A world away, Joyce and her caring aunts decided it was best not to tell Wendell his mother had passed away. He was very close to his mother and they believed news of her death would break his heart and will to live. His aunts sent him letters, signing their correspondence in his mother's name.

When Wendell came home, he started life again, though he never married. He lived in Portland, Oregon, for most of his life, where he worked as an executive with Schenley Industries, a liquor giant that held significant interests in whiskey during the twentieth century. He never spoke about his war experiences and was always kind to people with Japanese heritage. In fact, he hired mostly Japanese men and women to help with housework, and often provided financial assistance for their education.

Serving in San Diego during World War II

Back in San Diego, local citizens and the U.S. Armed Forces welcomed spring in 1945 with characteristically pleasant weather. Gene had grown used to life in the Navy.

He was luckier than other servicemen who were either dodging bullets or were prisoners of war like his brother-in-law. Gene was assigned to the relative safety of the USS *Sacramento* engine room, where he had very little personal space.

A few years earlier, the *Sacramento* had seen action in Pearl Harbor. She opened fire on Japanese aircraft that were attacking "Battleship Row," the ill-fated line of anchored battleships. In San Diego she was a gunboat, no longer in service for battle, but used to train gun crews. She pulled a large target, far enough behind the ship that other warship crews could safely practice shooting. From time to time, Gene took a small craft out into the ocean to put an overturned target back in place following bad weather.

As part of Gene's duties as machinist's mate 1st class, he made sure the engine, shaft, and propellers were functioning properly. Periodically, as the engine turned the propeller shaft during tumultuous storms, the propeller popped above the water and shook the ship violently.

While the days seemed long, his time on the ship had a deep impact on Gene's life. More than half a century later, at age ninety-seven, Gene still wore his custom-made USS *Sacramento* shirt and matching baseball cap day after day. He waved his hat to a sold-out crowd at the Ogden Pioneer Days Rodeo in the summer of 2017, where he was honored for his military service.

But Gene didn't know what the future held on March 22, 1945. If he had picked up the newspaper that day, Gene might have been interested in reports about U.S. Marines on the island of Iwo Jima, where they'd landed a month earlier. Perhaps he saw an advertisement for a cartoon character named Sylvester the cat, who debuted that day in the cartoon "Life with Feathers."

News likely did little to calm Gene's nerves. His pregnant wife was 800 miles away, due to have their first baby any day. He thought of her, and was glad she had the support of her aunts back home. He wished he could call to see how she was doing, but calls home had to wait.

Alan Eugene Hall is born

While Gene performed his daily duties at sea on the USS *Sacramento* on March 22, the cry of a baby son was heard, back in his mountain hometown.

Joyce and their new baby were on the fifth floor of what was known as "the Dee": the Thomas D. Dee Memorial Hospital at 24th Street and Harrison Boulevard in Ogden, Utah. Traditionally, hospitals were places where sick people went to die, but modern medical practices made hospitals more welcoming environments for mothers to give birth.

On that Thursday afternoon, Joyce lovingly held her first-born son, all seven and a half pounds of him. She admired his chubby little body and blond hair with awe and wonder. Jaundiced, his soft skin had a yellowish hue, but she could barely see that. He was hers! She felt her heart burst with this first taste of a mother's infinite love.

Long anticipated, he was the first grandson for the Hall and Hansen families. Joyce named him Alan Eugene Hall. "Alan" came from a popular movie star at the time, Alan Ladd, known for his ruggedly handsome appearances in Western films. "Eugene," of course, was in honor of his father.

"It all began with my mother," Alan says. "She was really happy with me. I was her pride and joy."

Joyce wanted Alan, born in the midst of war, to experience the goodness the world had to offer. "My mother was the ultimate benefactor who gave me everything I would become," Alan says. "She infused in me a sort of innate ability to be whatever I wanted to be. She helped me feel I belonged. I was accepted. I was loved."

This motherly support guided Alan through childhood, young adulthood, and into his adult life as he pursued his passions and interests.

Hundreds of thousands of people would one day associate the name Alan E. Hall with leadership, entrepreneurship, philanthropy, service, and education. His future included grand honors in front of applauding audiences. His signature would authorize thousands of university degrees. He would give fifty public speeches a year and write hundreds of articles on business for *Forbes* magazine and Utah newspapers. He would appear in the media spotlight as an expert of his trade. Thousands would raise their arms in ward and stake conferences to support his priesthood leadership. Indeed, big things were coming to this baby. But for now, he was all hers.

Joyce's closeness with her first child was evident to others throughout his life. In fact, Alan was nicknamed "Joyce's boy" by family and friends. Decades later, grown-up Alan teased his mother, saying he would run for governor of Utah someday with the slogan "Vote for Joyce's boy!"

Building a family life after the war

The war ended when Alan was almost six months old. Gene returned, and the young Hall family started life together again in Utah, this time in Salt Lake City.

Like many of his veteran comrades, Gene took advantage of the G.I. Bill to fund his education by enrolling at the University of Utah. The family of three moved into married student housing at Stadium Village, the former military barracks located east of today's Rice-Eccles Stadium. Gene started studying to be a pharmacist in the fall of 1946.

One of Alan's first memories was receiving a surprise gift left for him by an unknown benefactor on their doorstep: a small blackboard and chalk. "It was for me, and I remember just how thrilled I was with that blackboard," Alan remembers. "I drew whatever I wanted on it. The recollection that someone had thought well of me resonates deeply today."

Another lasting memory from this time was being warned by other children he should never go down to the nearby university reservoir. They said a whale would swallow him up. Their cautions scared the trusting boy so much that he never got too close to the hazard, not even with his parents. "I think the reservoir's still there, just to the east of the university's football stadium," Alan says with a smile. "It was probably just a water supply for lawns."

When Alan was about four, his dad took him to the Deseret Museum in Salt Lake City to see dinosaur bones. "That was a treasured moment for me," Alan remembers. "I loved being with my dad." Alan's involvement with Gene was very minimal, because he was often working and studying.

Gene dedicated most of his waking hours to his studies while Joyce stayed home with Alan. Their second son, Randy, was born August 5, 1949.

It was at this time Alan had a horrific dream he remembered vividly for several decades. He saw himself on the highway, traveling from Ogden to Salt Lake. He looked up at the hill in North Salt Lake, where he spotted dump trucks carrying rocks from the gravel pit. "In my mind's eye, they were racing out of control. In the middle of the night, I awoke crying. It was a very disturbing dream. Thankfully, my parents were there to calm me," he recalls.

Like any good mother, Joyce constantly watched over Alan and told him to be careful around the nearby canal, to hurry home for dinner, and go to bed on time. He spent hours outside with his friends, playing Superman with a towel as his cape and neighborhood games like hide-and-seek.

The Halls didn't have a television, but they did have a radio, featuring shows like *Amos 'n Andy* and *The Green Hornet*. Sometimes his family went to the movie theater to see the latest blockbuster. *Bambi* was a memorable silver-screen experience for Alan.

In 1950, Gene graduated magna cum laude with the first graduating class of the University of Utah College of Pharmacy. The Hall family lived frugally, making do with what they had. When Gene got his first job at Lever Brothers Pharmacy, located on State Street and about 30th South in Salt Lake City, his wages were modest. The family of four moved to the west side of Salt Lake City, into a simple home in a new neighborhood with lots of young children. Soon Alan's dad had scraped together enough money to purchase a new car, a green Studebaker.

"My dad loved that car, but for most people, it was just the ugliest thing," Alan remembers. The family attended church in an old LDS chapel on 800 West, arriving in the green Studebaker every Sunday.

Televisions were a luxury only the wealthiest families could afford. A friend in the new neighborhood let Alan watch their black-and-white television. "That was the first one I ever saw," Alan says. "I watched *Howdy Doody* and football games, and even General Conference." LDS General Conference sessions began to be broadcast on television in the intermountain area in 1949, when Alan was four years old.

Alan started kindergarten in the fall of 1950. As part of the daily routine, his teacher gave the kids juice or a snack and told them to rest quietly on a blanket. "I remember that with fondness as a peaceful moment for me," he says. "It was a blanket from home, so I was connected to my mom."

Restful moments didn't last long for the fidgety boy. "I recall that I was noisy (as I always have been)," Alan says. "I was very sociable so I probably talked with everyone while we were resting."

The winter of 1951–1952 set snowfall records that still stand for the highest levels in the Salt Lake area. Later in May, the snow caused an indoor flood. For the last weeks of the school year, the children used a temporary school building for their classes.

At one point in their Salt Lake home, the Halls had a pretty cocker spaniel named Sandy. Alan had a great affection for the dog. When she was hit by a car and died, he was devastated. "It was probably my first experience with death of any sort and it upset me profoundly," Alan says. "To this day, I have not bonded with another pet, although my family has had many over the years. The thought of losing another beloved animal friend is something I choose not to suffer again."

Early lessons in right and wrong

When Alan was five years old, he had a curious friend, a girl about his age. For reasons only known to history, when playing together one day they took off their clothes, getting stark naked. "She was just as curious as I was," Alan says. "My mother found us and punished me severely. She was furious."

Although usually a gentle mother, on this occasion Joyce hit Alan with a yardstick several times—hard enough that he never forgot it. "She was going to make sure I knew that was an error and should never do that again."

On another occasion in elementary school, Alan remembers his father's discipline. Like his friends, Alan rode the bus to school. He heard other kids using swear words and crude language. "Somehow, I learned how to give people 'the finger.' I didn't even know what the heck it meant." When playing with a neighbor kid after school one day, Alan flashed "the finger" at him in frustration. When his dad found out about it, instead of giving Alan a lashing, he simply said, "That isn't the right thing to do, so don't do it anymore." It was a powerful lesson in corrective gentleness that Alan has never forgotten.

"The light guides us home"

On a late winter afternoon in Salt Lake City, Joyce was missing ingredients to cook supper. She sent her six-year-old son to a nearby grocery store. Alan took a shortcut and traveled across an open field behind his house to buy the needed supplies.

With his purchases in hand, Alan began the return home following the same path. During the summer, the field grew alfalfa; in the winter, there was nothing but pointy stubble. As he approached the middle of the field, the sky became dark and a dense January fog surrounded him. He stopped moving in the blackness. The cold chilled him to shivers and he wondered how to make it back to his warm home. Terrified, with tears running down his cheeks, he remembered his parents taught him to ask God for help when in trouble. "I carefully knelt down on the frozen stubble and pleaded with my Heavenly Father to get me home," he recalls.

Back at home, Joyce started to worry about her son's safety. She saw the fog covering the field and the entire neighborhood, and with motherly instincts she turned on a yellow backyard porch light, hoping it would guide her little son home. Looking up from his prayer, Alan saw a dim yellow light in the distance, shining through the fog. "I knew God had answered my humble prayer and I began to walk in the direction of the light leading me to the safety of my beloved home."

As an adult, Alan has told this story on many occasions, teaching that divine light is what guides us to our heavenly home. "We are guided by the light of Christ. Our task is to happily follow it," Alan says. "For me, as a young child, that experience set a foundation that God is there and He does hear and answer our prayers."

In November 1952, Alan's first sister, Joan, was born in Salt Lake City. Gene and Joyce longed to return to Ogden, where their extended family and friends lived. That opportunity came soon after Joan's birth, when Harold Driver, grandson of one of the original pharmacists in Ogden, asked Gene to work in his pharmacy. The Halls were delighted to accept his invitation; they would be home, and Gene would no longer need to work on Sundays.

The Hall family moves back to Ogden

The family of five moved in temporarily with Gene's parents, Howard and Florence, while Gene built a home on 35th Street. His grandparents' home, located approximately at Jefferson Avenue and 23rd Street, had two levels and a basement with a coal furnace. Out behind, there was a large garage, nearly the size of a barn. A grocery store owned by a Dutch family stood kitty-corner from their house.

Gene taught Alan to ride a second-hand bike in front of Grandma and Grandpa Hall's house. He held on as Alan learned to balance. It was a large red bike, too big for Alan at the time, but he vividly remembers the thrill of speed. "It was the most exhilarating and liberating feeling to be able to ride by myself. Every spare moment, I was on it," he recalls.

The house was full. Alan's grandparents lived there, as well as his immediate family, plus other relatives who were transitioning between school and work. "I loved being around my cousins, aunts, and uncles," he says. "It was a joyous time for me to be near so many fun acquaintances."

Alan attended second grade at Washington Elementary School, located nearly ten blocks away on Washington Boulevard and 33rd Street. His teacher was Mrs. Gibson, a middle-aged brunette. "She was very kind to me," Alan recalls. "I can still see her caring face in my mind."

Happy childhood with his family

Around the start of third grade, Alan's family moved into their new home. He spent the rest of his childhood living at 725 35th Street, near the local cemetery, Aultorest Memorial Park. The entire house had three bedrooms and totaled about 800 square feet on one level. His parents had one bedroom, Alan and Randy shared another, and Joan had the third bedroom, which she later shared with their little sister, Karen, who was born October 16, 1957. Exactly six years to the date later, Nathan was born, making for even cozier quarters. He was eight months old when Alan left on his mission to Central America. The family shared one bathroom, a small living room, and a kitchen area. There was no garage or carport.

Looking back, Alan recognizes it was a tight space for that many people, but most of his peers' homes were even smaller. Wealthy people on the east side of Ogden had larger homes, but the Halls were content and happy with what they had. "For us, this was a happy home," Alan says. His family lived there from 1952 to 1965.

As the Halls were a middle-class family, Alan and his siblings didn't have a lot of toys or personal possessions. Christmas was modest for the family; the children did not ask for much. When Alan reached Scouting age, he was given a flashlight for his birthday and had a real interest in tents and camping. "It dawned on me that it probably was important to have a sleeping bag," Alan says. He requested one for Christmas, and his parents struggled to find funds for it. "I remember we drove to Salt Lake to some sort of an Army surplus store, where they bought a second-hand mummy bag for me."

The daily family routine looked like this: Joyce woke up the children, and they'd all eat breakfast and get ready for school. "Our clothes were always washed and pressed," Alan remembers, "and Mom always had some kind of treat for us when we came home." Then the kids were expected to do their homework. His mother did most of the cleaning around the house; the kids were expected to do a few chores, but not many. "I vacuumed, but I don't remember making my bed," Alan says. "I don't even know if I picked up my clothes."

Gene's career in pharmacy and teaching

Alan's dad worked as a pharmacist in Ogden at Driver Pharmacy, headquartered in the First Security Bank building in downtown Ogden on 24th Street and Washington Boulevard. "I don't think he was terribly happy with the money he made as a pharmacy employee," Alan recalls. Gene went back to school, this time at Utah State University, to obtain a degree in education. He planned to become a junior high school teacher.

To make ends meet, Gene now had two jobs. He taught Latin and Spanish at Mound Fort Junior High during the day and worked as a pharmacist on weeknights and Saturdays. To Alan, it felt like his dad worked all the time. "He just wasn't around much. He saw his role and duty as a provider for his growing family. That was just the way it was."

Learning lessons at school

Alan spent third and fourth grades at Washington Elementary. "I have really fond memories of that time," Alan says. "I had no cares, no woes. I was healthy. I never broke a bone or got sick, with the exceptions of having my tonsils removed and a hernia repaired." Dr. Leslie Smith removed Alan's tonsils in his office, using a pungent ether cloth over Alan's nose. "Besides that, I was happy and living life to its fullest. You know, as I think about earth life, that's what we'd all really like it to be— always happy."

In third grade, Alan started to recognize differences between boys and girls. It was the beginning of a life-long admiration of the opposite sex. "I adored all the girls in my classes at school. The first one I noticed was a very pretty dark-haired girl named Margie Holstein." He laughs. "Along with my classmates, I teased her about being a cow. Even so, I was smitten by her."

"I loved to go to school because I liked to be around my friends. Being with them filled me with joy. My citizenship rating was always awful. I loved visiting with everyone. I was never quiet." His report cards verify this. At parent-teacher conferences, teachers told his mother, "He's a very fine boy, but he should be more quiet and studious."

Alan's mother sent him to school with lunch every day. Most of the time it was a little sack lunch with a banana, orange, peanut butter sandwich, and chips. The kids sat outside on the grass when the weather was good, and inside when it was too cold. One day, his mother didn't have time to pack a lunch, so she gave Alan two quarters to buy something at a local corner grill, where kids could order a burger and fries or a grilled cheese sandwich. "During the lunch hour, I overcame my fears and went to the cafe and ordered something to eat with my fifty cents. I'd never done that before on my own," Alan says. "I hardly knew what to do, but learned quickly I could do it."

His teacher, Mrs. Folkman, "seemed to have a higher regard for my friend who was a fine artist," Alan remembers. "And if you know anything about me, you know I need to feel accepted. I need to feel loved and appreciated. This kid had her affection. I didn't."

Alan really wanted to impress this teacher. He concocted a scheme to win her heart with his own work of art. One afternoon while at home, he found an impressive ink drawing of Ogden High School that had been drawn by his uncle, Donald Hall. On the following day, Alan proudly showed it to Mrs. Folkman, saying he had drawn it himself. "She could see through that falsehood pretty fast," Alan recalls. "She patted me on the head and said, 'Alan, sit down.'" Her detached reaction concerned Alan. "I knew I had done a terrible thing. Guilt and pain crushed my soul."

Discovering sports and hobbies

During the summer, Alan played in an empty area in the cemetery near his home, where he built a makeshift baseball field. To practice pitching, Alan hung an abandoned car tire on a section of a chainlink fence to represent the strike zone. "I molded a pile of dirt for a pitchers' mound some sixty feet away from the tire to replicate the distance from the mound to home plate." Alan practiced pitching, hour after hour, learning to throw strikes.

He joined a Little League baseball team in fourth grade. Short in height at the time, he began as a third baseman. By sixth grade he'd grown a few more inches and became a pitcher. His team, known as

"Farmer's Grain," was good. They won the city baseball championship when he was twelve years old.

"I started to be very competitive in sports," Alan remembers. "I wanted to be the best at whatever I did." He showed interest in basketball and occasionally watched NBA games on TV. There were no sports camps for kids at the time, so it was up to him to learn to shoot on his own. He didn't have a basketball standard or hoop at his home, so he'd practice shooting into a tall garbage can in his back yard.

"The very first time I actually played in a game, I was in fifth grade. Along with a few classmates, we played in a tiny old gym at Quincy Elementary School," Alan says.

Beyond sports, Alan's mother introduced him to a variety of new experiences. "She wanted me to have every chance to find out what I really wanted to be, and what was going to make me happy in my life," Alan says. She enrolled him in dance lessons, but "those didn't go very well." Same story with violin lessons. She dressed him up in her seal fur coat to be Smokey Bear in a skit for Cub Scouts. She encouraged him to participate in pinewood derbies. She got him involved in the Hinchcliff's Drum and Bugle Corps. Alan remembers marching down Washington Boulevard playing a tune on the bugle during the Ogden Pioneer Days Parade. (Decades later, he often rode a horse down the same parade route as chairman of the Ogden Pioneer Heritage Foundation.)

In fourth and fifth grades, the school district sent Alan's class temporarily to vacant Weber College buildings in downtown Ogden while their new school, T. O. Smith Elementary, was under construction. The new building opened its doors during Alan's sixth grade year. At recess, the boys threw a football around and played kickball and softball, while girls preferred four square or hopscotch.

Fears of the bomb and polio

Two life-threatening world events occurred while Alan was in elementary school. Teachers and parents said Russians planned to kill Americans by dropping hydrogen bombs on cities in the United States, including Ogden. The U.S. government sent comic books to schools featuring Bert the Turtle, who urged students to hide under their desks in the event of bombings.

Alan, along with students across the nation, practiced "duck and cover" drills in their classrooms to be prepared for an attack. "Often, a test siren wailed and we scrambled under our tiny desks," Alan recalls. These exercises gave a false impression of safety. Had a bomb exploded nearby, no one would have survived. "I am sure I was not the only child who suffered fearsome nightmares of being vaporized by an enemy we didn't understand," Alan notes.

Another worrisome threat was polio, a crippling disease. Two young married adults in his neighborhood had contracted the disease, and there was talk about who would be next. Polio was incurable, according to the Centers for Disease Control at the time. The crippling and potentially deadly infectious disease caused by a virus could spread from person to person, invading the brain and spinal cord and causing paralysis. In the early 1950s, polio outbreaks caused more than 15,000 cases of paralysis each year in the United States.[4]

Alan remembers going with his mother to visit Mrs. Whitney, a young neighbor who had contracted polio. She lay inside a medical device known as an "iron lung" to help her breathe. "It looked like a coffin. It seemed she was a prisoner without an escape route. It was horrifying to see her so helpless," Alan recalls.

In 1955, Dr. Jonas Salk developed the first effective polio vaccine that could end the dreaded disease forever. Alan still remembers the day in April 1956 when he marched into the school's gym to be inoculated. "Hundreds of us rolled up our shirt sleeves to expose a bare arm for a saving shot," Alan says. "I can see the scene now in my mind. Teachers shouting commands. Kids crying. Nurses sanitizing skin with alcohol, followed by a swift and painful shot that we all feared."

Gospel learning and baptism

Alan's parents, Gene and Joyce, were united in their dedication to The Church of Jesus Christ of Latter-day Saints. Gene served in the local congregation's leadership as a member of the bishopric. "My dad was very much converted and happy to serve in any capacity. My mother was known for her compassion and care for others. She taught us to love one another and put the gospel in action by serving those in need," Alan says.

The Hall family attended church services on Sundays in the Ogden 28th Ward, located on Adams Avenue and 38th Street. At the time, Sundays involved three separate meetings: Sunday School at 10:00 a.m., Priesthood and Relief Society meetings at 11:00, and Sacrament meeting at 7:00 p.m.

"Sometimes I got in trouble in my Sunday School and Primary classes," Alan says. "A male teacher threw me out of class because I was talking too much to my friends. Now I understand how hard that was for my poor teachers."

After being all dressed up for morning meetings, the family came home for lunch. Alan's parents set a standard of keeping the Sabbath Day holy. However, with seven hours until the next church meeting, it was hard to keep children sitting reverently all day. "On Sunday afternoons, I played," Alan says. "I played football, tennis, and baseball. But I'd always come home to dress again in my Sunday clothes and go back to church. I was pretty quiet in Sacrament meeting because I sat with my family."

Alan was baptized a member of the Church on March 26, 1953, by his father. "I remember going under the water and coming up again. My grandfather, Howard Hall, confirmed me and invited me to receive the Holy Ghost," Alan recalls. "I remember what a sweet moment that was."

2

Junior High and High School

Prior to junior high school, all of Alan's friends lived in the boundaries of his neighborhood—those he saw at church, at the playground, or in elementary school. In seventh grade, Alan met new kids from other neighborhoods, which expanded his social circle. These girls and boys from vastly different backgrounds and ethnicities quickly became great new friends.

"I couldn't wait to see my wonderful new friends in class each day. I lived for that splendid moment," Alan says. "My relationships with interesting people were, and always have been, a significant part of my life." Alan has fond memories of being in classes with Anne Lynch, Uffe Traden, Al Belt, Margie Montoya, Deann Herrick, Frank White, Dave Halverson, Lana Stephens, Bruce Nilson, Ace King, and Gary Close.

Alan's junior high teachers pushed him to learn. He was expected to memorize facts in most classes, like anatomy. "I used flash cards to study new terms and memorize details. I could tell you where every bone was in the body," Alan says.

In a school setting, students primarily use their eyes and ears to learn. Alan felt a need to use his other senses in an integrated fashion to increase his ability to learn new concepts; he wrote review notes, repeated aloud to himself new ideas, and shared new learnings with his peers. "I sought to internalize new facts and connect them to what I already knew about a topic," Alan says.

He enjoyed having a variety of subjects taught by multiple teachers. "Thankfully, my instructors encouraged me to ponder, think, and be creative," Alan says. "I did really well at math and wasn't too bad at most of the sciences." He enjoyed a literature class, where he was taught to compose poetry and to write book reports. He discovered his life-long favorite book, *Les Misérables,* by Victor Hugo. He enjoyed it so much that he used it for his book report in ninth grade, then again in tenth, eleventh, and all the way through his senior year!

Alan got to know his junior high teachers outside the classroom, like the shop teacher who coached his basketball team and his health teacher who coached football. As educators had done throughout his entire academic journey, junior high teachers chided talkative Alan from time to time, telling him to be quiet. He was never sent to the principal's office or expelled, but remembers in-class discipline.

If he stepped out of line in gym class, his teacher punished him in front of his giggling peers. "You'd bend over to touch your toes and a teacher would hit you with the paddle," Alan recalls. "And boy, it would sting and leave a purple bruise." At that time, it was a common practice to physically punish children for bad behavior—cause for quick social-media backlash and legal action today. "In some families, discipline was the belt and it got really severe for some people," Alan recalls. "A lot of kids in my age group grew up with adults being very abusive to them." Fortunately for Alan, his parents were never abusive.

Learning about the birds and the bees
In the late 1950s, the widespread philosophy was that educating teens about reproduction would lead to sexual experimentation. Most school administrators kept reproductive instruction embedded in other academic subjects. For example, "the discussion of character building,

relationships, money management, marriage, and childbearing was part of home economics classes."[1] This left many teenagers, including Alan, with big questions about how babies were made.

Teenage theories about kissing and sex were whispered in the hallways at Alan's school. "As early as seventh grade, you could walk into a classroom and feel hormones swirling around," Alan says. Students shared foolish, false stories about the "birds and bees" that were far from the truth. "Sadly, there were no maturation classes during my generation and no mature guidance around romance, courtship, or sexuality," Alan says.

Alan's parents sidestepped a direct "birds and bees" discussion, too. When Alan was about twelve, his father sat down with him to review the "Articles of Faith," penned by the latter-day prophet Joseph Smith to define the religion's beliefs in 1842. "My dad's goal was to get to the 13th Article of Faith because it talks about being chaste. I had no idea what chastity was," Alan remembers. "I got the gist, but there was no conversation about it again." His mother taught Alan to treat young women with honor and protect them, but that was as far as Alan was taught about sexual intimacy or romance.

Despite lacking an adult confidante he could talk to, Alan intuitively knew when something was wrong. One of those moments happened with a good friend, who showed Alan pictures of naked girls in *Playboy* magazine.

One day, his friend's mom found where he hid copies of Miss June, Miss July, and Miss August. While the two boys sat in the living room watching a basketball game on TV, the boy's mother entered the room with the magazines in her hands. "I was so embarrassed, I hoped I might disappear into a vast underground sink hole in the floor beneath me," Alan says.

She didn't yell, curse, or scream. She looked them in the eyes and said, "Boys, you two hold the priesthood of God, and I believe He doesn't want you looking at these pictures." With wisdom and love, this kind woman taught two teenagers a never-to-be-forgotten lesson on chastity.

Another time, a girl in Alan's high school geometry class brought to school a steamy romance novel, *Lady Chatterley's Lover* by D.H. Lawrence. She turned to Alan, pointed to a passage, and asked him to read it. "It was about a sexual encounter," Alan says. "I was shocked and speechless. Thereafter she would wink at me with a beguiling smile."

As a former bishop and stake president, Alan recalls his own youthful follies when he meets with teenagers. "When I interview the youth in my stake, I tell them they are sexual creatures, with God-given and approved procreative powers. The important thing is to understand how to control this special gift before they are married."

He counsels parents to be upfront with their children about sexuality. This is especially important in an age of "sexting," easily accessible pornography, and blatant sexual behavior on primetime TV. "You need to know what your kids are hearing and seeing," Alan says. "Have a clear conversation before they reach sixth grade."

A kid who loved the spotlight

During junior high, Alan learned more about his interests, strengths, and weaknesses. For example, he was driven by a need to be liked. In the spring of eighth grade, Alan ran for student-body historian. He made election posters he hung in the hallways and spoke in an assembly where he encouraged his classmates to vote for him. Although he came in as a finalist after the primary, he did not win the election. "Being popular was important to me," Alan says. "I lost to a friend named Johnny Hansen and another close friend, Bruce Nilson, was elected student-body president. I felt rejected."

Every year, student leaders honored a student in a school assembly with the title of "Mr. Popularity." It was the biggest accolade a student could receive. When Alan won the title in ninth grade, it was the highlight of his young life. "I treasured that Mr. Popularity trophy and what it meant. If you look at me today, I haven't changed. I still need praise."

The highs and lows of junior high sports

Alan tried out for the basketball team in seventh grade. With high hopes, he went down to the gym to see who made the team. His name was not on the list. "That killed me," Alan remembers. "Some of my friends made it. I didn't. I wasn't going to let that happen again. I was going to work harder to make it."

The summer following seventh grade, his parents sent him to BYU in Provo for a three-week basketball camp for boys. He stayed with his uncle, Tracy Hall, then a chemistry professor at BYU, who had seven children. "This was a home where the kids had mush every morning for breakfast and were very disciplined by their mother," Alan says. "But it was a thrill to be there."

During the camp, Alan went to the BYU campus five days a week to play in the Field House, where Coach Stan Watts taught the fundamentals of the game. "It was a blast. They taught me how to dribble, shoot, and pass the ball. I really learned how to play basketball," Alan says. At this impressionable age, he saw how great coaching made him a better player. "That set in my mind that if you're going to do something really well, you better receive first-class instruction from people who are experts in their field," he says. He attended BYU's basketball camp three summers in a row.

When he tried out for the Washington Junior High Trojans basketball team in eighth grade, his time at the basketball camp paid off. He made the team and played in a few games that year. The Trojans had a decent-enough team, with its share of wins and losses. "We'd have bad games," Alan says. "Part of athletics is learning how to lose with grace as well as win with dignity."

By ninth grade, Alan was a starting guard and team captain. After a basketball practice one day, Alan and his friend Bruce Nilson unknowingly damaged the gym floor. While showering, they used wet towels to build a dam that blocked the shower exit. Their idea was to make a swimming pool. Once completed, they splashed around, naked, in several feet of warm water. "The problem was the dam broke and we were unable to stop the flood. We had no idea of the long-term damage the rushing water caused," Alan says. "It seeped underneath the wooden basketball floor, where the moisture warped the floor. Looking back years later, I probably should have paid to replace that damaged court."

Alan tried his hand at other sports, too. He played on the junior high football team, where he was tailback on a single-wing offense. His tasks were to throw or run the ball and sometimes to hand off to another running back. "I didn't like to run," Alan recalls. "I wasn't that tough and hated getting tackled. But I did like to throw passes." His favorite receiver was Henry Owens. Their best play was when Alan threw the ball down field as far as he could. Henry, the fastest runner on the team, always caught it. Henry was later an all-conference running back at Weber State.

In one heartbreaking game, Alan was called to play strong safety on the defense team. The Trojans played Central Junior High, a competitive team that season. One of Central's fullbacks got the ball and ran through Washington's defensive line, right into Alan's territory. "It was my job to stop him, and the kid ran right over me! I didn't tackle him and he scored a touchdown," Alan says. "I still remember feeling like an utter failure."

Alan's third sport was baseball, and he played on the junior high team. His forte was pitching, due to all those hours of practice after elementary school in the nearby cemetery. "I could throw a fast ball and a curve ball, but other pitchers were better than me," he remembers.

After ball practice each day, he walked the few blocks home. He'd pass by the grocery store on the corner of 34th and Washington, where delicious smells lured in the hungry athlete. He'd often treat himself to a fresh donut.

Alan's dad never saw him play a single ballgame. Since games were always at the end of the school day, they were during Eugene's work hours. Alan's mom attended a couple of games during his teenage years, but not many, since she was caring for his younger siblings. Actually, most parents didn't attend games at his school, and student athletes preferred it that way. "When the dads showed up, they'd try to curry favor with the coach, or tell their kid what to do. Most of us didn't want our parents there," Alan says. "It was our way of being independent in our own world."

Growing up in a time of racial tensions

In 1954, the U.S. Supreme Court unanimously overturned the "separate but equal" doctrine in the landmark case *Brown v. Board of Education,* which called for the desegregation of schools.[2] This decision served as a catalyst for the expanding civil rights movement, which came to national prominence during Alan's junior high days in the late 1950s.

A railroad town, Ogden attracted diversity, but its residents were predominately white. What did teenage Alan think about people with a different skin color? "I wasn't discouraged from having friends who were black," Alan says.

Ace King, an African-American athlete who was on Alan's junior high football team, approached Alan decades later with a complaint about how he felt Alan had treated him in childhood. He remembers being Alan's friend, but never being invited to Alan's parties. The truth of Ace's words stung. "I never thought I was biased against my friends who were Mexican or African-American, but my behavior showed otherwise," Alan says. "I decided from then on, I'd go out of my way to be more sensitive and aware. In my world today, I have many friends from a variety of ethnicities."

Insensitivity to racial differences was common at that time, though most were unaware of it. As an active member of the South Ogden Utah Stake, Alan participated in stake road shows. When Alan was in seventh grade, Geneva Peterson directed a musical play for youth. "I can't believe we did this, but we were white kids with our faces painted black," Alan says. "I sang this song called 'Mississippi Mud.' I still know the lyrics today." He wasn't aware of racist implications; he just knew he was having fun. Alan remembers it being a thrill to go to road show rehearsals, be with other kids, and travel to perform.

Church activities, Boy Scouts, and priesthood duties

"It was fun to be a member of the Church, participate in the youth activities, and grow in the gospel," Alan says. He sang in a priesthood boys choir and particularly remembers practicing the hymn "The Morning Breaks." He was a home teacher (it was called "ward teaching" then) and visited a few families each month with an older gentleman in the ward. Alan learned to give a spiritual message and offer a prayer during these visits. He also visited ward members to collect fast offerings and tithing, a duty of Aaronic priesthood holders.

Alan was fortunate to be surrounded by many neighbors who were friends of his parents. Most of them were young couples living in their first homes and raising young children. Each in their own way supported and assisted Alan in his many activities. He recalled special feelings for the Wright, Sato, Avondet, Buckner, Waterfall, Page, Bolton, and Van Drimmelen families.

Alan's participation in Boy Scouts was interlaced with church activities, as they were the same group of leaders and peers. For Alan's first Scout camp, his parents bought him a backpack. When fully loaded with gear, the pack weighed sixty pounds. "I couldn't carry it at all," he remembers, "but I learned to love the mountains, fishing, and camping."

One time on a Scout trip to the world-famous, primitive Wind River Range in Wyoming, he rode in a truck with an admired Scout leader in his ward. To Alan's astonishment, his leader pulled out a cigarette, lit it, and started to smoke. Smoking is prohibited in the religion's Word of Wisdom. "I was stunned," Alan remembers. "But it didn't change my regard for him. He said he needed to smoke, and I wasn't going to judge him."

The habit of looking past people's faults stayed with Alan. "Even today, I figure it's not my place to judge," Alan says. "Everyone sins. Nobody is perfect. We're all children of God trying our best to be good."

From the time Alan was twelve until his sixteenth birthday, he returned each summer to the Wind River Range with his peers and Scout leaders. He recalls the night of August 17, 1959, when his tent and the ground nearby suddenly began to shake. He later learned that a 7.2-magnitude earthquake near Yellowstone, Montana, had caused the earth to move in his campground—even though he was 125 miles from the epicenter. Scouts in the Wind River mountains were unharmed, but twenty-eight campers near Hebgen Lake were buried alive by a massive mountain landslide.

During his teenage years, Alan attended Mutual, a church-sponsored weekly youth activity night. He looked forward each week to being with his friends Gary Close, Oletta Yost, Pamela Taylor, Russell Lawrence, Dennis Simpson, and Ricky Brunson. Once he and his friends could drive cars, have part-time jobs, and be on the high school teams, they stopped attending Mutual activities.

Likewise, Boy Scouts wasn't prioritized the way it was for the next generation. For example, many of the youth in Alan's age group did not earn the Eagle Scout award. "I achieved the rank of Life and nothing more. Earning an Eagle wasn't a priority for our leaders, so it wasn't for us," Alan says.

Alan remembers the very first Sunday he passed the Sacrament. "I spilled the water tray all over the stake president. He was sitting on the stand in front of the congregation," Alan recalls, shaking his head. Little did young Alan know he would be the stake president one day. "Now when a deacon approaches me with the Sacrament, I put my hand under the water tray to keep it level."

From an early age, Alan learned to lead his peers as he followed the direction of adult supervisors. He served as president of the deacons quorum, and organized passing the Sacrament, collecting fast offerings, and other responsibilities. "Church leadership was a training ground for me on how to work with others and lead in an organized way," Alan says. "How many young men in the world get a chance to lead at the age of twelve, thirteen, or fourteen?"

Alan's lifelong affinity for public speaking began during his youth while serving and participating in church. He remembers giving one talk about the seagulls that saved pioneers from losing their crops to crickets. "They prayed for God to save them, and He sent the seagulls," Alan says. "That was my first talk. It was two-and-a-half-minutes long. I was five years old and I remember asking God to help me with my talk."

Meeting the prophet and getting a patriarchal blessing

In seventh grade, Alan came face to face with the prophet of The Church of Jesus Christ of Latter-day Saints. White-haired David O. McKay was from Huntsville, Utah, a short drive from where the Halls lived. One Saturday, President McKay was scheduled to speak at a park in Huntsville. Young men showed up in droves with their fathers and leaders to hear the beloved prophet. A stage was set up with a platform, podium, and audio system. Alan's stake president, Kefford Peek, was in charge of conducting the meeting and asked Alan to give the closing prayer.

"I'll never know how I got that assignment, but there I was," Alan recalls. "After President McKay's talk, I wandered up to the pulpit and said the closing prayer into the microphone, which gave delayed feedback from the sound system. When I spoke, I could hear my voice a few seconds later, which confused me a little bit."

President McKay pulled Alan aside after the prayer for a quick chat. He looked right into Alan's young eyes. "It was like he looked into my soul. I felt it was an interview of my worthiness," Alan says. "Here was the prophet of the Lord talking to this little seventh-grade boy. That has stayed with me all these years."

Another significant spiritual event in Alan's youth was receiving his patriarchal blessing. Every baptized Latter-day Saint is entitled to receive a special blessing from God via an authorized church leader known as a patriarch. The blessing provides inspired direction for individuals during their lifetimes. Alan received his blessing when he was sixteen; the promises in it have comforted and directed him ever since.

A rough welcome to high school

Alan attended a sophomore orientation at Ogden High School, where both his parents were alumni. "The campus was magnificent," he recalls of the tour. "It is even more so now."

New students were led to a field, where a rope was laid out perpendicular to a firehose, aimed to spray the losing side of a tug-of-war. All the seniors lined up on one end, unsuspecting sophomores on the other. "The idea was the older upperclassmen would pull you through the rushing water. But instead, they dropped the rope and then began to attack us," Alan says, smiling. "We were running for our lives!" That was the last year the rope pull was allowed.

Alan's junior-high reputation as Mr. Popularity didn't protect him from further initiation. Big-ego seniors let Alan know where he fit in the new pecking order. "I went from ninth grade, where I was really something, to the big school where the older guys looked like Greek gods," he says. "On the first day of school, they pulled my Levi pants down, sat me on the running drinking fountain, and pulled my pants up over my wet underwear. The message was loud and clear: 'Welcome to Ogden High. Don't mess with us. We are in charge here.'"

Attending LDS seminary classes at a church building near the high school campus was much more peaceful and welcoming. Alan enjoyed the daily one-hour instruction on gospel topics he and his friends received from beloved teachers. "I loved the calmness and positive environment of the seminary. Everyone was friendly and happy," Alan recalls. He graduated from the program after attending classes for three consecutive years. He still reveres Lynn Poulson, one of the teachers who cared for his welfare.

Alan found his way through the school campus, with 2,000 kids for him to meet. He met new friends everywhere he went. He still visits with his high school friends on a regular basis. Close to sixty alumni meet quarterly for lunch in Ogden, and he has chaired his high school class reunions three times.

Sophomore year, dubbed "Happy Feet Hall"

Alan had the typical sophomore classes, like math and English. He was also required to attend a daily Army ROTC course. Every day, he attended military training for an hour, learning rifle shooting and various military strategies. Sophomore boys were required to wear a military uniform once a week. It was green, hot, made of heavy wool, and itched horribly. Alan hated it. His mom sewed a silk lining in the pants to make it more comfortable.

As a teenager, Alan didn't worry much about style. He wore Levi's to school every day, along with white-and-orange saddle oxfords. "All the boys wore Gant shirts, a very popular brand. But I didn't have money for them," Alan says, "so I wore whatever my mother could buy."

Instead of focusing on clothes, he concentrated on becoming a good athlete. "Life was good for me because I was successful in basketball," Alan says. He made the sophomore basketball team, and his team played high schools from around the state. One day, some upperclassmen took Alan's Converse basketball shoes and wrote "Happy Feet" with an orange magic marker on them. It was done more to be funny than to harm, and Alan didn't mind being the center of a joke if it got him noticed. The nickname stuck for the rest of Alan's life.

During his sophomore year, one of Alan's teachers suggested he coach a sixth-grade basketball team. "That was a defining moment. Somebody I respected trusted me to do something worthwhile," Alan says. "That little team won the city championship because it was made up of a lot of coachable players." Although it was fun to see his team win, Alan learned winning wasn't everything. "Athletics became not so much about the victories as it did the opportunity to participate and give it your best, work together as a team, and have discipline."

During his sophomore year, Alan took a driver's education class and learned to drive his parents' stick-shift car. The vehicle was meant for his dad to drive to work, so Alan rarely got a chance to use it. From time to time, he might drive it to church or run an errand for his mother, but the car wasn't his. Why did he want wheels? So he could date girls.

"I really enjoyed visiting with the pretty girls in my classes. Oh, how I wished I could take them on a date!" Alan says. "But I was poor, had no car, and they lived so far away." A little brunette named Dixie Hess made his heart flutter, but he couldn't date her without a car. "She was the most beautiful thing I'd ever seen. She looked just like Natalie Wood, star of the hit movie *West Side Story*. I was smitten with them both."

Twenty miles south of Ogden, the amusement park Lagoon hosted big-name performers like the Beach Boys. "I dreamed of taking my cute classmates to see the Kingston Trio, Johnny Mathis, or The Lettermen," Alan says. "But that year, I just sat home and wished I could."

A messy start in his first real job

The summer after his sophomore year, Alan had his first taste of making money. While his mother had paid him for a few small jobs around the house and his great-grandmother offered a nominal fee to mow her grass, Alan got his first real job in the summer of 1961. Dale Harris, his mother's cousin, agreed to pay Alan to help him build his new home.

One evening, Dale asked Alan to make mud to secure several wooden posts. Obediently, Alan filled a wheelbarrow with dirt and water. He mixed it thoroughly with a shovel, and wheeled it over to Dale.

"What is this?" Dale asked. "It doesn't look like mud."

"Yes, it's mud," Alan answered.

"Where did you get it?" Dale asked.

"Over there," Alan pointed to a hole in the ground.

Dale started to laugh. "He laughed so hard we had to quit and go home," Alan remembers. "In construction terminology, 'mud' was cement. He'd pointed to bags of cement, but I had no idea what he meant, so I mixed a batch of real mud. It's a story my family still tells today."

Later in high school, Alan worked at Ogden Roofing and Supply, located between 28th and 29th Streets on Grant Avenue. He got the job through a connection at church and worked there Saturdays and after school when he wasn't playing ball. During the summer, he worked full time, six days a week. He drove a lumber truck, delivered materials, and sold products. "I moved sheetrock and lumber, and got pretty strong and tough," Alan says. "I worked as hard as I possibly could."

In these first jobs, he learned about different personality types, and other lessons from mentors. His boss, Harold Ence, taught him to secure lumber with strong knots. He also picked up some colorful words. "I worked around older men who lived a Western, cowboy lifestyle," Alan says. "At work, I heard all kinds of new expletives and crude stories. I was self-disciplined enough to never use foul language at home, but on the job, I said 'hell' and 'damn' with some enthusiasm!"

This spurs a more recent memory of Alan swearing. After attending the Horse & Hitch Parade in July 2015, Alan stopped at McDonald's to get ice cream with his young grandsons. "I said, 'This is the best damn ice cream I have ever tasted.' They laughed so hard they almost wet their pants!" Alan says with a chuckle. "They had never heard their religious grandpa swear before. When I swear now, it's only for humor. I said it for their reaction, which I got in full measure."

How did Alan spend his hard-earned money in his teenage years? He'd pick up new blue jeans and a few new shirts, but never had enough money to buy a letterman's jacket. "But I did get a student-body officer sweater and still have it today," he says. He used the rest of his money to buy favorite albums of popular singing groups.

Freedom on wheels

During Alan's junior year, his Grandfather Hansen died. It was January of 1962. "I was crushed by his passing. I loved my grandfather,"

Alan says. Grandfather Hansen had worked at a local favorite sweet spot, Farr's Ice Cream. On most Saturdays, he brought the Hall grandchildren popsicles or ice cream.

After Alan's grandpa passed, there was a silver lining in the sadness. As the oldest grandson, Alan inherited his grandfather's 1948 Dodge. Alan fixed it up, and though it wasn't the fanciest car in the high school parking lot, to him it was freedom on wheels. For a seventeen-year-old who wanted to take girls on dates, it was the grandest inheritance possible.

Student-body officer and Boys State delegate

Alan made the varsity basketball team his junior and senior years, thanks to Mark Ballif, head coach. They won about half their basketball games, but never went to state finals or won any championships. Today, Alan continues to associate with the remarkable young men with whom he played ball. He often thinks of good times he had with Bruce Nilson, Dean Wiese, Kent Martin, Bob Johnson, Henry Owens, Terry Monson, and Vestell Wright.

Alan's dreams of high school popularity came true in the spring of his junior year. He ran for student-body historian as "Happy Feet Hall," and won. "And that, for me, was one of the most glorious moments of my life," he says smiling. He was now among the best-known kids on campus. He ran student activities with fellow student-body officers Craig Anderson, JoAnn Burdett, and Anne Lynch.

That same summer, he attended Boys State, a week-long leadership and citizen program sponsored by the American Legion. Teachers and administrators at his school nominated Alan and a dozen other boys to represent Ogden High at the program, held at Utah State University. The boys stayed in the dorms, heard speeches by the Utah governor and lieutenant governor, attended classes on civics, and played in the afternoons. "It was great fun. I met these smart teenage leaders from all over the state," Alan says. "My world continued to expand with more new friends. Looking back, winning the election and then going to Boys State were enormous boosts for me."

With a car and popularity, Alan's confidence grew with girls. He started dating his first girlfriend, a friendly little brunette with a beau-

tiful smile. Diana lived close to the high school, and Alan visited her
regularly. She was his first kiss. In fact, they got pretty good at kissing
during his senior year. "We liked to make out," Alan says with a grin.
"That was the most fun thing I'd ever done; I mean, it was just glorious."

One summer night, while the young pair was sitting in Alan's car
in front of Diana's house, her dad came out and knocked on the car
window. He held out two popsicles and said, "I think you two need to
cool off."

"We wanted the earth to open up and hide us," Alan says. "We were
so embarrassed!"

They learned their lesson from the popsicles. "We didn't do anything
bad," Alan says. "I thought about it—but didn't. We just had a fun senior
year together." For Christmas, Alan bought Diana a present. "I'd never
done that for any girl before. I didn't even know how," Alan says. "My
mom suggested I buy her a teddy bear, which I did. I thought it was a
wonderful gift and I think she liked it."

Senior year as a big man on campus

Senior year was everything Alan dreamed it would be. He had a
pretty girlfriend, was a student-body officer, captain of the basketball
team, led assemblies, and participated in public events. Every day
he was getting attention, even beyond the world of the Ogden High
campus. His picture was in the local newspaper as the captain of the
basketball team.

"Had I died and gone to heaven?" Alan says with a gleam in his eye.
"Life was good, really good. I think at the end of the day, my popularity
came as a result of wanting to be a friend to everyone."

Alan learned to look for those who needed a friend. He learned
to connect with people from every walk of life, and could get along
with anybody. He paid special attention to those who were often
overlooked. For example, Alan always said hello to one young woman
named Charlene, who had some disabilities. Later in life, Alan
taught his children and grandchildren to reach out to kids who were
disadvantaged, those who "aren't the popular ones, the pretty ones, the
athletes, or the scholars."

In his final days of high school, Alan sat in the hallway to sign yearbooks. A teasing charmer, he put the same romantic note in every girl's book: "I can't help falling in love with you." The words came from a popular Elvis Presley love song. Of course, the girls loved it.

At the graduation ceremony in May, the graduating class sang the school song, dressed in caps and gowns. "It killed me to graduate," Alan says. "I had mixed emotions because it was the end of an era. We were leaving the nest."

On that final school day, Alan and some friends hiked Malan's Peak, a steep climb east of the high school, to celebrate the symbolic summit they'd reached in their lives. Feeling on top of the world at 6,980 feet above his home town, eighteen-year-old Alan didn't know the summer ahead would include the darkest days of his life.

CHAPTER

3

Crossroads Year

A couple of weeks after graduation, Alan embarked on an adventure-turned-nightmare that would haunt him the rest of his life. Uncle Tracy Hall invited Alan and his fourteen-year-old brother, Randy, on a rafting trip down the Colorado River. The expedition was planned for the young men in Tracy's Pleasant View 3rd Ward in Provo, where he was a counselor in the bishopric. He thought his nephews from Ogden would enjoy the trip.

Tracy volunteered to be the bishopric representative and act as chaplain. "Tracy had always wanted to go on a rafting trip down the Colorado River and he was just as excited as the boys were," wrote Ida-Rose Hall, Tracy's wife and Alan's aunt, in her account from personal experience and stories she was told.[1] Darrell Taylor was Scoutmaster.

The trip had attracted the attention of the press. Twenty-four-year-old reporter Dorothy Hansen from the *Deseret News* came along to write about the trip. She knew it was a historic time for the Colorado River, which would soon become Lake Powell after Glen Canyon Dam's completion later that September. She was delighted to cover a special feature story.

Monday, June 10, 1963

At 6:00 a.m. on June 10, the Scouting caravan left Provo, beginning the journey south in a bus. Alan, Randy, and two of their cousins, David and Tracy Jr., were thrilled to be together. It turned out Tracy Sr. got the flu a few days before the trip and was unable to travel with the youth of his ward.

"Tracy got out of bed, even though he was still ill, and all of us went down to the church to see the boys off on their river trip," wrote Ida-Rose. "After a group prayer, the boys and their leaders boarded the bus. The bus rolled out of the church parking lot and started for Southern Utah."

Chase Allred went in Tracy's place. Disappointed to miss a once-in-a-lifetime adventure, Tracy returned home.

Most of the boys on the trip were from Provo; some were from Salt Lake City and Ogden. It took nearly six hours to arrive at Escalante, Utah, where they left the bus and ate lunch. At that point, their packs were loaded into the back of a two-and-a-half-ton cattle truck, on top of heavy rubber rafts provided by an expedition company.

Forty-six people, including Scout leaders, Scouts, and the reporter, climbed aboard to ride on top of the gear. Three more rode in the cab, bringing the total to forty-nine. The rollicking Boy Scouts and leaders overloaded the truck. Boy Scouts of America rules prohibited riding in an open truck, but the leaders believed such a special adventure was worth the risk.

Alan found his spot on the left side of the truck, toward the front. Randy sat near him, closer to the truck's interior. "We were all sitting down in the back of the truck, singing and joking," said Charles Pope, a twenty-eight year-old Scout leader from Provo, in a *Chicago Tribune* article.[2] It was a beautiful summer day. According to weather reports, the high temperature was 82 degrees.[3]

"There were only a few clouds in the sky," Alan remembers. "We didn't go very fast up and down the winding and a dusty desert road." Their destination was Hole-in-the-Rock, sixty-two miles southeast of Escalante in Kane County.[4]

The geological wonder, a historic LDS pioneer site, had been a deceptive shortcut for weary pioneers looking to shave several hundred miles off their long journey toward Blanding, Utah. The pioneers widened the downward path with pick axes, shovels, and limited quantities of blasting powder. Leaders had planned for the Scouts to hike down Hole-in-the-Rock with all their equipment, then launch the rubber rafts into the river.

Their driver, Ernest S. Ahlborn, fresh off an LDS mission, was an employee of SOCOTWA (South Cottonwood Ward) Expedition Corporation, the company providing the tour. He maneuvered the overflowing truck along the multiple curves of the road, his passengers taking in views of Escalante's famous mountain range. "Every once in a while, we would see some interesting Southern Utah rock formations," Alan recalls.

A few minutes after 3:00 p.m., thirteen miles from their destination, they came to a steep hill in a washed-out gully. As the truck started up the steep grade, the driver struggled to reach the top of the ridge. "I could hear the gears grinding and noted the driver wasn't able to shift to a lower, more powerful gear," Alan says.

Unable to gain traction, the vehicle started rolling back down the road. According to a 1993 *Deseret News* article, "the brakes, later found to lack fluid in the master cylinder, didn't catch."[5] The driver tried again, but the weight and speed were too much to overcome. In a matter of a few terrifying moments, the truck rolled backward 124 feet and flipped over a thirty-five-foot embankment, "spilling people and gear into the sandy gulch."[6] Screams rang out in the raging crash. Scouts and leaders landed underneath the upside-down truck and beneath its heavy contents, later giving the gully a new name: Carcass Wash.

"I can remember flying through the air. What saved me was a small depression in the sandy creek bed. I landed where the contents of the truck were over me but not pressing hard on my body," Alan remembers with tears in his eyes. "I must have been unconscious for a moment."

He called for his brother Randy, but heard no response. He heard the crying of people in severe pain. He called again for his brother. Still no answer.

In a rush of adrenaline, Alan struggled with all his might to escape the weight of the gear on top of him. Once free, he saw the mayhem. Eventually, the death toll included seven Scouts and six adults. Twenty-six were injured. Ten Scouts, like Alan, escaped with only minor injuries. "For the next little while, we tried to figure out how to help the injured," Alan said. He helped remove the heavy rubber rafts and packs from the truck, which were crushing people. Some were pinned in the wreckage for almost an hour.[7]

As the equipment was removed, Alan saw his brother's body for the first time. His heart sank. "My brother was gone," Alan says. "I picked Randy up and carried him over to the shade of a desert tree, and wept. I sat there and cried."

On its way to the bottom of the culvert, the truck had rolled over some of the occupants who jumped out of the vehicle and pinned victims beneath it when it came to rest. In sum, eleven were killed on the spot. The young female news reporter from the *Deseret News* died en route to the hospital. The thirteenth victim died two days later.

Two hours until help arrived

The group was far from civilization, with no phones or way to get the help they desperately needed. One of the adults approached grieving Alan and said, "You know, there's nothing you can do for him now, so please help us rescue others."

Alan realized this was a crucial moment to help comfort and rescue those who needed it. "I was probably in shock because of the experience and the heat," he says, "but I did what I could."

Two Scouts, Brian Roundy and Tom Heal, left the wreckage to seek help. After four miles of walking with broken ribs, they found a rancher who radioed for help. It took hours for the sheriff's deputies and state policemen to reach the scene, and a fleet of private and chartered planes was hastily mobilized to fly the more seriously injured to hospitals in Provo and Salt Lake City.

"During the two hours before help arrived, those who were able helped pull those injured from the mess of supplies and equipment," wrote Ida-Rose in her 1963 account. "I think they must have grabbed the many sleeping bags and used those to lay the injured Scouts on. There was no mention of this in the newspaper reports, but I surmised this to be the case, because our own sleeping bags were blood stained."

One of the state road workers, Worthen Allen, was first to the scene. He later reported to the *Deseret News*: "I immediately drove there in a station wagon. It was an awful thing to see. They loaded me up with seven and I immediately drove back to Escalante, where the injured persons were transferred to ambulances and taken to Panguitch and Richfield hospitals. It was the worst thing I've ever seen."[8]

Alan didn't know anyone else in the group besides Randy and his two cousins. David had black eyes and a mild concussion, and Tracy Jr. suffered only bruises and stiffness.

Dr. Cook, despite his own injuries and losing his brother in the crash, helped the wounded with a few medical resources he had with him. "He worked ceaselessly for thirteen hours, far into the night, treating the wounded and stopping the bleeding," wrote Ida-Rose. "Even after everyone had been removed from the accident site and taken to the Panguitch hospital, he kept going from patient to patient, without any rest."

A BYU professor was crushed. "As we pulled him out, he was screaming. The accident had broken nearly every bone in his body," Alan remembers. Miraculously, he survived after surgery.

News of the accident

Over the rest of the afternoon and evening, news of the tragic accident made its way north to the families of the Scouts.

"I do not remember the exact moment, but sometime in the afternoon, Tracy came downstairs into the room where I was," wrote Ida-Rose. "I could tell from his face that something was very wrong. He told me that there had been an accident! Bishop Free had called him. Some of those on our Scout trip had been killed and some injured. No names of the injured, survivors, or the dead had been released by the police at that time! And no other details of the accident were available."

Ida-Rose and Tracy called Joyce and Gene Hall to alert them of the news. "The worst part of the whole terrible ordeal was the waiting—not knowing where the Scouts were or in what condition," wrote Ida-Rose. "The rest of the day we were glued to the radio waiting for news."

The police released the names of the injured and dead as soon as they had the accurate information. "Over the radio, we heard our nephew, Randy Hall, fourteen, had been killed," Ida-Rose wrote. "It was terrible for Joyce and Gene to receive the news of his death that way."

Rescue efforts for the survivors

That evening, rows of cars and trucks arrived at the accident site, hauling the survivors out, some who'd been pinned for several painful hours. Rescuers began removing those under the truck one by one, jacking up one side of the truck.

"The next thing I knew, I was in the Panguitch hospital overnight. I must have scraped my ear, but no other injuries," Alan says. He received a phone call from a reporter from Ogden's *Standard-Examiner,* who interviewed him for a front-page article about the accident.

The following day, the highway patrol stopped drivers who were on their way north, asking for help. They waved down a family, who volunteered to drive Alan the several hours home. In the car were a mother and father and their kids, although Alan doesn't remember much more about the drive. "I was pretty somber the whole way home. I don't think I talked much. I didn't have much to say," Alan remembers. When they arrived at his driveway, his parents came out. "They were crushed beyond imagination. On the news the night before, reporters had implied we both had died. So they were glad to know that I was okay, but grief-stricken that Randy was gone."

Going on without Randy

"I wanted to die," Alan says. "The grief and mourning in our home was intense." He felt survivor's guilt and, as the oldest, bore deep shame that he wasn't able to save his younger brother.

"Those who lost brothers felt they had to somehow make up for what their brothers hadn't had a chance to accomplish," wrote Ida-Rose, likely referring to Alan.

As news spread about the accident, the Hall family had many visitors, including Randy's classmates, Alan's friends, Ogden High teachers, and church members. "Everybody wanted to comfort us, and in some ways it worked, and in other ways, it was just too much," Alan says. "I've learned I have to be careful when I comfort others when tragedy strikes."

Joyce was beside herself with grief. She was expecting her fifth child in October, and the toil of emotions was too much for her to bear. "She had a hard time going to Sacrament meetings after he was killed," wrote Ida-Rose. "Randy had been his deacons quorum president and it was hard for her not to see Randy passing the Sacrament with the other boys." Joyce's doctor finally coaxed her into seeing a therapist, and she started taking anti-depression medication. Alan's dad became the emotional support for the family.

In Provo, church leaders held a mass memorial in the Tabernacle to honor the deceased. Randy's body was delivered to the Lindquist Mortuary in Ogden for funeral services, and Joyce asked Alan to pick out a burial suit for Randy. Alan went to Tanner's for Men to pick out a suit. Nate Tanner, the owner, told Alan that the family would not have to pay for the suit.

The day of Randy's burial was painful. "To see him in that coffin was so hard on me," Alan says. "My mother didn't let my sisters, Joan and Karen, come at all. They never saw him." Although Joyce was trying to spare her young daughters the pain of a loss, Alan's sisters told him fifty years later that they had never been able to gain closure or properly go through the grieving process.

Alan wept and prayed often after the accident. He desperately needed comfort and asked God to give him peace. "I never lost faith, nor was I angry," Alan says. "In time, peace came to my wounded soul as I realized that death is what it is: a passing to a better place. We have to die to return to God."

Eventually, Alan went back to work, but was depressed the rest of the summer. "I didn't want to do anything," he recalls. "The guys I worked with were kind and gave me space, but I was struggling." He still had his girlfriend, but he didn't want to see her. Getting through each day was painful. It was a hellish time to endure.

Alan found comfort in his patriarchal blessing. "It was a great source of strength to me to read God had promised to preserve my life until I fulfilled my life's work on this earth," Alan says. "I was also reassured I am part of an eternal family and that one day I will be with my beloved brother again."

A prophet's call for temple work

Eugene and Joyce Hall, along with the other parents who lost children in the tragedy, were invited by President David O. McKay to visit with him at the Church Office Building in Salt Lake City. It's unknown if Joyce attended, but Alan remembers his father going to the meeting. In this special gathering, the prophet invited the parents to do their deceased children's temple work and do it quickly, because their boys had work to perform in the spirit world. Shortly thereafter, Eugene went to the Salt Lake Temple and vicariously performed sacred ordinances for Randy.

"It wasn't until later in life I read in the 138th section of *The Doctrine and Covenants* why that was done," Alan says. "In this scripture, Joseph F. Smith has a vision of the resurrected Savior in the spirit world. While there, He organized groups of missionaries from among many faithful spirits who were clothed with power and authority to teach the gospel to those in spirit prison." When Alan read that, he realized that his brother had also been clothed with power to teach the spirits of men and women who have died without the knowledge of the restored gospel of Jesus Christ.

Randy was buried in the family burial plot next to his Hansen grandparents in the Ogden Cemetery, remembered by a little flat headstone. At first, Joyce refused to put a marker on Randy's grave. That was the first thing her therapist insisted she do to heal. "Until she did, he felt that she would not let herself admit Randy was really dead," wrote Ida-Rose. "All that time, I thought she had taken his death beautifully. She finally told me how difficult Randy's death had been for her."

Decades later, Alan found notes on Randy's grave from his classmates who described him as a remarkable young man. "They wanted our family to know that they also missed him," he says.

Alan and Jeannie take their grandchildren to Randy's grave every year to tell them his story and keep his memory alive. "I know where Randy is. He's doing a great work among God's children in the spirit world. I look forward to seeing him one day," Alan says.

To perpetuate Randy's memory, Alan and Jeannie created the Randall M. Hall Scholarship Fund in the late 1990s. The scholarship targets young men or women who are good students, fine leaders, and athletes. Each year, the family presents the award to a deserving student who may use it toward tuition at Weber State University or Ogden-Weber Technical College.

Sad story told in stone

Alan returned to the scene of the accident for a memorial dedication on the thirtieth anniversary of the tragedy. It was his first time back. "It's a painful place to visit," Alan says. "But it's important to visit the site because it's sacred ground where so many lost their lives."

Eugene and Joyce did not attend the dedication. It was too painful. "They had a hard time getting someone to say the dedicatory prayer," wrote Ida-Rose. "They asked Bishop Free, but he couldn't handle it emotionally. They asked Chase Allred, but he wasn't sure his legs would be up to the terrain. Tracy finally accepted."

The accident site is a two-hour drive south from Escalante on a dirt road. Cars can't go much faster than twenty miles per hour due to the gravel and rocks on the road.

Survivors Tom Heal and J. Lee Colvin had committed to build a memorial someday to honor those who were lost. After three years of collecting donations from nearly every survivor and families of accident victims, including Alan and Jeannie Hall, the sandstone monument was erected and dedicated on the thirtieth anniversary of the accident. The sad story told in stone bears an inscription with these words:

IN MEMORIUM

JUST PRIOR TO THE CREATION of Lake Powell, a party of 49, including Explorer Scout Post 36 from LDS Pleasant View 3rd Ward, Provo, Utah, set out on an expedition to run the Colorado River rapids between Hole-in-the-Rock and Glen Canyon. Riding in an open truck, they reached this point at approximately 3:15 on the afternoon of June 10, 1963. The truck stalled as it ascended the grade on your left, and its brakes failed. Rolling backward, it overturned and rolled down the steep embankment on the other side of the sharp curve from this monument. Seven Scouts and six adults lost their lives in this tragic highway accident, the third worst in Utah's history.

In loving memory of those who perished:

Gary Lynn Christensen, 14

Lynn Louis Merrell, 15

Robert Cook, 29

Randy Wayne Miller, 14

W. A. "Bill" Creer, 39

Marvin Poschatis, 29

Joseph William Erickson, 16

Gary Lynn Rasmussen, 15

Gordon Henry Grow, 15

Dr. Martin J. Shaw, 51

Randy M. Hall, 14

Dr. Harvey Darrell Taylor, 45

Dorothy Hansen, 24

Erected and dedicated June 10, 1993, by the families and friends of those who perished, in cooperation with Kane County and the U.S. Bureau of Land Management.

After the dedication and back in Escalante, he asked local citizens if they remembered the event. Older folks remembered it like it had happened yesterday. To learn more about the event, they were invited to visit a small museum in Escalante with information about the accident. They also suggested the Halls visit a Mrs. Jones, whose husband had been on the rescue team.

Alan went again with Jeannie and several of their adult children and their spouses to the accident location on the fiftieth anniversary of the accident, in remembrance of his brother. "As I read the memorial plaque, I noticed more adults had died than I thought, and the death of so many teenagers just about wiped out that ward's Young Men program," Alan says.

First year at Weber State

Weber College, a two-year school in the fall of 1963, was located only a few blocks from the Hall home. It was the convenient choice for Alan's higher education and let Alan enjoy some stability before serving a mission. Alan's parents and all his relatives had attended Weber, so it was a family tradition and familiar territory.

"My first semester at Weber was emotionally challenging. I needed to find a way to focus on school, adapt to changes in my family, and plan for my future," Alan says. "My world had changed drastically in ninety days. Where I had been a big guy on campus, in college I was a small fish again." At the same time, he was adjusting to a new baby brother. The Halls' youngest child, Nathan, was born October 16, 1963, just after Alan began college, while he was preparing mentally and spiritually to leave home and serve a mission.

Alan decided to be a dentist and chose classes in chemistry, algebra, and biology to prepare for that profession. Traveling on the road as a player on the college freshmen basketball team, Alan struggled to attend class and study. He got straight Cs that first semester. "Looking back, I realize I was also still emotionally depressed from the death of my brother," he says.

On campus, above Harrison Boulevard on 38th Street, there were four new one-story buildings, numbered 1, 2, 3, and 4. There was a small building called the Temporary Union Building, dubbed "the TUB" by students, which was an old army barracks that served as a general meeting place for students.

The day JFK died

After a few weeks at college, a national tragedy shook Alan's world again. It was November 22, 1963. John F. Kennedy, president of the United States, was shot in Dallas, Texas. The youthful, charismatic president had been an American idol. "It was shattering for me. I remember walking across campus when somebody told me the president had been killed. Within moments everything on campus was closed. People were sent home—everybody, including the faculty, immediately left the campus," Alan remembers. "All of us turned on our television sets to see what in the world had happened. Over the next week, we never turned the TV off."

The country was in shock. Television had been JFK's ally in winning the American vote and keeping the world's favor after gaining the presidency. For example, he was the first U.S. president to conduct live, non-edited press conferences. He attracted 65 million viewers (out of 183.6 million Americans) in his first post-inauguration broadcast. *Time* magazine named him "Man of the Year" in 1962, with an article that detailed how his image as a youthful, handsome, charismatic leader led to his popularity: "Kennedy has always had a way with the people . . . a quick charm, the patience to listen, a sure social touch, and an interest in knowledge."[9]

During all of this, a stunned and grief-stricken American public relied on TV anchors as sources of fact. After nearly three years of presidential service, television immortalized Kennedy's memory. Details of the Dallas shooting came out in the media, followed by murder allegations against Lee Harvey Oswald, who was taken into custody.

"Before our very eyes as we watched TV, the assassin who killed the president, Lee Harvey Oswald, was shot by a man named Jack Ruby," Alan says. Even more upsetting, Oswald was in police custody when Ruby shot him. As the cameras rolled, Oswald was being escorted through the police basement to an armored car that was to take him to a county jail. Ruby stepped out from the crowd and fired his .38 revolver, fatally wounding Oswald. Alan saw that moment, and remembers the emotions he felt vividly. "All of a sudden, I felt the world was falling apart. It was such a cloud over my college studies and so traumatic for me. I couldn't do homework."

In the coming days, America watched JFK's state funeral. On the Sunday after the assassination, his grieving family walked behind a flag-draped coffin as it was carried on a horse-drawn caisson to the U.S. Capitol to lie in state. Hundreds of thousands lined the streets to view the guarded casket. Representatives from more than ninety countries attended.

A brief but memorable collegiate basketball career

Weber College's assistant athletic director, Gary Compton, had been Alan's football coach in junior high. He knew Alan had been the captain of the basketball team at Ogden High, and mentioned the possibility of a scholarship if Alan played for Weber College.

Alan tried out and made the team. The freshman basketball coach, Don Spainhower, offered him a full scholarship for winter quarter, valued at $50. "I was thrilled to make the team and have my tuition included," he says.

Beginning in December, the freshman team started to practice and play a few games. For away games, the team traveled in an old, black hearse. "I don't know where the college found it, but we would travel to Snow College, or Utah State, or to BYU in this strange, long, black vehicle with no windows," Alan says. "We didn't think twice about it being a hearse."

When playing out-of-state teams, such as Montana State, Alan and his teammates traveled by plane. Alan's first time in the air was one of these trips, in a Douglas DC-3, a propeller-driven plane. On one memorable trip from Ogden to Montana with the varsity basketball team, Alan and his friend Barry Ball were continually throwing up as the plane flew north on a windy January day over the mountains. When the plane landed, two sick and very pale players didn't move from their seats. "Coach Dick Motta walked back to where we sat with multiple vomit bags on our laps. He looked at me, then Barry, and exclaimed, 'Barry, you are the first green African-American I have ever seen,'" Alan remembers.

While Alan was not a starter on the team, he played in games from time to time. "I was known as a shooter, and that was all I did. I could hardly wait to get the ball and launch it," Alan says. "On one occasion, we had an inner-squad game and I scored the most points, which was wonderful."

In one memorable game in Logan, Alan watched the second-leading basketball scorer in the nation, Wayne Estes. Utah State University's muscular six-foot-six-inch star forward impressed Alan. "He was a big, fleshy, solid kid. He didn't look like a basketball player," Alan remembers, "yet this guy was a scoring machine!" He held the school record for career points per game at 26.7.[10]

Later, when Alan was on his mission, Wayne Estes unknowingly came across a downed electric power line in the snow. It was a fatal mistake; he died of electrocution. "It was a huge tragedy in Logan," Alan says. Wayne Estes had been a local hero with such a bright future, expected to be drafted as a first pick to the L.A. Lakers.

The very last night the team played, in March 1964, they went to Provo to play the BYU freshman team in the George Albert Smith Field House. BYU's varsity played Arizona that night and the two freshmen teams were scheduled to play against each other before the main event. It was on the very floor where Alan learned to play basketball as a teenager in summer camps.

"That great BYU freshman team, which was undefeated and scored more than 100 points a game, beat us by 50 points that night in front of 10,000 fans," Alan recalls. "I still vividly remember stealing the ball from one of their All-American guards and racing toward our basket at the other end of the floor, only to meet a six-foot-eleven-inch BYU center, Craig Raymond. He swatted my shot high into the stands, to the delight of cheering fans."

At their home games, Alan's team was lucky to have fifty people watching, so it was quite a rush to play in front of such a large crowd. Despite that embarrassing moment and the crushing score, it was still a highlight for Alan to play in that historic venue.

Alan had a brief but memorable collegiate basketball career. Following his mission, he chose to pursue other interests and didn't play again on the school's team.

Preparing for a mission amidst times of turmoil

In March 1964, Alan started the rounds of interviews with church leaders to become an elder and submit mission papers. Alan received his call that spring and learned he would serve in the Central America Mission, which included Guatemala, El Salvador, Honduras, Nicaragua, Costa Rica, and Panama. Never having been outside the country or much beyond neighboring states, he wasn't conversant in world geography. "I thought, 'Am I going to Kansas? Is that Central America?'" The paperwork listed Alan's mission home in Guatemala City, Guatemala, a Spanish-speaking mission. He'd taken Spanish in junior high and high school, but was not fluent.

Alan's dad ordained him an elder in the Melchizedek priesthood and Alan prepared to receive special ordinances in the temple. There were no temple-preparation classes at the time. "My dad helped me understand the commitments I would be making to be more like Jesus Christ in my thoughts and actions," Alan says. "I remember the special day I visited the Salt Lake Temple to receive my endowments."

Serving a mission for two

"I wanted to serve a mission. And in a way, I wanted to do it for my brother Randy as well," Alan says. "I was going to work harder than the average guy because I was doing it for two."

Alan's missionary farewell was held on a Sunday night in June 1964, with family, friends, and many ward members in attendance. Alan selected a few special people in his life to speak, and he spoke as well. He remembers talking about Randy and the accident.

Alan and his mom purchased the required missionary suits and accessories for the Central American climate and geography. Alan would serve for twenty-seven months, with three of those months in Provo to learn Spanish. Previously, calls were for thirty months, since missionaries learned their mission language on the job, without the three-month language instruction missionaries receive in the modern Missionary Training Center.

He left in June, almost a year after the accident. Alan's parents drove him to Salt Lake City for a week in the Salt Lake Mission Home, which was then located north of the Salt Lake Temple. "I spent a week there with all these missionaries (not many sisters) who had come from all over the country," Alan says. "We slept in bunks, ate at a cafeteria, and had a full week of training. We were taught gospel lessons, attended the temple, and heard General Authorities speak. It was a very spiritual and happy environment."

At that time, missionaries were set apart by members of the Quorum of the Twelve Apostles. Alan was set apart as a full-time missionary by Elder Howard W. Hunter in the Church Office Building in Salt Lake City.

After a week in Salt Lake, Alan and other foreign-language missionaries were sent to Provo to live in BYU's Helaman Halls and learn their mission language. There were no students in the dorms that summer, only missionaries, and the program was called "the Language Training Mission."

They started in a business building on campus, receiving language lessons from returned missionaries. Then the missionaries switched to an older building south of campus, notably called "Allen Hall." This training went on for three months. "To advance, you had to have lessons memorized in the language. It was hard work. I don't think I've ever studied that hard in my life," Alan says. "I can remember memorizing line after line."

At night, a native Spanish speaker or a returned missionary evaluated and certified the language competency of new missionaries. Fortunately, Alan learned quickly. An apostle of the Lord had promised help with learning the language. "The blessing worked," Alan says. "I learned to be proficient in Spanish as I studied it from early morning to late at night, seven days a week."

He was learning with a cohort of missionaries that would go with him to Guatemala, several young men and a few young women. "We formed a tight-knit group. We helped each other daily and we were spiritually and emotionally united," Alan says.

During that ninety-day timeframe, Alan thought of home in his spare moments. More precisely, he thought of the girl he left at home. "I was suffering from our separation. I would write Diana little love letters often and send them to her," Alan recalls.

Alan had dental braces at the time and went home with special permission to have the braces removed. Diana came to see him and they shared a tender kiss in the parking lot. "Later during my mission, I learned that was the last time I would see my first love," Alan says.

When it came time to leave for Guatemala, Alan and the other missionaries were driven to the Salt Lake City International Airport, which then had a single terminal. Their families were there to see them off.

At the airport the day he left for Central America, Alan and a good friend, Paul Checketts, who also was going to Central America, sang "Ye Elders of Israel" with two other missionaries to their families and farewell-wishers. "We were so excited to have everyone there to support us. We were all weeping by the time we boarded the plane," Alan remembers. "It was a heart-pounding moment to kiss everybody goodbye and then embark on the greatest adventure a nineteen-year-old could ever have."

Many years later, Alan realized the great sacrifices his mother had made while he was away. "She worked in the cafeteria at Weber College," Alan remembers. "She went to work to earn a paycheck to pay for my $150-a-month mission expenses. I choke up now thinking about her undying willingness to bless her family, no matter the circumstances." In one year, she had lost a son, given birth to a new baby boy, and now was supporting her oldest son while he served his mission.

As the Western Airlines plane rose into the Utah sky, Alan wondered about the next two years of his life in a strange land far from his beloved home. He would soon find out.

CHAPTER

4

Missionary Service

Missionaries for The Church of Jesus Christ of Latter-day Saints dedicate themselves full-time to being witnesses of Christ, setting aside school and career as they serve in a church-assigned location. Nineteen-year-old Alan left behind dating, basketball, and even his own first name. In Central America, Alan was known as Elder Hall, except by some in his mission area, who affectionately called him "Corredorcito," meaning "little hall."

Never having been outside the United States, Alan quickly noticed significant changes between Ogden, Utah, and his new environment. The weather was hot and humid. Instead of a high desert landscape, Alan saw a lush green countryside. Instead of towering mountains, there were magnificent active volcanoes. The food was a Latino diet with ample beans and rice. Everyone spoke Spanish, which was hard to understand.

Even more intriguing were the people. Everywhere he looked, Elder Hall saw beautiful smiling people with brown skin, dark hair, and dark brown eyes. As a tall blond with blue eyes, Elder Hall stood out in the crowd.

Mission President Terrence Hansen greeted Elder Hall and a dozen other new missionaries at the Guatemala City airport and drove them to the mission home, where they slept their first night. After a hearty Guatemalan breakfast, Elder Hall was sent to his first area assignment in San Salvador ("Holy Savior"), capital of El Salvador.

Getting accustomed to missionary life

Elder Hall's first companion was Elder Knight, a young man from Huntsville. He had only three months left until the end of his mission and seemed to have lost motivation to work. For example, Elder Knight asked Elder Hall to give all the lessons to investigators. This quickly put pressure on Elder Hall to learn Spanish beyond the minimal phrases he'd learned in Provo.

After all that training, Alan was eager to get to work. They spent hours and hours knocking on doors, hoping to find people to teach lessons about Christ. "During those first few weeks, we'd have some lessons from time to time," Alan says. "Out of necessity, I really learned how to speak Spanish quickly." He and his companion woke up early and did not come home until late. Elder Hall felt exhausted every day.

Embarrassing moments popped up as he learned Spanish. For example, during one dinner Elder Hall asked the landlady if she had any milk: "¿Tiene usted leche?" Worded that way, he was literally asking, "¿Do you have breast milk?" Likely smiling, she corrected the red-faced missionary with the proper phrase: "Hay leche?" which means, "Is there milk?"

Living conditions in Central America

Elder Hall and his companion lived in a two-story apartment building similar to a hostel. Residents slept in their own rooms, which were all on the second floor. The first floor was a community gathering place with a living room where they ate. "Back then, my companion and I slept in the same bed," Alan says. "Through my whole mission, except for maybe a couple of times, I always slept with my companion in one bed."

Elder Hall wrote an inspirational thought on a large piece of butcher paper, which he taped on the wall to remind him: "*When the going gets tough, the tough get going.*"

Throughout Alan's mission, he never made a meal, washed his clothes, ironed his shirts, or even made his bed. For the most part, missionaries stayed with members of the Church and paid them for rent and other services, such as meal preparation and ironing their clothes. "Their help freed us to have more time to proselyte versus doing domestic chores," Alan says.

Elder Hall recognized the vast differences in the comforts he enjoyed in the United States compared to the people in San Salvador. The Salvadorean families lived simply, with homes measuring only a few hundred square feet. Most homes had dirt floors; cement if they were lucky. The homes were often made of adobe bricks and cement. Without reinforced iron supports, tenants were at high risk as houses often crumbled during earthquakes.

Earthquakes were common and frequent in San Salvador. The city was known as the Valley of the Hammocks because of the swaying nature of the tremors. "They weren't jagged quakes; they rolled back and forth," remembers Alan. "At dinner, I was used to holding my drinking glass so juice wouldn't spill out during earthquakes." One time, during a big earthquake, Elder Hall jumped out of a second-story window down to the street below, fearing he'd be crushed if the building came down.

He was right to be cautious. In May 1965, a few months after Elder Hall's time in El Salvador, a large earthquake in San Salvador killed 125 people, injured 500 more, and left an estimated 48,000 homeless.[1] Decades later, earthquakes are still the norm in the area. A check on earthquaketrack.com shows there were at least 120 earthquakes in El Salvador in 2018.

Elder Hall was exposed to hardships he'd never imagined in his Northern Utah hometown. He was alarmed and frightened by what he saw: unimaginable poverty so severe, people were dying of malnutrition. He saw prostitutes on the street for the first time. He saw gangsters and violent crime. Some parts of his mission are still known as centers for murder.[2]

Besides getting adjusted to regular earthquakes and corruption, Elder Hall adapted to a new diet. "We ate different food, like cow tongue. It was strange for me," Alan remembers. He lost weight on his mission. His basic diet in Central America consisted of *plátanos,* a type of boiled banana, with rice and black beans. Occasionally, he ate beef and chicken.

Teaching the gospel of Jesus Christ

As he prepared for each day, Elder Hall packed his Spanish scriptures, a projector, and a little flannel presentation board with small felt figurines of Jesus, Joseph Smith, and other leaders of the Restoration. When they found a willing listener and an electrical outlet, they beamed pictures against a wall. "We showed a filmstrip, which included music by the Mormon Tabernacle Choir. As we sat there, the room just filled with the Spirit," Alan says. "It touched people's hearts and mine."

Elder Hall particularly remembers teaching a short, stout man named David. "He was an alcoholic, but he knew the gospel was true and wanted to get past his drinking," Alan remembers. "The next time we visited him, David said, 'I've had a dream, and I saw the Savior. I saw him in a white robe with a red sash.'" That was answer enough for David. He stopped drinking and was baptized.

A new chapel was being built in San Salvador in the center of town. From time to time, missionaries helped with construction. Once a week they collected letters from home at the main post office. "As often as possible we bought éclairs from a German pastry shop," Alan remembers. "Our parents sent money to us for expenditures. We'd pick up our monthly living allowances from a nearby bank. I learned to take care of myself, get around town, and manage my finances. I started to feel good about my independence in a foreign country. I was getting the hang of it!"

It helped that Alan's grasp of the language was improving each day. Before the chapel was completed, he gave his first church talk in an old home with a big living room. "Talk about stressful, trying to give a talk in Spanish! After a lot of prayer and fasting, I was able to do it," Alan says.

After three months on his mission as a junior companion, Elder Hall received a surprising call from his mission president. He informed Alan that he would train a new young missionary from Idaho.

Assuming this responsibility after only three months was unprecedented in his mission.

A pivotal decision moment

In addition to stress about his new responsibilities, Elder Hall worried about his girlfriend back home. Things weren't going well with their relationship. "Diana's letters were getting few and far between and they weren't as loving as before," Alan recalls. He had written her faithfully every week of his mission. The mail service had a two-week delay between countries, so everything he read from her was a couple of weeks behind. He also received regular letters from his mom, who sometimes mentioned Diana.

"I was far, far away, and it drove me crazy I couldn't see her," Alan says. "Plus, I just didn't know if I could do this new assignment worrying about how she felt about me. I didn't want Diana to forget me or leave me." One night, he found a private place to pour out his heart to God for help and ask if he should stay or go home.

Most missionaries experience crossroads moments, and this was a big one for Elder Hall. He pondered going home or staying. In the end, he decided to trust in the Lord. He prayed for help to overcome things beyond his control. "Thankfully, the Lord blessed me with peace and a desire to continue as planned. I felt assurance that no matter what might happen with Diana, my life would be a happy one," he says.

Focusing on missionary work helped the most. With his new companion, Elder Hall forgot about his own worries and went to work meeting, teaching, and baptizing people.

First Christmas on the mission

Alan and his companion went to a member's home for a Christmas Eve dinner. "That first Christmas on my mission, far away from my dear family, was painful," Alan says. "My companion and I were both new to the country and missing home. But a great meal and being around a wonderful loving family helped us overcome our holiday blues."

Another three months passed and Elder Hall heard again from the mission office. He was being transferred. "It was a bit traumatic for me to leave again, after having established relationships with my companion, the members, and the community, as well as getting familiar with the area," Alan recalls. He was sent to Mazatenango, a city about three hours southwest of Guatemala City.

Mazatenango, Guatemala

Elder Hall's new companion in Mazatenango, like his first senior companion, didn't want to be on a mission—or even leave their apartment. Mazatenango's sweltering heat didn't help. "A shower did us no good because ten minutes later, we were wet with sweat again," Alan says. "We were always sticky, hot, and tired."

While in Mazatenango, Elder Hall met a family that was the cornerstone and strength of the local church community. The father was the branch president, or leader of the congregation. He helped the missionaries with proselyting by introducing them to possible investigators.

Proselyting came with surprises for young Elder Hall. For example, Guatemalan women breastfed without covering up. When Elder Hall gave a lesson and a baby needed nursing, bare breasts did their motherly job. It was quite a shock for the chaste nineteen-year-old to see. "The women weren't embarrassed at all. It was just how they did things," Alan says. "I eventually realized I needed to adjust to their culture and not worry about it."

Missionaries had free time only once a week, a day known as "P-day," or preparation day. One P-day, a missionary in Elder Hall's zone rallied the other elders to take a three-hour train ride to the Pacific Ocean. "We played football on the beach, which was fine, but it was against the rules to swim," Alan explains. "Some of the elders threw the ball way out into the waves and swam out to get it." Elder Hall, however, stayed on the beach.

A dozen or so rebellious missionaries formed "The Santa Ana Jeep and Surf Society," dubbed for their surfing and Jeep-riding adventures. How did the mission president not know about their insubordination? "You have to remember, our mission covered six countries from Guatemala to the bottom of Panama, distance-wise more miles than from New York to Los Angeles," Alan says. Email and cell phones did not exist at the time, so the mission president did what he could to keep problematic missionaries nearby. "There were a few elders who were doing inappropriate things and were sent home."

It's not that missionaries were banned from having fun—they were just expected to adhere to mission rules. For example, President Hansen permitted missionaries to see movies. Elder Hall saw "The Sound of Music" in Guatemala City. "I loved Julie Andrews and her beautiful voice," Alan says. "After that, everywhere we went, we were singing."

James Bond also was a missionary favorite. "Thunderball," the fourth in the James Bond series starring Sean Connery, came out in 1965. "After seeing the movie, we bought suits that looked like Bond's clothing—not a good idea. Due to the humid weather, we never wore the jackets," Alan says.

Every so often, missionaries heard new popular American music over local radios. The top billboard song "Downtown," by a young British singer named Petula Clark, became a favorite song for Alan. The Beatles were still big, and the missionaries sometimes heard them singing as they passed by homes where people were listening to the radio.

"For the most part, we were very isolated; we didn't know what was going on in the world," Alan says. "We didn't watch the news on TV or read the newspapers. Our lives were centered on fulfilling our assignments of preaching the gospel of Jesus Christ to the people of Guatemala."

Writing and receiving letters, including a "Dear John"

While serving in Mazatenango in March 1965, nine months after leaving on his mission, Elder Hall received a dreaded "Dear John" letter from Diana back home. "She was engaged to another fellow," Alan says. "I wept. I was devastated by the news and depressed. It was another personal loss of someone I loved."

Joyce Hall, knowing her missionary son would be heartbroken, reached out to the mission president's wife to make her aware of the situation. In response, when Elder Hall came to the mission home regarding a transfer to a new area, Sister Hansen took Alan aside and offered him motherly encouragement about moving on.

Elder Hall faithfully wrote his mom once a week. Joyce kept each letter and compiled a list of all the converts her son baptized, which totaled eighty people. The best records of his mission are those letters.

Another hard letter to receive on his mission was news that his Grandmother Hall had passed away in May 1966. Not being able to say goodbye was hard. He missed being there to mourn with his family or talk about his memories of her.

The work continues

The only true cure for a broken heart is work, and Elder Hall put his might, mind, and strength into it. In one neighborhood where they were walking, Elder Hall and his companion found a family of eight that made mattresses for a living, using coils and fabric. "We've been waiting for you," the father told the missionaries when he opened the door. "I saw you coming in a dream. I know exactly who you are. I've seen your faces. I know why you're here and we welcome you." The elders taught the family the gospel lessons and they joined the Church.

Another time, a man said to Elder Hall, "I had a dream last night and I saw a gentleman, an older man. I don't know who he is and I don't know why I had this dream." When Elder Hall opened his flip chart with the pictures of church leaders, the investigator stopped him at the picture of David O. McKay, the prophet at the time. He said, "That's the fellow I saw in my dream!"

In these experiences, Elder Hall learned the Lord communicates with some of his children through dreams and visions. When they are illiterate, God blesses them with other kinds of spiritual manifestations.

Day after day, Elder Hall's love for the sweet and kindhearted people of Guatemala grew. "I learned we were indeed true brothers and sisters, children of God, all part of a grand family," Alan says. "I had tender feelings and an affection for these dear people and wept when I was transferred to another city."

In one month, Alan baptized twenty people; he was the top-baptizing missionary for that month. "We were fasting, working long hours, and never came home until late at night," Alan says. Pushing himself so hard on spiritual work took a physical toll on Elder Hall. One night, he fainted.

President Hansen put Elder Hall in a private hospital in Guatemala City to get treatment for his medical condition. He was diagnosed with Hepatitis A and jaundice, which had turned his skin a yellowish hue. The mission president came to visit and said, "When you return to missionary work, you can't work that hard again. Try not to push yourself beyond your limits. Remember to pace yourself. There is no rush."

After two weeks in the hospital, Elder Hall was still not well when he was discharged. The mission president invited him to stay at the mission home to recuperate. "I was very weak, tired, and listless. I had lost a lot of weight," Alan says.

While living in the mission home, Elder Hall learned that President Hansen knew his uncle, Dr. Tracy Hall, since they were both BYU professors. "It dawned on me that because of their friendly academic ties in Provo, President and Sister Hansen had more than a special interest in my welfare," Alan says. "In many loving ways, I was more than a missionary to them. I was a favored family friend."

Quetzaltenango

When he had recovered sufficiently, Elder Hall was sent to a city called Quetzaltenango, northwest of Guatemala City. It's also known by its Mayan name, Xelajú or Xela (pronounced "sheh-lah"), and is the second largest city in Guatemala, situated near several volcanoes in the Sierra Madres. Days are warm and nights are cool in this high mountain valley. "Some people believe it's where the waters of Mormon were located," Alan says, referring to a scene in *The Book of Mormon* where believers were baptized.

Around Quetzaltenango were villages of indigenous Kaqchikel and K'iche people, who still wore traditional Indian apparel and brought their products into town to sell: dresses, materials, and produce. Elder Hall didn't teach them, as other missionaries were assigned to speak their native languages.

"I met this beautiful girl in Quetzaltenango," Alan says. "She was an Indian girl about eighteen years of age, and her name was Marta Sac

Estacui. I couldn't believe how pretty she was." When he taught her the gospel lesson, Elder Hall learned Marta had had lovers. "That was maybe one of the worst moments of my mission—to see this beautiful girl, who had such a good heart, living a wicked life," Alan remembers. "It became an Atonement moment for me. I realized she could truly repent of those sins and move forward, clean and pure." He later baptized Marta.

District leader and assistant to the mission president

At the one-year mark of his mission, Elder Hall served as the district leader, with responsibilities to oversee six sets of missionaries. He was also training a new companion from California. "He'd been a wild kid back home but had repented. His girlfriend sent him a 'Dear John' only six weeks into his mission, and he told me he was leaving," Alan says. "There was nothing I could say to convince him to stay. He went home."

Elder Hall had another learning moment with his next companion. One cold night, Elder Hall was shivering in his own bed. In the middle of the night, he felt his companion put a large woolen blanket on him. "I still remember that special moment," Alan says. "He had to be as cold as I was, and yet he gave up his only blanket so I would be warm. I will never forget the feeling of gratitude I had for him and the lesson of love he taught me."

Also in Quetzaltenango, Elder Hall made an important decision. They were living in the house of a woman who brought a variety of lovers into her home. "I didn't know if she was a prostitute, but I knew what she was doing was wrong," Alan says. He approached her and said they couldn't live under her roof any longer. She refused to change, so Alan and his companion moved to another apartment.

Aside from needing to find a new home, things were going well for Elder Hall and his companion. After a missionary conference, President Hansen took Elder Hall aside and said, "You're coming back to Guatemala City to be my assistant in the newly formed Guatemala-El Salvador Mission." Surprised and excited for the new assignment, Elder Hall packed his bags for the biggest transfer of his mission.

Tracting days behind him, Elder Hall spent the rest of his mission in leadership roles. He traveled with his mission president to every branch conference and district conference in Guatemala and El Salvador.

Elder Hall taught local members how to run a church congregation. Although he was young, he knew enough to help locals lead fledgling branches. "That was a singular moment, because the president had enough trust in me to have me speak in church, train a branch president, and set people apart," Alan says. "It was especially fun for me to fly, drive, and go places with the mission president. I learned better Spanish from him; he was a Spanish professor, after all." Elder Hall wrote a weekly letter—in Spanish—to branch presidents about the principles of church leadership. He also assisted in leading missionary zone conferences.

Elder Hall lived with the mission president's family and formed close relationships with them. The Hansens had two beautiful daughters in elementary school, Christine and Angela. The girls reminded Elder Hall of his own sisters at home. Their two sons became friends with Elder Hall, too. The oldest son, Terry, was about eighteen years old and preparing to go on a mission himself. The younger son, Michael, was fifteen. "I'd take him with me when I drove a van to run errands. Missionaries did not have cars; you were either on foot, on a bus, or riding a bike. I'd let him drive from time to time, a favor that thrilled him," Alan says.

On one occasion, they visited an Indian village called Patzicía, the place of the very first baptism in Guatemala. Elder Hall was sitting next to the mission president on the stand, ready to start a branch conference, when President Hansen nudged him and said, "Look at that older fellow sitting on the front row."

There sat Daniel Mich, wearing indigenous clothing and sandals of leather with bottoms made from tires. This weathered man, with gnarly feet and wrinkles, was the first member of the Church in Guatemala. President Hansen shared Daniel's story with Alan.[3]

Nearly a century earlier, an apostle named Orson Hyde had gone to the Holy Land, where he climbed the Mount of Olives and dedicated the land to missionary work. In his blessing, he asked the Lord to inspire the "kings and the powers of the earth" to help "restore the kingdom unto Israel."[4] If they did, he prayed the Lord would bless their countries with the restored gospel of Jesus Christ. In May 1948, the United Nations voted to recognize the State of Israel, and Guatemala voted in favor of it.

Missionaries from Mexico soon entered Guatemala. They struggled getting anyone to listen, until they met Daniel Mich. He was working in his field and decided to hear what they had to share. He had a spiritual experience so vibrant it prompted him to action. He was baptized in 1948, and became the very first convert in the country. After the local community learned of his church membership, he was ostracized and threatened by bullies who sought to injure or kill him. Warned by the Spirit of the Lord on numerous occasions of impending danger, Brother Mich was protected from harm throughout the rest of his life.

Looking at the weathered face on the first row, Elder Hall thought, "Here's one of the more faithful people in the world sitting right in front of me. He's a true Saint and disciple of Christ. I am sure he qualifies for the Celestial Kingdom." It was thanks to Brother Mich and other early LDS pioneers that the Church is in Guatemala. The Central American Mission, headquartered in Guatemala City, was organized in 1952, and the Church gained recognition in Guatemala in 1966.[5] As of May 2019, the country has forty-nine stakes, six missions, and two temples.

Although time seemed to pass slowly in his first year, the second year of Elder Hall's mission sped by. "When the day came for me to go home, I didn't want it to be over," Alan says. "Those two years changed me forever. My life had direction, a foundation of strength, and a clear purpose. I learned the restored gospel was true, powerful, and could be a blessing to all; that God lives and Jesus is my Savior and Redeemer. I experienced what it's like to love others: the people, my companions, and God."

Before he left, he visited a tourist marketplace to buy mementos to help him remember the mission. He bid farewell to the Hansens, whom he loved with all his heart, and boarded the plane for home. "They had become my second family," Alan says.

Honoring the Hansen family

In the summer of 1966, President Hansen completed his time as mission president in Central America and returned home to serve as the president of the Language Training Mission in Provo. In 1974, at the young age of fifty-three, he passed away unexpectedly following surgery. Alan was shocked to hear the news and attended his funeral with other returned missionaries. Twenty years later, his wife Glenna Hansen passed away from cancer. "I cherished my relationship with these two wonderful people," Alan says. "They were like family to me. I loved them deeply."

In the Hansens' honor, Alan and Jeannie set up a scholarship at BYU for Central American students who need financial assistance.

Lifelong love for Guatemalans

Alan and Jeannie have given back to the people of Guatemala by helping to fund a micro-loan program in Guatemala City and El Salvador called Mentors International (MI). Guatemalans can borrow money from MI to start or grow a successful business. A loan might be to buy a bicycle for a delivery business or a sewing machine for a seamstress. The Hall Foundation helps fund Weber State University's certified sales training programs in Guatemala, El Salvador, Nicaragua, and Peru. The sales training courses dramatically help the students find excellent employment opportunities with local businesses. The goal is to provide them with the skills to make them self-reliant and prosperous.

Forty years after his mission, Alan returned with Jeannie to visit Guatemala again. "We flew to Guatemala City and saw it had changed in so many ways," he says.

The Halls asked a local church leader to be their driver so they wouldn't look like wealthy tourists. "I was concerned for our safety," Alan says. "We traveled to Lake Atitlan and visited the historic city of Antigua. We took photos of the open-air Indian market in Chichicastenango and enjoyed a meal of rice and black beans. We enjoyed speaking Spanish to the people we met along the way."

They also visited places of spiritual significance. The Halls attended the beautiful Guatemala City Temple, dedicated in 1984. They looked for the mission home where Alan had spent many months, but were disappointed to learn it was gone.

"The people I knew couldn't be found. They had moved or had passed away. All those special things I so desperately wanted to see were gone," Alan says. "Time marches on. Things change. We can never go back to what once was. Thankfully, I have splendid memories of my missionary service; I will never forget the wonderful people and the powerful experiences. It is a time in my life I will cherish forever."

Four key lessons from Alan's mission

As a stake president, Alan has taught departing missionaries four key principles:

1) Love your companions and make sure to serve them.
2) Love the people. Let your heart be full of affection for them.
3) Love the Lord. Know He's there and keep His commandments.
4) Be obedient to the mission rules.

Then he says, "Remember these four points. When you come back and I release you from your missionary calling, I will ask you to tell me if you accomplished these goals."

When missionaries return home to resume their lives, Alan tells them, "I trust you will always remember, recognize, and be forever grateful you had the unique opportunity to serve God and His children for two years. Also keep in mind that your sacrifices and those of your parents will bring you and your family the greatest blessings God has for those who love Him."

Returning to life back home

When Elder Hall arrived back in Salt Lake City, he transitioned back to being "Alan"—but a new and improved version. "My family noticed I was different," Alan says. "I was more knowledgeable, experienced, wiser, self-reliant, and independent; not the immature teenager of the past."

While he was away, Alan's family had moved to South Ogden from the home he knew as a boy. He remembers lying in bed his first morning home, looking up to see a young child staring at him.

"It was little Nathan, now three years of age," Alan remembers. "He had no clue who I was, and asked our mom, 'Who is he and when will he be leaving?'"

As he prepared to start classes at Weber State, Alan signed up for an archeology class. In Guatemala, he'd enjoyed digging up long-lost artifacts (some of which he still owns), and thought he might want to become an archaeologist. "That lasted one class," Alan says. "I couldn't see archaeology providing an income to support a family."

He took a class from Dr. Stratford, a psychology professor, who told returned missionaries they were all self-centered and arrogant. "We, of course, thought we knew everything, and he wanted to make sure that attitude was corrected," Alan says. Eventually, Alan chose to major in psychology, the study of the human mind and behavior.

There were some adjustments to living back in his parents' house. One night he came home at two in the morning and found his mother sitting in a chair in the living room. "She said if I was going to stay in her house, I had to live by her rules," Alan says.

Whether rebellious or just absentminded, Alan came home late one night past his mother's curfew. Her response? She'd placed all his earthly belongings on the front porch. In the dark of the wee morning hours, Alan was stunned to be kicked out of the house. He gathered up his clothes, books, and other personal items and drove to his step-grandmother's house, where he sheepishly knocked on the door and asked to stay.

A couple of days later, Alan's dad came to get him. He invited Alan to come home and live by his mom's rules, which were meant to keep him safe. "Thankfully for both my mom and me, I agreed to obey her wise rules and be home before midnight," Alan says.

Back in the dating scene

It had been more than two years since Alan had been on a date. Coming home as an eligible returned missionary meant pretty girls were no longer off-limits. A young woman named Cheryl attended Alan's missionary homecoming. He'd never met her before, but Gene and Joyce Hall knew her parents from their days as students at the University of Utah. She caught Alan's eye. "Cheryl was about nineteen years old and gorgeous! She was the first girl I took out after my mission," Alan says.

They started dating, and Alan regularly made the almost hour-long drive to her home in Salt Lake City, near Skyline High School. They became good friends quickly, and in short order, she expressed a desire to be his wife. "For my part, there was no way I was ready for that commitment," Alan says. In the meantime, he started taking other girls on dates.

Charismatic and confident, Alan courted girls he knew from high school or new girls he met at Weber State. "I started to date everybody as fast as I could," Alan says. "Unfortunately, as Jeannie will tell you, I picked up a reputation for being a 'Cookie Monster.'" That was a term for someone who kissed without commitment.

He met a beautiful girl named MaryAnn, a neighbor of his Hall relatives in Provo, Utah. She was a tall, cute, vivacious blonde who was a sophomore at Brigham Young University. "We started dating and I began driving to Provo on a weekly basis, while at the same time I was driving to Salt Lake regularly to see Cheryl," Alan says with a smile. Soon enough, Cheryl found out. So did MaryAnn.

Despite his affection for Cheryl, Alan broke up with her. "I knew she wasn't the girl for me and decided to end the relationship as gently as I could," Alan says. He met with Cheryl's parents and talked to them about his decision to move on.

"They had hoped I would be their son-in-law and part of their wonderful family. When he talked with Cheryl, she burst into tears and was inconsolable," Alan says. "My decision had broken her tender heart."

As he got more serious with MaryAnn, Alan made the trip many times from Ogden to Provo to see her. "I loved her. I believe she loved me, but I knew she was waiting for a boyfriend who was on a mission," Alan says. They dated during Alan's sophomore and junior years of college and became inseparable. He drove to Provo weekly to see her, always with a plan to enjoy fun activities together. On the weekend, he stayed at Tracy and Ida-Rose Hall's home as their guest. The Halls lived next door to MaryAnn's parents and knew them well.

Alan hoped to marry her. He deeply loved the tall beauty and her family, and it seemed her parents approved of him. In February 1968, Alan carefully broached the idea of marriage. To his disappointment,

MaryAnn told him she had other plans. He left Provo that day brokenhearted, suffering yet another personal loss.

In time, Alan started dating again, looking for an eternal companion among the wonderful young women at Weber State and Utah State University. For a few weeks he dated Linda, a lovely cheerleader from Utah State University. They went horseback riding and boating together and always had a great time. "I really liked her and looked forward to being her friend," Alan says. "I also periodically dated Andrea, a beautiful young woman every boy at Weber State wanted to marry. I took her to see the Miss Weber State pageant in April 1968, and I saw for the first time the girl I would marry a year later. Her name was Jeannie Nowak."

5

Meeting and Marrying the Love of His Life

Alan registered for a summer psychology class at Weber State in 1968, as did Miss Jeannie Nowak. Jeannie was involved in the music department, and Alan hadn't crossed paths with her in any previous classes. Along with hundreds of other admirers, Alan had seen Jeannie from afar when she competed for Miss Weber State, a local competition for the Miss America scholarship pageant. He had taken a date to the program, where they watched Jeannie win the crown. "I knew she was the campus queen, but we had never met," Alan remembers.

Jeannie had graduated from Skyline High School in Salt Lake City in 1966, and that summer her parents moved to Ogden. Wishing to continue her education and meet new people, she began attending Weber State as a seventeen-year-old freshman. The Weber State campus was literally on the other side of the family's backyard gate, making for a convenient commute to class.

Her parents wanted her to attend a college out of state and avoid the influence of members of The Church of Jesus Christ of Latter-day Saints. They were devout Presbyterians and had a low regard for LDS doctrines and practices. Jeannie's summer was happily occupied with singing performances and a role in a college musical. When she was offered a full tuition scholarship, she decided to be a Weber State Wildcat. Her parents accepted her decision, noting that Weber State was far less expensive than the private school she had planned to attend out of state.

Luckily for Alan, she stayed. In the summer of 1968, he sat right next to beautiful Jeannie in that psychology class. "She asked about my girlfriend, and told me she was engaged. She had a diamond ring," says Alan.

As the summer continued, Alan was smitten by Jeannie's personality and enjoyed their conversations, but figured she was off the market to date. "I was certainly interested in her, but I could not see any future relationship beyond just being friends," he says.

First date gone wrong, then right

Alan and Jeannie were nothing more than classmates that summer. They both began their senior year in the fall of 1968, and had another psychology class together. Alan was still dating lots of girls. Jeannie returned the engagement ring that summer because she was attracted to a certain someone in her psychology class. (Alan didn't find out *he* was the reason until later.)

Every year at Weber State, the student association sponsors Homecoming events. One day, the vice president of the men's association, a mutual friend, encouraged Alan and Jeannie to attend an outdoor Homecoming activity that afternoon. They agreed to meet after their last class. Unfortunately, the school cancelled the event when a fall thunderstorm suddenly drenched the campus, disappointing them both.

That evening, the phone rang at Alan's house. He remembers the date—October 16, 1968—because it was Nathan's and Karen's birthdays, and they were all celebrating. A family member picked up the phone and handed it to Alan.

"Hello," he greeted the caller.

"Hello, this is Gertrude Hickenlooper from the complaint department at Weber State University," said a woman in a high-pitched, funny voice. "I am filing a complaint against one Alan Hall, who stood up one Jeannie Nowak at the Homecoming event today."

Alan protested, "No, I didn't! It was cancelled because of the rain!"

The voice on the other end of the line began laughing, and Alan was relieved to hear it was Jeannie.

"I'm just teasing," she said good-naturedly.

Delighted with another opportunity to spend time with this captivating girl, Alan suggested they study together that night for a psychology test the following morning. Once the family party ended, Alan rushed to Jeannie's house, and they drove to the college library.

They found a quiet spot, but Jeannie wasn't interested in studying.

"All she did was playfully stare at me," Alan says. "It was great fun being close to this heavenly beauty, but I really needed to study!"

When the library closed around 9:30 p.m., Jeannie asked Alan if he would like to take her home to eat some delicious cookies she had baked. Alan quickly agreed. "For the most part, I was just being polite," Alan says. "I was in awe of her. She was drop-dead gorgeous, and she intimidated me. I'd never been around a young woman quite so dazzling."

They arrived at her house, where Alan met Jeannie's mom and dad, Henry and Betty Nowak. Alan didn't know it yet, but Henry was raised in a Polish-Catholic family. Betty grew up Protestant. Together, they'd converted to Presbyterianism, and raised Jeannie and her sisters to believe Presbyterian tenets. The Nowaks were dedicated leaders in their local Ogden Presbyterian congregation, where members were wary of those belonging to The Church of Jesus Christ of Latter-day Saints. Her parents had read literature against the Church and didn't believe its members were Christians.

The Nowaks were both educated professionals. By day, Jeannie's mother worked as an elementary principal; she later researched education concepts, earned a doctorate in education, and served as a Weber School District administrator. Jeannie's father, Henry, was literally a rocket scientist who worked at Hercules. He was just shy of a PhD in chemical engineering.

These were smart parents, but all Alan knew at the time was that he felt butterflies around their oldest daughter. They made their way into the kitchen, and she got out the cookies.

"I saw she'd used one of those Pillsbury pre-made batches, where you break and bake them," Alan remembers. Wanting to make sure her hair and makeup were just right, she hadn't had time to make them from scratch.

As the pair sat at the kitchen table with sweet bites and sweet talk, their conversation turned to religious beliefs. As he gazed into Jeannie's bright blue eyes, he learned she taught Sunday School in her Presbyterian church. Similarly, Alan taught the teenagers in his ward. Her smile widened when he said religion should be more than just a Sunday activity, but an everyday way of life.

"I could tell that idea pleased her, and I had this overwhelming feeling of love come over me for her. It was apparent she felt the same way for me. I'd never fallen in love with someone who fell in love with me at the same moment," Alan says.

He reached over and gave Jeannie a little kiss. He gently told her he had wonderful feelings for her. "She had the same feelings for me," Alan recalls warmly. "And I went home that night knowing I was going to marry that Presbyterian. How was I going to tell my mother?"

Well, Alan did tell his mother. Being a big tease, he told her a crazy story about the woman who had won his heart. He'd seen Jeannie recently perform in the college production of *The Threepenny Opera,* a dark, melodramatic musical that features the world of crime and corruption in a large city. Jeannie had played the madam of a house of ill repute, where she managed the affairs of prostitutes who worked for her. With this in mind, he told his mother he had fallen deeply in love with a prostitute.

"She knew I had a sense of humor and forgave me, but couldn't wait to meet this interesting young woman who was a member of a different faith," Alan says.

Jeannie's journey of faith

After that first kiss, Alan and Jeannie went to the Homecoming football game on Saturday afternoon. Jeannie was so excited to go, and bought a beautiful new winter coat to impress Alan. "After that date, we were inseparable, together night and day," Alan says.

Throughout that fall semester, Jeannie felt a strong desire to learn more about The Church of Jesus Christ of Latter-day Saints, not because of her love for Alan but for her own sake. "When you know Jeannie well, you know that when she has something she's going to do, nothing gets in her way. There are no barriers," says Alan.

A central truth in the Church's theology is the idea that families can be together forever, even beyond death. Rather than "until death do us part," Church members believe marriage can be for eternity. For a marriage to be "sealed" in a temple ceremony, both husband and wife must be worthy (as determined by a church leader) to enter the temple. Because Alan had set his sights on being married in the House of the Lord, dating someone of another faith hadn't been an option for him in the past. Jeannie was his one exception.

Without telling Alan, Jeannie contacted missionaries in her area to start the lessons. "When I found out she was doing that, I backed away a little bit because I wanted her to find out for herself and not be swayed by me," Alan says. The stake mission president, Ron Wright, taught Jeannie. After going through several lessons, Jeannie understood intellectually about Church doctrine and principles, but hadn't yet had a personal spiritual confirmation. President Wright told her, "You know in your heart this is true, but you try intellectually to disprove it."

After two lessons, he told Jeannie that when she really wanted to know, she could come back. He was aware that the year before, Jeannie had played the lead role in Weber State's production of *Finian's Rainbow*. He also knew Petula Clark had just starred in the movie and that it was premiering in Salt Lake City. President Wright invited Alan and Jeannie to go to lunch the next day at Hotel Utah (now the Joseph Smith Memorial Building) and then see the movie with him and his wife, Sharon. Jeannie cleared it with Alan and the four of them went to lunch and the show.

At lunch, President Wright asked Jeannie to sing "The Lord's Prayer" in a student ward Sacrament meeting the following day. Having participated in high school and college singing groups, Jeannie had attended and performed at numerous LDS meetings. This was her first time attending with Alan and not in a family ward. Protestant worship services had always been reverent and quiet, because little children were sent off to Sunday School. This was the first Sacrament meeting she had attended without little ones in the congregation, and because of this, it was totally quiet and reverent. Immediately after the Sacrament, Jeannie sang. The Spirit was very strong.

As Jeannie sang, Alan saw a glow of light around her. "When she finished the solo she came back and sat by me, and I asked if she was all right," Alan says.

She whispered to him, "As I sang the words 'Thy will be done,' the Spirit of God witnessed to me that this is His true and living Church." Then she said something that forever changed their lives: "I know the gospel is true and I want to be baptized."

This personal revelation and desire to be baptized created a deep wedge between Jeannie and her parents. She'd always been close with them and her sisters. Now, in her parents' minds, she was rebelling in the biggest way. It was embarrassing and painful for them to have one of their children "lured" into the popular faith of the area. "Jeannie was about as obedient to her parents as a person could be, and well known in her Presbyterian congregation," Alan says. "Her conversion was a blow to her parents and to the local Presbyterian community." Her father asked her to wait six months. She respectfully replied that she had received a witness of the Spirit and could not put it off.

Alan baptized Jeannie a member of The Church of Jesus Christ of Latter-day Saints on Thanksgiving morning, 1968. Her twentieth birthday was one week after her baptism. When she awoke that morning, under her bedroom door was an envelope with a note from her mother saying her daughter was dead. There also was a baptismal certificate enclosed from the Protestant church her family attended when she was five years old in Texas.

It was a very dark and painful time for the Nowaks, Jeannie, and Alan. Her parents were terribly hurt and unhappy about Jeannie's decision. They were sure she was joining the Church because of Alan. They clearly saw he was a wonderful young man, but didn't think anyone should lure their daughter from the faith of her birth. In truth, she had not chosen to be a member because of Alan, but because of the powerful witness of the Holy Ghost.

Two days after her baptism, her parents invited their Presbyterian minister to the house to persuade her to steer clear of the LDS Church. Although her parents didn't kick Jeannie out of the house, they severely restricted her. "All their communication after that was not in person or verbal, but via notes under her bedroom door," Alan says. Despite the hurt, Jeannie felt peace and deep compassion for her parents. She knew she had chosen to honor her Heavenly Father and the testimony she had received of the Holy Ghost.

They forbade Jeannie from talking to her younger sisters, Michelle and Patti, who were about fifteen and eleven at the time. The Nowaks thought they were too impressionable and could be influenced by their wayward older sister. They were both baptized years later, although Patti left the Church after a few months.

For the rest of Henry and Betty's lives, Jeannie did her best to honor her parents, love them, and go out of her way to be kind to them. Over time, her goodness softened their hearts, but they never embraced their daughter's faith.

Relationship stress for the young couple

The disapproval from her family put a strain on Alan and Jeannie. They were serious about each other, but not yet engaged, and still living under their parents' rules. "We had more stress than I think a lot of couples have. Normally, you just hope things work out so your in-laws, your parents, and everybody is happy for you and your fiancée," says Alan.

This was a very challenging time for Alan. The parents of the girls he had previously dated admired him greatly. The Nowaks acknowledged he was an amazing young man but were furious that he had seemingly taken their daughter away from them. "Thankfully, my parents embraced Jeannie and we were always welcomed at my home," Alan says. "My mother taught Jeannie how to prepare delicious meals and my dad showed her the attributes of Godly love."

Jeannie later returned this kindness to Alan's dad by serving as his daily caretaker until he was 98. Gene lived with Jeannie and Alan for thirteen and a half years; during that time, Jeannie tended to his every need and saw that he was showered, properly dressed, and well fed. She cared for him as though he were her own father. Gene turned 98 on December 31, 2018.

"Jeannie's a spiritual giant," Alan says. "She prays with my dad, sings with him in the morning, and makes certain he is treated kindly and all his needs are met. If there's anyone I know who gives Christlike service, it's my wife."

Alan's first (and last) singles trip to Hawaii

Soon after Jeannie's baptism, in December 1968, Alan went to Hawaii for a week with a college-sponsored student tour. He'd saved money to go with his friends and other Weber State students and faculty. He wished Jeannie could come, but she had commitments with the music department during December. "We didn't want to be apart, but I was pretty excited to go," Alan says.

The weeklong trip was organized by Fishburn Travel and was very inexpensive for cash-strapped students. For example, when they arrived in Kauai, the group slept on the gym floor of an LDS chapel to save on hotel costs.

The students didn't care where they slept. They were in Hawaii! "All the scenery was magnificent. It was so green and the water so clear," Alan remembers.

Although he wasn't engaged yet, Alan seemed to know it was his last hurrah as a single man, and he lived it up. The group toured the beaches from the film *South Pacific*. They took a river tour through the mountains where Elvis Presley filmed *Paradise, Hawaiian Style* a couple of years earlier. When they went to the island of Oahu, he rented a 1968 convertible Mustang for sightseeing. He loved the feeling of the wind whipping through his hair as he drove to the Polynesian Cultural Center.

Alan returned home in time for the holidays, where a waiting young woman hoped he'd give her something special.

Finally, an engagement ring

All Jeannie wanted that Christmas was an engagement ring. She really thought that's what Alan was getting her and had good reason to think so—they had gone ring shopping and he told her she was going to receive something for Christmas in gold and crystal.

When she opened a package from him with perfume in a beautiful glass bottle with a gold lid, she smiled and tried to be grateful.

"I did tell her the time would come for our engagement, but it needed to be on my terms," Alan says with a smile. Alan teases Jeannie that it was the first and last time he ever had any say in their marriage.

He did give her clues. He said it would be at twelve o'clock, but did not say whether that meant noon or midnight. He also said it would be by something green and a white stone. (She started carrying a white stone with her whenever she was with him.)

New Year's passed.

Valentine's Day passed.

Still no ring.

Then on Sunday, February 16, 1969, Alan took Jeannie to the South Ogden Stake conference service at the Ogden Tabernacle. "At noon, following the services, I walked her out to where the Church had announced plans to build the new Ogden temple," Alan says.

He knelt down on one knee, looked at her with all the love he could offer, and said, "Jeannie, what time is it? Twelve noon. What's the color of the grass? Green. The white stone?" He explained that the white stone was both the Tabernacle and the new temple to come.

Full of tender emotions, he presented her with the engagement ring she had been hoping to receive. "We hugged, kissed, and wept. It's a moment I will cherish forever," Alan says, smiling. "Thankfully, she agreed. Yes, she would marry me!"

He had kept that beautiful ring in his sock drawer at home for several months. He kept looking at it, knowing it was for his beloved sweetheart, Jeannie.

Where did Alan find money for the ring? His mother gave him the cash. She collected in full the thousand-dollar life insurance policy she'd purchased when Alan was born. "Jeannie and I went to find something special and we picked it out together," Alan says. "The ring that holds the diamond has an antique motif and there are two separate gold bands, one on each side of the diamond. It's symbolic to us: One side is me, one side is her, and the middle ring is the Lord."

Decades later in their marriage, when their kids were grown and married and family finances were of little concern, Alan went to Farr's Jewelry to surprise Jeannie with an upgraded diamond ring. "All her daughters and daughters-in-law have huge diamond rings," Alan says. "And hers is nice, but it's certainly not like theirs."

He bought Jeannie a larger diamond stone. It was magnificent and cost $28,000. She made him take it back. Not that she wasn't grateful, but to her, the original ring has greater value.

Alan's wedding ring has an antique motif and features yellow gold and black. On the inside of his ring, Jeannie had the following words etched into the metal: My Heart Eternally Thine, June 11, 1969.

Pressure-cooker engagement

Despite the excitement of their upcoming marriage, it was a tense time for Alan and Jeannie. The United States government was drafting young married and single men to serve in the Vietnam War. "Our engagement was a pressure cooker for us. We had emotions boiling up in every direction with the war, our parents, and Jeannie's adjustment to a new religion," Alan says. He was feeling increasingly nervous about the responsibilities of being a future husband.

One night on a date, sitting in Alan's Mustang, he told Jeannie he wasn't sure if he was ready to get married. In tears, Jeannie handed him the ring and jumped out of the car. Alan was shocked.

"I loved her and wanted her as my wife. It didn't take long to figure out my mistake. I left the car and ran to find her," Alan says. "I caught up with her a few hundred yards away. She was running to her home."

Sitting in his car, Alan apologized to her for being such a fool and asked her to forgive him. "I pleaded with her to give me another chance," Alan says. "Thankfully, she agreed to keep the engagement ring and to move forward with our plans to be married."

Vietnam War raging

To add to the stress, Alan was about to be drafted by the U.S. government. "We were worried I'd be called up and sent to Vietnam," Alan says. "We saw the American soldier death counts on TV every night, and that scared us."

At the time, the Vietnam War separated families across America. Lonely wives missed their husbands, and children missed their fathers. Alan wasn't the only one hoping to avoid the draft. Anti-war protests erupted on college campuses and in public squares. "Some young men moved to Canada to dodge the draft. If the U.S. government caught them, they were put in jail," Alan remembers.

In the beginning of the war, names of all American men of draft age were collected by the Selective Service System.[1] Before even meeting Jeannie, Alan had taken a military health exam at the local draft board. Made up of community members, local draft boards had a life-altering power to decide who stayed and who was drafted. Men were qualified or disqualified based on that exam. Alan was in prime health, so he was required to carry around his A-1 draft card.

"Knowing I was healthy and available, I constantly worried when I'd be called," Alan says.

Alan and Jeannie didn't want to be separated so soon after their marriage. Together they explored options and came across the Peace Corps. It was President Kennedy's new program dedicated to the progress and peace of developing countries. Congress approved the Peace Corps as a permanent federal agency within the State Department, and JFK signed the legislation in September 1961.[2]

"To be honest, our first interest in the Peace Corps was about delaying the draft so we could have time together after we were married," Alan says. "However, we also looked forward to serving the people in the area where we would be assigned, as well as serving our country."

Alan went before the local military draft board after getting engaged and said, "If you'll let me serve my country as a Peace Corps volunteer in a peaceful setting, you can have me one year later and I'll go to Vietnam. But please give me one year to be a husband."

They granted his request. "Their response was unheard of as most married men were being drafted to the battlefields of Asia," Alan remembers.

Seeking another exception

The timing of the war presented another obstacle. The couple had set a date to be married on June 11, six and a half months after Jeannie's baptism the previous November. To qualify for a temple recommend and to be married and sealed in an LDS temple, the Church policy is that one needs to be a faithful, church-going member for at least one year following baptism. That left Alan and Jeannie with only one option: a civil marriage. At the time, however, a couple who married civilly had to wait a year to be sealed in the temple. Alan and Jeannie wanted to be sealed before going into the Peace Corps.

Alan and Jeannie went to see their individual stake presidents. Alan's stake president was Kefford Peek, a humble leader who worked as a postal clerk. Jeannie's stake president was the famous architect Keith Wilcox. "President Peek called the Church Office Building and made an appointment," Alan recalls. "So the three of us went to see the first counselor in the First Presidency of the Church: N. Eldon Tanner."

In downtown Salt Lake City, President Tanner, a former Canadian businessman, looked deeply into Alan's eyes. To Alan, it seemed as though the apostle were peering into his soul. "He was an intimidating gentleman. We explained what we wanted to do about marriage and the Peace Corps," Alan says. "He interviewed both of us thoroughly and individually. He wanted to understand our maturity and commitment to the gospel."

President Tanner told Alan and Jeannie he'd take the issue to President David O. McKay and President Marion G. Romney of the First Presidency. President Peek received a letter the next week that granted Alan and Jeannie permission to be sealed in the temple.

Henry and Betty Nowak were not happy. Like most parents, they wanted to participate in their daughter's marriage ceremony. They couldn't attend the temple because they were not members of the

Church. To include Jeannie's parents, the young couple wanted to have a civil ceremony (which the Nowaks could attend), and then be sealed in the temple the next day. The couple worked with President Peek to send another correspondence to the First Presidency to ask for permission to be married civilly and not have to wait a year to be sealed. President Peek also made a phone call, explaining the sensitive circumstances.

"So we were asking for permission before her year mark to be sealed," Alan says. "On top of that, we were asking permission to be sealed in the temple the day after a civil marriage ceremony." Both requests were granted and the couple moved ahead with wedding planning.

Many years later, the Halls had dinner with Elder James E. Faust, then a member of the Quorum of the Twelve Apostles. Alan told him about the special exceptions they were granted for their temple marriage. "Well, Alan, that is highly unusual," said Elder Faust.

Years earlier, before he was called to the Quorum of the Twelve Apostles, Elder Faust knew of a widower stake president living on the East Coast who wanted to be sealed to his fiancée. She'd been a member of the Church for ten months. They had a Salt Lake City trip planned to attend General Conference, and hoped to be sealed during the trip. Despite being only two months from her year mark, their request to church authorities was denied.

"Who was the prophet who granted your request?" Elder Faust asked.

"President David O. McKay," Alan replied.

Elder Faust smiled and said, "Alan, he loved the boys of Weber County."

History only knows the reasons behind the Halls' special exceptions. Decades earlier as a young man, David O. McKay had been assisted with college tuition by Aaron W. Tracy, former president of Weber College. Aaron Tracy is a relative of Alan's (after whom he would later name his first son), and perhaps his late relative's good turn was passed in full circle when Alan really needed it. Or did President McKay remember Alan from when he gave the closing prayer as a deacon in Huntsville, Utah, several years earlier? Or perhaps President Tanner's X-ray vision into the hearts and souls of both Alan and Jeannie helped him be a strong advocate for the young couple.Whatever the cause, being married and sealed in the temple at the start of their marriage was a blessing that Alan and Jeannie cherish. They both wanted the power and protection of temple covenants as they served abroad in the Peace Corps. "There would be powerful forces, both good and evil, happening in our lives, and we wanted divine intervention wherever we lived," Alan says.

Graduating together from Weber State

The young pair graduated from Weber State College together on June 7, 1969, both with degrees in psychology. Alan, with a love for people and gift for conversation, considered being a counselor. With a wedding and a year of Peace Corps service fast approaching, however, a career was not the first thing on his mind.

Jeannie, age twenty, graduated as the number-one student in the psychology department. She was recognized with an award, "Woman of the Year," the equivalent to the modern-day Crystal Crest Award, Weber State University's highest honor.

The graduation was held outside in the football stadium. Graduates sat on the bleachers on the east side of the stadium, and President William P. Miller conducted. An interesting family note: Dr. Miller had been influenced by Alan's relative, Aaron Tracy, to pursue a career in higher education. He followed his counsel and eventually served as the president of Weber State for eighteen years, the longest tenure of any Weber president.[4]

Sitting there as one of many graduates, Alan couldn't have known that decades later, *he* would be the chairman of the Weber State University board of trustees and sit on the stage at commencement multiple times. Did he imagine he would be a future commencement speaker? In December 2016, he shared some experiences and wisdom with more than ten thousand students, parents, and faculty in the Dee Events Center. (See his remarks in Appendix II.)

During their graduation procession, Alan and Jeannie made their way across the stage. Alan opted for a golf shirt under his graduation robes, instead of the traditional shirt and tie.

After the ceremonies, Alan and Jeannie celebrated separately with their families. The Halls and Nowaks weren't friendly with each other, even though the wedding was only four days away. While Alan and Jeannie and their families attended graduation ceremonies, neighbors of the Nowaks worked miracles in the Nowaks' back yard for the wedding reception on June 12.

Wedding day, round one

As he had thousands of times before, Alan dressed downstairs in his parents' home. This special day, his own wedding day, was different. After putting on his tux, tying his tie, and brushing his teeth, Alan paused for a brief moment to reflect on the occasion before him. He looked at himself in the mirror and thought: *This is it. My single life is over. After twenty-four years with my parents and family, I'm leaving this home of my youth, never to return.*

It struck him profoundly in a way he remembers decades later. "Up until then, I was carefree, doing as I pleased, making decisions on my own," Alan says. "After that day, it would change. I would be in a partnership and make decisions with Jeannie."

In an intimate, small ceremony with parents and siblings and a few close friends, Alan and Jeannie were married civilly on June 11, 1969, in an upscale restaurant in Ogden called the Mansion House. Quinn McKay, an LDS bishop and dean of the Weber State Business School, officiated at the ceremony. He'd been approved by the Nowaks because of his academic status. He was also a relative of David O. McKay, the prophet of the Church, which pleased the Halls. Jeannie walked down the aisle to the musical lilt of Felix Mendelssohn's "Wedding March." Quinn performed the ceremony, and they were invited to exchange rings. Alan's little brother, five-year-old Nathan, was the ring bearer.

After the civil ceremony, the wedding party went upstairs to the restaurant, where the Nowaks hosted a wedding dinner. After the dinner, Alan and Jeannie drove to Logan, Utah, with their friends David and Lana Halverson. They had reservations for two rooms: Jeannie would stay with Lana, and Alan with David. They planned to stay overnight in a hotel and be sealed the next morning in the Logan temple.

As they tried to check into the hotel, the receptionist informed them their rooms were not available—they had been given away to someone else. They had arrived later than planned and it was Utah State University's graduation weekend. "What a disaster! Not the best way to start married life," Alan says.

After driving all over town looking for other rooms and making numerous calls from hotel lobbies, David suggested they stay overnight at his relative's home in Smithfield, Utah, a town close to Logan. He called his uncle at nearly midnight and described their plight. Alan and David slept in one room, while Jeannie and Lana slept in another. "Jeannie and I shook hands. Nervous as could be, we didn't even kiss," Alan says with a smile. "Neither of us slept well. We were excited for the morning and our future together."

Wedding day, round two

The next morning, June 12, they awoke early to go to the temple. Alan's family and friends were there to greet them. "There I was, with this beautiful girl I loved with all my heart," Alan says. "It was a heavenly experience to see each other dressed in white, kneeling across the altar in the House of the Lord."

They looked into each other's eyes and pondered being together forever. "We have a deep and profound love for each other," he says.

The officiator, temple president Elvie W. Heaton, invited Alan and Jeannie to make sacred covenants, then had the pair stand and kiss. Finally, he invited them to exchange rings.

After the sealing, friends and family drove to nearby Perry, Utah, for a wedding party luncheon at Maddox Steak House, hosted by Alan's parents. "I thought it was spontaneous, but my mother had planned it. Unbeknownst to us, she had not invited the Nowaks and they were upset and angry," Alan says. For the next twenty years, there were strained relations between the Halls and Nowaks.

After returning to Ogden to their parents' homes, the couple dressed and prepared for the backyard reception. That evening at the Nowaks' home, Alan and Jeannie were thrilled and surprised to find that the

Primary and Relief Society presidencies of the 73rd Ward of the Weber Heights Stake had provided cookies and brownies elegantly served on trays to go with peach sundaes.

Several hundred friends from college attended the reception. Both sets of parents were pleased to also see their friends and relatives. Jeannie worked diligently to keep costs low: She made her own wedding dress, train, and veil, and she had prepared pre-scooped vanilla ice cream topped with canned peaches. She persuaded a willing photographer to take photos at no cost.

As the night continued, a summer rain started, and the party ended quickly at 9:00 p.m. Jeannie and Alan cut the wedding cake, changed their clothes, and waved goodbye to well-wishers. They climbed in Alan's 1965 baby-blue Mustang, and with fanfare waving them off, drove away as a married couple.

Alan and Jeannie stayed in the wedding suite at Ogden's new Ramada Inn on 2433 Adams Avenue for their honeymoon night. "I'd never seen a naked girl before and she'd never seen a naked boy," Alan says. "There was a Bob Hope movie on television that night and we both laid there watching it, wondering what was next."

Honeymooners in Island Park

The next morning, the plan was to drive to the Nowaks' cabin in Island Park, Idaho, for the week. But Alan's little blue Mustang wasn't working. "So that's how we started the next day of our married life: with a dead battery!" Alan says.

They bought a new battery and started on their trip that afternoon. There was no freeway at the time, only a state road, so it took more than five hours to reach their destination. By the time they arrived, it was near midnight.

"Jeannie didn't know the way to the cabin—she'd only been there a few times with her parents. We knew it was tucked behind lodgepole pines in the center part of the island," Alan remembers.

There were no street lights or easy-to-find signs, so they kept driving around the island, in the black of night, trying to spot a little sign that said, "Nowaks' Nook." Alan was exhausted and frustrated and thought they should have just stayed at the Ramada, but they had no money. The cabin was free.

Finally, they found the tiny cabin, opened the door, and went to bed. In the morning, they saw they were in the middle of nowhere. There was no television, no radio, and no phones. "It was just the two of us," Alan says. "Being on a honeymoon, it was all about getting used to each other in an intimate way, which was very strange."

Alan and Jeannie both look back at that first week of marriage with great humor, realizing how innocent and inexperienced they were. "We were there for a week and got bored. You can only do so many things so many times," Alan says. "So we called up our best friends, the Halversons, and asked if they wanted to join us."

The Halversons came to the cabin and had a room in the loft. "We didn't see them very often. They stayed in their room. It turned out, Lana got pregnant at the cabin while on *our* honeymoon!" Alan says. "Nine months later, while we were in the Peace Corps, she had a baby boy."

More than a year later, after returning from the Peace Corps, the Halls invited the Halversons to the Island Park cabin a second time ... and nine months later they had another baby boy! "They decided to never stay with us again," Alan says with a smile.

Post-honeymoon, pre-Peace Corps

Coming back from their honeymoon, Alan and Jeannie stayed in the Nowaks' basement for a couple of weeks. The basement didn't have an oven, so they made do with an electric frying pan. Jeannie was cooking meals and returned again and again to a favorite casserole with noodles, tuna fish, mushroom soup, green beans, and crushed potato chips on top. "I think I had that ten thousand times!" Alan says with a chuckle. Meal preparation was limited to only one pan.

Staying with her parents was not their top choice, but it was free. They only needed a place to stay temporarily before their Peace Corps assignment at the end of June. It was such a happy time, they didn't think much about their future or careers. "I didn't worry about our income," Alan says. "I just thought we'd earn it somehow."

6

Peace Corps Year in Brazil

A decade earlier, prime-time media had portrayed happy families in a traditional mom-dad-kids scenario, like those in *Leave It to Beaver* or *I Love Lucy*. In the 1960s, however, that image seemed quaint. For several reasons, young people in the '60s made a statement. This was personified by peace-loving, long-haired hippies promoting an anti-establishment agenda and sexual revolution. "The movement was rapid; very rapid," Alan remembers. "It was the revolt of teenagers against their parents, driven by Hollywood, the media, and the music industry. They all evolved to drive a counter-culture change."

While school administrators had hardly allowed whispers of the word "reproduction" during their high-school years, sex became a free-for-all public discourse during Alan and Jeannie's college days. Songs from the controversial 1968 Broadway show *Hair*, which featured profanity, drug use, nude scenes, and depictions of free love, became anthems of the anti-Vietnam War peace movement. "We saw people in big cities on the news promoting free love and drug use, but it seemed so far away," Alan says. "We were this young, happy, monogamous, religious couple, mostly unaware of the outside world."

Reporting for Peace Corps training

For two young conservatives, Peace Corps training in 1969 was an eye-opening experience. The majority of the trainees were liberal, anti-war, and anti-government. In late June, Alan and Jeannie reported to Alta Ski Resort in Salt Lake City for twelve weeks of Peace Corps training. They all lived in the dorm-style Alta Peruvian Lodge. "Our fifty classmates were a potpourri of diversity, from Jewish kids to Hispanics to Harvard scholars," Alan says. Most were single, but there were a few married couples.

The trainees were assigned to serve in Bahia, Brazil. Day and night, they trained for Peace Corps work, studied Portuguese, and learned about Brazilian culture. The Peace Corps hired LDS instructors from the Language Training Mission.

Like Spanish, Portuguese is a Romance language rooted in Latin, so there were a lot of commonalities for Alan, who was fluent in Spanish. However, it was more challenging for Jeannie, who had studied Spanish in school for three years but had never used it in a Latin American country.

Consider the life changes happening for the twenty-year-old bride. A recent college graduate, Jeannie was adapting to a new faith, new husband, new language, and a new living situation, preparing for an unknown future. "In many ways, she was relying on me to make sure we'd be all right," Alan says.

Alan and Jeannie had little time alone together. They were living in dorms, with shared restrooms down the hall, and a community cafeteria for all meals. "We were different from a typical married couple who has privacy in those first honeymoon months," Alan says. "But we continued to develop our relationship. I was trying to get used to living with a woman. She was trying to get used to me. I don't recall disagreements, but we had a lot of stress on us to pass language proficiency tests. It wasn't easy."

Some trainees were "de-selected" from the program and sent home for lack of progress with the language. Some were considered too emotionally unstable to handle the rigors of a foreign assignment. The pressure was on Alan and Jeannie to meet the high standards of proficiency and maturity.

A psychiatrist checked their emotional stability to ascertain their ability to survive the severe personal and marital strains of living in a third-world environment. "Jeannie reminded me we could survive any challenges as a couple if we honored God and kept our sacred commitments to each other," Alan says.

To ease the stress, Alan and Jeannie took evening walks, hand in hand. It was a beautiful time to be at the resort, with cool nighttime temperatures and gorgeous mountain surroundings. On the weekends, all the trainees were supposed to stay at the lodge, but the Halls slipped away in Alan's blue Mustang. "We literally sneaked out of the dorm to drive home to see our relatives, attend church, and enjoy a home-cooked meal. Sunday nights we'd drive back to the dorm and slip back in through an open window," he recalls.

As the twelve weeks came to an end, the Halls qualified for the next segment of the training in Bahia, Brazil. They sold Alan's car and found a ride to the Salt Lake City airport with four suitcases of clothing and supplies to last them a year. They were on their way to an adventure of a lifetime.

Arriving in Brazil

Alan and Jeannie remember their first international flight together, to São Paulo, Brazil. "Over the Andes, I was sick as a dog, throwing up as the plane bounced along through rough weather. Jeannie was doing her best to nurse me through it," Alan says. From São Paulo, they traveled by plane to Rio de Janeiro, then to Salvador, the capital of the State of Bahia. "It was a couple of really long days, and we were weary."

When the Halls arrived in Brazil, Peace Corps administrators greeted them. They soaked in new sights, sounds, tastes, and smells. Although Alan and Jeannie arrived in Salvador in mid-September, the tropical rainforest climate brought temperatures in the 80s and thick, humid air. A bustling coastal city, Salvador was founded in

1549 by Portuguese settlers, and the population consisted mainly of multiethnic descendants of European colonists, South American tribes, and African slaves brought centuries earlier to the first slave market on the continent.

The city was diverse, with cathedrals and colorful colonial architecture, beaches boasting white sand and palm trees, and markets serving spicy African seafood. "Some of the locals practiced voodoo and others Catholicism," Alan says. "It felt like a different planet."

Speaking of planets, it had been a landmark summer for space exploration. The world was focused on the man on the moon and his auspicious American flag. Everywhere Alan and Jeannie went, they were asked about Neil Armstrong and President Kennedy: "Did he really land on the moon? Do you like JFK?"

Since John F. Kennedy was Catholic, devout believers in Brazil had pictures of him posted on their walls, with burning candles underneath. "He was Saint Kennedy to them," Alan says. "Catholics loved him."

Additional training in Feira de Santana

The Halls were assigned to a little town called Feira de Santana for their additional training. They lived with a local family. Every weekday for approximately six weeks, they met in a rented office space with Peace Corps administrators who trained the volunteers in Portuguese and Brazilian culture.

Peace Corps volunteers were not paid a salary, but received a monthly stipend for room, board, and essentials—just enough money to meet basic financial needs.They also were paid eleven cents an hour per person, which was to be used for education following their Peace Corps service. Between them, Alan and Jeannie saved almost $2,000.

The Halls had virtually no privacy living with their host family. "In fact, we rarely enjoyed alone time," Alan says. "Our hostess was a kind and generous woman. She went out of her way to take care of us. She actually let us sleep in her bed."

Unfortunately, the bed was short in length and the Halls' feet hung over the edge. The mattress was made of straw and very uncomfortable. The bed was also home to scores of fleas who feasted upon the young couple during the night. In the mornings, their legs and arms were covered with itchy red sores. "In time, we learned to apply ample flea powder to the bedding, and to wipe our legs, arms, and trunks with rubbing alcohol before we went to bed. We smelled badly but the fleas were repelled by it," Alan says. "All of us shared one common bathroom at the back of the house, which was also home to large hairy spiders and fast-moving green lizards."

Their hostess made them breakfast and dinner. At first, being fed authentic Brazilian meals felt like a feast for the couple. The problem was her limited repertoire. Night after night, she served pumpkin soup and bread for dinner. For breakfast, she served greasy eggs over-easy with rice, beans, and bread. This was the menu week after week. "I felt like if I had another greasy egg, I might scream," Alan says.

One morning, Alan lost his composure and threatened to never eat a greasy egg again. He pleaded with Jeannie to make him a scrambled egg without grease. Jeannie proceeded, in front of the hostess, to cook Alan a scrambled egg, which he ate with pure delight. "I am afraid I broke the kind heart of our hostess as she watched me inhale my breakfast," Alan says. After that, Jeannie cooked Alan's eggs each morning.

The Halls were surprised to learn their hostess had a daughter with severe disabilities living in the home. "I'll never forget one day being in the kitchen when a previously unnoticed bedroom door was open. Something caught my eye and I looked in to the shadowy space. To my amazement, there lay a frail little girl wrapped in a worn blanket," Alan says. They never asked about her condition. They concluded the mother loved her and cared for her, but not in their presence.

The spies of Governador Mangabeira

As part of their training, Alan and Jeannie took a two-hour bus ride to Governador Mangabeira, a town in Bahia founded in 1962. They were assigned to learn as much as they could about the thousand or so residents and to write a report to Peace Corps administrators about their experience. When they arrived at their destination, they rented a room in a dilapidated hostel and organized their approach to learning about the small community.

They talked to everyone as they walked the town's dusty streets. They met homeless people, nuns, business owners, teachers, government workers, mothers, students, and children. As they spoke to the citizens, they wrote down notes to remember what they had heard. They were unaware the local police chief was quietly following them, suspicious of two chatty note-taking Americans on his turf.

One morning after Alan and Jeannie had been in town for a few days, the police chief appeared unannounced at the hostel and told the proprietor he wanted to see the two Americans. "As he began to speak, I could smell alcohol on his breath," Alan says. "There was no doubt in my mind he was drunk, especially since he mumbled his words incoherently."

He was, however, quite able to declare that he was convinced they were spies and terrorists. With a gun in his hand, he commanded Alan and Jeannie to leave the building and follow him outside. "I was sure he had every intention of shooting us on the spot," Alan says. "It was a terrifying moment. There was no way to change his mind or escape from his grasp. I shouted to Jeannie to run to our room and lock the door."

Luckily, a businessman from Rio de Janeiro was staying at the same hostel and overheard the frightening conversation. He was bilingual and spoke excellent English. He diplomatically approached the chief and calmed him down. In a convincing manner, he told the officer the Halls were good friends of President John F. Kennedy and that he had sent them to help Brazilians.

"They're fine," he said. "Don't worry about them."

His authoritative words seemed to briefly placate the chief. After a short pause, the chief told the man the Halls should leave town immediately. With utmost gratitude, the scared pair thanked their rescuer, gathered their belongings, and boarded the next bus out of town. "As we headed back to Feira de Santana, I kept thinking to myself that the Lord had been watching over us and placed that man in our midst to save us," Alan says.

Living and serving in Itajuípe

After six weeks of training, it was time for the Halls to travel to their assigned city, where they taught the people leadership skills. "We

were to teach leaders how to understand public needs and engage the
population in solving universal problems that affected all citizens," Alan
recalls. "It didn't take us long to learn electric power and sanitation were
major concerns to the people in general."

After a grueling eight-hour bus ride from Salvador, Alan and
Jeannie arrived in Itajuípe, a rural town of about 2,000 residents. The
community smelled of sweet dark chocolate and was their home for
nearly a year. Most residents were farmers who worked on large cacao
(chocolate) plantations that were owned by wealthy Lebanese families.
Workers harvested, dried, and sacked large quantities of cacao on a
daily basis. Throughout town, there were multiple warehouses filled
with large gunnysacks of cacao beans ready to be shipped to major
chocolate confectioneries worldwide.

The couple's living conditions were challenging. They lived at number
43 Rua Rui Barbosa, a small rectangular home approximately ten feet
wide by thirty feet long. The walls were made of adobe bricks and the roof
of clay tiles. There was one window at the front of the house, but it held no
glass. Solid wooden shutters were used to cover the opening. The cement
floor was painted red, and the living room had no furniture except two
stools. The water supply for the shower came from a rooftop basin that
caught rainwater. There was a small bedroom with a custom-made bed,
built by a local carpenter to fit Alan's height. "We put a mosquito net over
the bed to protect us from mosquitos, spiders, and other strange creatures
that fell from the ceiling at night," Alan says.

Next to the bedroom was a cramped kitchen with a propane gas
stove and miniature refrigerator. "We did not have a washing machine,
so I washed our clothing, towels, and bedding by hand," Jeannie recalls.
"I scrubbed it all in a metal basin on the ground, rung it out, and hung
it on a clothesline in the back yard to dry."

The basic necessities of cooking, cleaning, showering, and even
sleeping took constant effort in their Brazilian home. "Without air
conditioning, it was hard to sleep during very hot summer nights. We'd
lie in bed and sweat profusely for hours," Alan remembers.

Unlike Friday-night dates back home, the young couple had limited
options for entertainment. They had a small collection of books and

their scriptures. If he could find a copy of *Time* magazine, Alan bought it. They did not have a television, personal computers, or the Internet, but they did have access to a record player and a few records. For connection to the outside world, they had a small radio. At night, they could listen to BBC broadcasts from London.

In town, there was a dilapidated movie house that featured foreign films. "We'd go every week to whatever show was playing. They were mostly cowboy movies in Italian. It was a filthy theater, with rats running around on the floor beneath our feet," Alan says.

Comforts of living in the United States seemed a distant dream. Air-conditioned grocery stores weren't an option—they didn't exist. The open-air market was available once a week, so Jeannie went on Fridays to buy food, weaving her way through hanging steer carcasses buzzing with flies. It made her sick to look at them. At first, she avoided buying any meat, but in time, she learned to select a good piece of beef that she placed in a pressure cooker until it was sanitized and tender. "The food was wild. We sometimes saw chicken beaks and claws in the soup!" Alan remembers.

Jeannie was uncomfortable with some aspects of the culture. At meals, Brazilian women never ate with the men. The sons and dads ate together, but mothers and daughters ate in the kitchen. (Women were not even allowed to open their own bank accounts in Brazil until the 1960s, when the Halls were first there.)

"I told them Jeannie would eat with me," Alan recalls. "It upset the men and surprised the women, but I told them that's how we do it in America. I didn't get a lot of pushback, other than Jeannie set a precedent and the women started wanting to do it too."

In addition to culture shock, the Halls faced serious health problems, ranging from irritating to serious. Man-killing snakes were everywhere and bug bites never seemed to stop itching. Jeannie regularly applied yellow iodine to flea bites. Her friend Fatima, seeing the yellow marks on Jeannie's legs, asked her, "Do white people have yellow blood?" Fatima was 14, but her kindness to the tall white stranger made her Jeannie's closest friend in Brazil.

Along with a constant skin rash, Alan developed a persistent cough that turned into bronchitis because of the humidity. "I couldn't get rid of it," Alan says. He went to see some Brazilian doctors, but they were little help. It wasn't until they returned to Utah's dry climate that Alan's cough finally stopped.

They also were concerned about the large snakes in town and were very careful to watch their steps. The village had poisonous snakes everywhere, slithering in from the surrounding jungle.

"Every once in a while, we'd travel by bus to a nearby town called Itabuna," Alan says. "In the early morning, the bus bounced along the highway. It bounced because the tires hit and rolled over scores of huge slithering reptiles spread across the warm asphalt highway."

Peace Corps work

Since its inception, more than 200,000 Peace Corps volunteers have served in more than 100 countries, with assignments including education, health, nutrition, HIV/AIDS training, agriculture, business, community development, forestry, and environmental protection. Their role is to give a helping hand to struggling communities, leaving behind lasting change. The Peace Corps assigned Alan and Jeannie to be community-development specialists, with the mandate of getting to know locals, learning their problems, and teaching them how to solve issues independently.

At first, the Halls focused on adjusting to their new environment. They continued to practice Portuguese and spent time meeting local shop owners and neighbors. "We were in a discovery mode, trying to understand the community and the people," Alan says. "We met the priests, the mayor, and lots of little kids. We weren't accomplishing anything other than just learning about them."

It seemed everyone they met in Itajuípe thought Alan and Jeannie were brother and sister, because they were both tall, blond, white Americans. "They could never figure out why we there," Alan says. "We taught some of the kids in town free English classes as we tried to determine how to best accomplish our mission," Alan says.

"One day, Jeannie and I were walking along the street, heading into a certain neighborhood, when several shop owners came out and stopped us," Alan says. "They basically said, 'That's a street of crime and prostitution. You don't want to go down there.' They were trying to protect us."

The Halls later learned most of the local men—even married men—frequented prostitutes. "In a way, it was their form of birth control, I guess," Alan says. "It was definitely a culture shock."

The Peace Corps didn't send them with a checklist of things to do; it was up to Alan and Jeannie to discover needs and enable the people to solve them. They were always looking for a meaningful project.

They often asked Brazilians how they could help make their lives better. When one has lived in harsh conditions all their life, it's hard to imagine anything better. Social problems were everywhere, and the Halls learned that certain parts of town depended on kerosene lamps because they did not have access to electricity. In third-world countries, kerosene lamps are widely used as a source of light, but they are extremely inefficient, dangerous, expensive, and pose extensive health and environmental drawbacks. The World Bank estimates that "breathing kerosene fumes is (like) smoking two packets of cigarettes a day, and two-thirds of adult females with lung cancer in developing nations are non-smokers."[1]

Bringing electricity to the poor became one of the Halls' community projects. They began by teaching residents of Itajuípe the democratic principle of petitioning. They invited informal community leaders to encourage their neighbors to sign a petition requesting that local elected government officials install electricity throughout the village. They spent many hours teaching leadership skills to the people with a hope that time-tested principles could benefit them long after the Halls left.

Sanitation was the most devastating problem in Itajuípe. The town had no underground sewer system to safely carry waste away. Instead, there were open-sewer ditches everywhere, filled with deadly microorganisms. Young children played near these filthy ditches and became infected with serious diseases. The local river was also polluted. Women washed clothes in the river alongside their children who swam in the infected water. The children often contracted *Schistosoma,* parasitic flatworms responsible for a group of infections considered by the World

Health Organization to be the second-most socioeconomically devastating parasitic disease after malaria.[2] Between the open sewers and the river, the sanitation problems annually killed many local children; they only had a fifty-percent chance of reaching their first birthday. "The main cause of death was lack of proper sanitation," Alan says. "Sadly, the locals were unaware of the hazards and believed their babies died from the influence of evil spirits." The Halls worked on a plan to solve this vexing problem.

Voodoo and spiritual survival

In the community where they lived, some locals practiced Candomblé, an Afro-Brazilian religion with elements of Catholicism, African mythology, and indigenous traditions. Believers performed rituals that included animal sacrifices and trance-like dancing, accompanied by percussive drum music. "There was a practice of black magic in our village," Alan says. "Devilish ceremonies were conducted by a high priestess, the *mãe-de-santo*, in the middle of the night outside of town in the jungle. She held great power over her followers."

At times, they felt the presence of dark spirits near them. "We had an episode one evening during the middle of the night when we experienced the influence of an evil spirit in our bedroom," Alan says. "I felt someone was very near my side of our bed and I could not move in any direction or speak. It seemed this wicked being had supernatural power over my entire body."

Fear overcame Alan and his heart raced wildly. Whoever or whatever it was, he wanted it to stop and leave at once. Even though it had control of him physically, Alan still had his ability to think and reason. Marshaling all the energy and strength he had left, Alan silently prayed: *In the name of the Lord Jesus Christ, and by virtue of the holy priesthood which I hold, I command you to depart.*

In an instant, the personage left, as did the feeling of darkness.

Once gone, Alan jumped out of bed and turned on every light in the house. He didn't sleep the rest of that frightening night. "Today, years later, as I reflect on that terrifying event, I now know why the First Presidency gave Jeannie an exception to be endowed in the temple and allowed us to be sealed before the start of our Peace Corps journey. It was to protect us from great evil."

Looking back, Alan gained a special awareness and knowledge of Lucifer's world of consuming darkness, which in a strange way reinforced his faith and knowledge of God's existence, power, light, and love for His children.

The couple depended on each other for spiritual nourishment. There wasn't a congregation of their church anywhere close; the nearest LDS branch was in Rio de Janeiro, 780 miles away. On Sundays, they read the scriptures and *Jesus the Christ* together. They greatly missed going to Sacrament services, Sunday School classes, priesthood quorum meetings, and Relief Society gatherings. They missed attending stake and general conferences and visits with other members of the Church. With nowhere locally to make a church donation, they saved their tithing and fast-offering contributions for when they returned home.

Carnival revelry

In Brazil, Carnival is observed usually five days prior to Ash Wednesday and the beginning of Lent. An annual tradition of the entire Brazilian community, Carnival was a jovial time for Itajuípe. People set out to eat, drink, and be merry. Many people in the small town where they lived took it to the extreme, generally because of too much alcohol.

For five days and five nights, people followed music trucks blaring bossa nova and samba music through the streets. School groups, clubs, and other organizations wore matching costumes or covered their faces and hair with white flour or makeup, dancing to the beat of the rhythmic music with wild abandon. Alcohol flowed freely, drugs were passed around, and sexual immorality was rampant. The wild parties ceased on Ash Wednesday and the forty-day period of repentance and abstinence began prior to Easter. After Carnival, a lot of repenting was necessary!

Echoes of war, all the way to Brazil

Although Alan and Jeannie grew weary of third-world living, they had fears of returning home. At least in Brazil, they were together. They didn't know if Alan would be shipped off to Vietnam upon their return to Utah. On December 1, 1969, the first Vietnam draft lottery took place with an announcement of an orderly way to draft new recruits. The U.S. military and Congress were losing the war and needed more troops to defeat the enemy in Asia.

The Selective Service put all the days of the year into blue plastic capsules and placed them in a large glass jar. An officer then pulled from the jar one capsule, September 14. That birth date was assigned the lowest number, 001.[3] All those born on September 14 would be the first to be called up to go to war, if eligible.

The officer then proceeded to pull from the jar the remaining capsules, giving each day of the year a number from two to 366, until all were removed. Based upon government calculations, each assigned number represented a certain number of young men between the ages of nineteen and twenty-six.

Alan and Jeannie listened to the BBC Radio broadcast that day to learn what Alan's lottery number would be. "I heard my number, 265," Alan remembers. "I wondered what that number meant to me and Jeannie. Would the U.S. government call my number, or would I escape the war and serve my country through the Peace Corps? Fortunately for me, the government didn't need those of us with the number 265," Alan says. "It appears the armed forces had enough men after 195 lottery numbers were selected."

Two trips to Rio

Every once in a while, Alan and Jeannie left Itajuípe and traveled to general Peace Corps meetings. They attended meetings in Bahia's capital, Salvador, where they stayed in the filthiest hotel they'd ever seen.

They also took a weeklong vacation to Rio to see the sights of the famous city and attend church. They boarded a bus for the long journey. "We slept on the bus and read books on the way to Rio," Alan says. "We found an inexpensive but clean boutique hotel where we felt safe. The hotel served delicious, cold milk. I hadn't had a cool glass of milk in months and loved every drop of it."

They toured Rio with wide-eyed wonder, seeing sights like the Christ the Redeemer statue and Ipanema Beach. They attended a professional soccer match at the world-famous Maracanã stadium, where they joined 200,000 rabid fans to watch Santos of São Paulo play Fluminense of Rio. The players and referees were protected from fans by a large, high fence that surrounded the field and a deep, waterless trench many yards wide. "We'd never seen so many screaming people in one place," Alan says. "The stadium had no seats. Everyone just stood and cheered for their team."

Attending church services was not on the typical tourist itinerary, but it was important to them. They attended church at an LDS ward in Rio, their first time among fellow Saints since they'd left the United States. "It was really nice to take the Sacrament and be around other members of the Church," Alan says.

Alan and Jeannie applied for graduate school in business and psychology when they returned home to Itajuípe. They traveled back to Rio, where Alan took the GMAT exam at an approved testing location. "We took the bus again for a grueling day-long journey," remembers Alan. "After that exhausting ride, I don't even know if I was awake for most of the test."

Building a marriage, planning a family

Deep in the Brazilian jungle, Alan and Jeannie were forced to rely on each other for support. "We were very alone without any other souls to guide us," Alan says. Jeannie had no close friends nearby. She missed speaking with her family and friends. Calling home was impossible, and their correspondence was restricted to mail. Every couple of weeks, they'd send handwritten letters home to loved ones, and did not receive responses for a few weeks. Jeannie's parents, still unhappy with her life decisions, didn't always write. When they did, they sometimes sent literature against the Church, which was painful for her.

"I am sure most American couples our age didn't have to experience the physical, emotional, and spiritual hardships we endured during that first year of marriage," Alan says. "It was tough on us individually and as a couple to live in such rough conditions."

Despite the struggles, they made happy memories. Almost like clockwork, warm rain filled the streets with water each afternoon. "I persuaded Jeannie to take a shower with me in a small courtyard with high walls behind the house," Alan says. "I said, 'Let's just run out there naked to get wet, then hurry back to soap up, and then quickly return to the downpour to rinse off.'" Decades later, Alan told that story to a church congregation and thought red-faced Jeannie would never forgive him.

Sitting in their little living room one day, Alan and Jeannie used a chalkboard to envision plans for their future family. They didn't know what life would bring, but they had big dreams. "We talked about wanting to have six children, and what we'd like to name them," Alan says. "For the most part, that's what their names are now."

They talked about spacing their kids, and how to fit in Jeannie's goal of a master's degree. "We thoughtfully planned the future, hoping one day it would all come to pass," Alan says.

For their first Christmas as a married pair, Jeannie formed a Christmas tree out of chicken wire. She decorated it with green crepe paper, colored Christmas-type ornament pictures from magazines, and lit a few live candles at midnight. For gifts, Alan gave Jeannie flip flops; she gave him a folding, webbed lawn chair. It was the only chair with a back that they owned and was a luxury to sit in after a long, hot day.

The Halls spent their holiday visiting a beautiful town called Ilhéus, nestled on the Atlantic Ocean. They enjoyed exploring its colonial architecture and beaches, including Millionaire Beach. They found on the outskirts of the city several abandoned box cars still connected to a rusting locomotive. It looked like a train that would have hauled cocoa beans from the plantations to the port. Alan was enthralled with the miniature size of the rolling stock. They swam most of the day in the bay where a large cargo ship had partially sunk. When night fell, they returned home with smiles on their faces and red sunburns.

Although they often wished for better living conditions, the young couple didn't want to leave their work undone and never considered the option of going home early. "We were there to see it through, no matter how tough it might be," Alan says. "I would not wish that experience on a couple, though. It was really difficult."

Preparing to return home

As their time to leave approached, the couple was eager to move on with their lives. They decided to return home to continue their education at BYU in the fall, and advised their Peace Corps supervisors that their tour of service would end in June 1970. "As we boarded the plane in Rio de Janeiro for the fifteen-hour flight to New York City, we were excited to be on our way. But we would miss the adventure of living in a foreign land and the incredible life-changing lessons we had learned," Alan says. "We would also miss the kind and loving Brazilian people who had carefully watched over us. And for sure, we would miss speaking Portuguese on a daily basis."

As the couple landed in America, they wept. "We wanted to kiss the ground beneath our feet. We were back in the United States and the land that we love. A few hours later, weary but greatly excited, we were greeted by loved ones at the Salt Lake City airport," Alan remembers.

As they drove from Salt Lake to Ogden, Alan felt they were no longer inexperienced newlyweds, but two seasoned, married young adults who could accomplish any magnificent dream they wished to pursue.

7

Graduate School and Growing a Family

When Alan and Jeannie returned to the United States, they had a few months before school started in the fall. After having such independence abroad, they didn't want to return to either of their parents' homes. During their first year of marriage, they had enjoyed privacy in Itajuípe and hoped for the same in a place of their own in Ogden.

Fortunately, they were offered an opportunity to house-sit for family friends who had a large home on the east bench in Ogden. For minimal rent, they could live there as long as they kept the home and yard clean and well maintained. The Halls stayed there while the homeowners toured Europe for several months with a daughter and son who had completed an LDS mission.

Jeannie returned from Brazil with more than memories. She was carrying their first baby, along with *giardia lamblia,* an intestinal parasite. The commonly prescribed drug for killing giardia posed a harmful threat to a growing fetus. Jeannie chose not to take the medicine. Out of concern for Jeannie, her father strongly encouraged her to have an abortion, but she absolutely refused.

Two grad students at Brigham Young University

During their time in Brazil, Alan decided he didn't want to be a counselor, the career path psychology majors generally followed. "With all the leadership training we performed, it struck me I might be good at business," Alan says. "I remember seeing my GMAT score, which was low in comparison to my peers. Today, BYU probably wouldn't let me in, based upon my unimpressive scores."

Alan and Jeannie moved to Provo, Utah, in August 1970, where they settled into their apartment at Wymount Terrace, housing for married students. That was their home for the next two years as they attended graduate school. Alan enrolled in the MBA program, and Jeannie enrolled in a master's degree program in psychology. She also worked as a graduate teaching assistant at BYU.

Obtaining an advanced degree was a full-time endeavor, and Alan was not permitted to work during the school year. The small amount that Jeannie earned as a teaching assistant helped cover their tuition and pay for rent, which was $80 a month. They also relied on savings from their eleven-cents-an-hour salaries in the Peace Corps. They spent about $2,000 to buy a used 1968 four-door Chevrolet. "It wasn't sporty, but it worked," Alan says. "We didn't obtain a student loan. We lived simply and survived on our own."

Although it was an exciting time in life, pressure was growing between expectations in their classes, callings at church, and preparing for the baby. After a year away from studies, the rigors of academia took a toll on Alan. "My first year was really frustrating for me. I hadn't had economics or accounting classes at Weber State," Alan says. "A lot of my classmates were engineers coming back to school to earn an MBA. They were all bright men who had been in business for a while. Taking business classes was all new to me and I hoped I could survive the program."

Weekdays were booked with classes, projects, and studying. When the weekend came, Sundays weren't a day for rest; they both actively served in the BYU 1st Ward. Alan had a leadership position in the elders quorum presidency and Jeannie taught in the Relief Society.

They rarely had time to make the ninety-minute drive to Ogden to visit family, but they did for Thanksgiving, Christmas, and special occasions. During this time, Alan and Jeannie set the pattern for celebrating the holidays: they would be with the Hall family on even years and the Nowak family on odd years. "We also decided who would say our daily prayers. I prayed on the odd days, she prayed on the even days," Alan says. "We still follow that pattern today."

As a student, Jeannie spent many hours doing research and teaching. To generate data for her thesis, she would enter punch cards into a room-sized computer in BYU's computer lab. In the MBA program, Alan spent countless hours in the classroom and library learning the principles of a successful business.

Sometimes demands and conflicts between their academic pursuits, family duties, and church responsibilities caused tension in their home. "I remember Jeannie and I having a disagreement over priorities one night when I became very upset. To calm down, I walked all the way around the BYU campus before I could come back home and be civil," Alan says.

To decompress and enjoy time together in their packed schedules, they'd meet at home for lunch and enjoyed watching their shared guilty pleasure, *General Hospital*, a popular TV soap opera. They didn't have time to watch anything else. They attended BYU football and basketball games for entertainment. Alan also played on the MBA intramural flag football and basketball teams, which kept him active in sports.

Their meals were rushed. "We had macaroni and cheese, Top Ramen, pork and beans on toast, cold cereal, and grilled cheese sandwiches with tomato soup," Alan says. "Every now and then, we'd make time for pancakes. We were poor college kids living on nickels and dimes."

The Marriott Center had just been built, so the couple watched the very first basketball game played in the arena. It opened in December 1971 to host the Cougar Classic basketball tournament. At the time of its construction, it was the largest university activities center in the United States.[1]

Living simply with antique decor

Starting their marriage in humble Peace Corps conditions gave the Halls a precious gift. They had perspective on how they wanted to spend their time and money. For example, they weren't willing to be shackled with consumer debt. They avoided buying furniture at a retail furniture store for the first two decades of their marriage. "Fortunately, Jeannie didn't need to have the finest furniture in town," Alan says. "We were not worried about what other people thought of us. We lived, in so many ways, very conservatively."

Alan and Jeannie liked the idea of owning items with history behind them. "We found that antiques were a cheap way to furnish a home," Alan says. "We took great pleasure in decorating our home with inexpensive antiques."

For their wedding, Jeannie gave Alan an antique telephone with a separate ear piece and microphone attached to a box, which complimented Alan's prized old butter churn and his grandfather's hundred-year-old pendulum wall clock.

Alan acquired the butter churn years earlier. He found it in Morgan, Utah, and liked it so much that he worked for a farmer for a few hours to earn it. Alan brought home the churn, replaced a few broken slats, and sanded it.

Another antique icon in the Hall home is an old church bench. Knowing her son's affinity for antiques, Alan's mother called and told him the old Ogden 1st Ward building was being torn down to make room for the new Ogden Temple site. With a borrowed lumber truck, he went to the church and asked if he could have a curved choir bench that was about to be thrown away. It took several strong men to lift the heavy, twelve-foot oak bench onto the truck. Thankfully, it was in really good shape. (But it still had decades of hardened chewing gum beneath the seat!) Alan took it home and told Jeannie they had a couch. She made a few cushions for it, and re-covered them several times over the years. They still have it today in their family room—gum intact.

With no money for nice carpet in their university apartment, the Halls fashioned their own floor covering. They went to a carpet retailer and asked if the manager would give them old carpet samples for free. They were happy with any color and style—all carpet types were welcome. The Halls organized the samples like a puzzle, putting them together in a creative way to fill the floor space. "We glued them on a nine-by-twelve room-size canvas," Jeannie says. "They looked like samples, but the result was soft and clean and much better than a red cement floor in Brazil or the linoleum of Wymount Terrace!"

At Deseret Industries, they found an antique four-poster bed with pineapples on the top of the posts. The bed frame wasn't wide enough to comfortably fit two people, so Alan took it apart and cut a piece of plywood for the headboard and footboard to make it larger. Then he sanded and painted it.

During their first year at BYU, the young Hall couple noticed in the newspaper that a church in Yakima, Washington, was selling its 1908 Estey pump organ for $150. Even without seeing it, they scrambled to find the money, which was nearly two months of rent. They pulled together the cash and sent the church a check for the organ. In about a week, a huge crate arrived at Wymount Terrace.

"I remember that day so distinctly. The package held this magnificent instrument. We had a crew of students help us get it into our little apartment. Once in the room, a friend who was an organ major played it," Alan says. "It delivered a very beautiful sound that made us smile."

They kept the organ in their living room, along with other treasures. "Our children grew up in a living room that was basically the poorest you could imagine, all dressed with inexpensive antiques: an old oak choir bench, a wooden rocking chair, a pump organ, a pendulum clock, a butter churn, and an old chest we painted purple and gold," Alan says. "Our kids didn't really know how frugal their mom and dad were."

Welcoming their first child

On March 4, 1971, in the early morning hours, Jeannie's water broke as she was sleeping. She rolled Alan over in bed and told him she was going to the laundromat. Being a get-it-done woman, Jeannie left to wash the linens; the student housing laundry facility was a two-minute walk away.

"Jeannie does not leave anything undone," Alan says. "That's her nature. She wasn't about to have a baby with dirty sheets on her to-do list."

However, sometimes babies don't wait. "I got the load through the wash and into the dryer. Before it was dry, I was in hard labor," Jeannie recalls.

At 4:30 a.m., Alan drove his laboring wife quickly to Utah Valley Hospital, the first fully staffed 24-hour emergency center south of Salt Lake City.[2] The doctor on duty had planned to give an epidural, but he didn't have enough time—red-headed Aaron Tracy Hall was born at 6:32 a.m.

"He came out with red hair! And I mean *really* red—red eyebrows, red everything. Who were his parents?" Jeannie says, laughing. "We were ecstatic with our firstborn son and marveled at the miracle of our perfect little boy."

That morning, several other babies were born in the same hospital. Without enough room to accommodate the new mothers, the hospital staff wheeled Jeannie into a room with four other mothers. "I was on a rollaway bed in the middle of the room with no privacy, and could hardly wait to go home," Jeannie says. "I came home the next morning."

The Halls had not considered getting medical insurance. Jeannie still has the bill: A grand total of $150 for the doctor and $150 for the hospital. "That was a big stretch for us, but we managed to pay it off," she recalls.

Bringing home their first child was an adventure. Neither Alan nor Jeannie had any training in caring for a baby. "Having a newborn was quite a new experience for Jeannie," Alan says. "Her mother could not help her with the baby. She lived in Ogden and worked full time."

Alan's mother, Joyce Hansen Hall, came to Provo for a couple of days to assist with the first grandbaby. She stayed with Tracy and Ida-Rose Hall, who lived a few blocks away. "We called Aaron 'Golden Boy' because he had this lovely tan-colored skin," Alan says. "My wise mother kindly informed us he had jaundice and that his yellow color would soon be gone."

Living in an apartment with cinder-block walls, the new parents did their best to care for their baby without disturbing neighbors. "When

Aaron cried, we worried he would bother families who were sleeping in apartments next door," Jeannie remembers.

In 1971, a new mom couldn't Google questions when problems popped up. Thankfully, Jeannie was friends with plenty of other young mothers who helped her, and the Nowaks had given them the trusted book *Baby and Child Care* by Dr. Benjamin Spock.

They took baby Aaron to see his great-grandfather Hall, who was living with Uncle Tracy and Ida-Rose. In his mid-eighties, he'd already been a widower for a few years and met a lady at the senior center. "He was a very happy-go-lucky guy," Alan remembers. "We had him and his lady friend to dinner occasionally. He passed away while we were in graduate school at BYU."

When it came time for Aaron to receive a name and a blessing, Alan and Jeannie returned to Ogden to perform this sacred ordinance. Surrounded by his dad and a few uncles, Alan gave his first son a family name. He was named in honor of Aaron Tracy, a noble relative and former president of Weber College.

 Soon Jeannie started attending classes again, bringing Aaron along in a little backpack. He went everywhere with her. "Back then, there were no car-restraint devices. Our children grew up without safety belts," Alan says. "Having a child changed our world immediately. Before, we did anything we wanted. Now, we were focused on caring for our sweet redhead. We were a little more constrained, but very happy to be new parents. Being poor students, we didn't buy Aaron new clothes. He wore hand-me-downs or gifts from family and friends."

Alan's first business venture

"I wanted to be successful in business, but never had a desire to work for a big global company, like Procter & Gamble or ExxonMobil," Alan says. He knew he wanted to run his own business, but BYU had no programs for entrepreneurs. Others in his program questioned his plans and wondered why he didn't want the security of employment with a big company. Alan replied, "It's just not who I am. I'd rather do something different."

The summer between his MBA program's first and second year, while his peers were interns at big companies, Alan started his own venture called Excelsior Advertising Agency. He'd seen advertising on the backs of benches at bus stops and wondered if he could apply the same advertising concept to golf courses. Thus, his first business idea took formation.

He found a manufacturer that made fiberglass golf benches in any color for $100 each. He then approached the 18-hole Provo Golf Course and offered the manager free use of the benches, for the life of the bench, if he'd let Alan place advertising on each bench. The manager agreed. Moving forward, Alan created a flip chart with statistics about the number of golfers who would see the signs each day.

Armed with marketing material, he approached business leaders at establishments like Bullock & Losee Jewelers and Given Ford. He signed them up for $1,000 per bench, and after his $100-per-bench expenses, he walked away with a $900 profit every time he sold an ad to a client. Within eight weeks, he made more than some future offers for a year's salary. The number of sales grew and he proudly brought home more than $2,000 a week. "In that one summer, I sold enough advertising to earn $16,000," Alan says with a smile.

Alan told his business professors about his business model. "Most of them pooh-poohed it as a silly idea, but one professor encouraged me to do it all over the country," Alan says. "I didn't. I wasn't yet ready to be a full-time entrepreneur. As a young father, I wanted to provide some stability."

Second year of the MBA program

Alan's scholastic efforts and relationship-building in his program slowly paid off. In the second academic year, Alan was elected class president by his fellow classmates. The MBA program director, however, wasn't as enthusiastic as the students. Although the director historically worked with the class president on events, fundraisers, and other initiatives, he did not work with Alan. "He had favorites among the students who were engineers, and never invited me to work with him," Alan says.

Alan also thought his English professor was prejudiced against him because he'd been a Peace Corps volunteer. "He viewed me as a liberal and a rebel. I remember coming home one night after receiving a C-on an English paper," Alan says. "I was so upset at the grade that in frustration, I threw our big rotary phone at our antique chest on the other side of the living room," Alan says.

Aaron was just a few months old when that happened. "I am sure Jeannie thought to herself, 'Oh, my poor child. You have a crazy father!'" Alan says. "That chest got dinged, as did the phone." In time, Alan calmed down and apologized for his anger.

That year, Dr. Chauncey Riddle, a celebrated BYU professor and dean of the graduate school, established the Graduate Student Advisory Council. "I attended the first meeting with the student presidents from the other graduate school programs, and they elected me the president of the council. I met with Dr. Riddle regularly to discuss various topics and to develop an agenda for monthly meetings," Alan remembers.

Despite getting better grades his second year, Alan wasn't resonating with the learning material in his MBA classes, which focused on how to move up the corporate ladder. In 2019, it's typical for workers to jump from company to company, even from career to career, but in the 1970s, most employees committed to the same company their entire work life. They progressed through promotions.

Alan made a decision before graduating that would define his career mobility differently from his MBA peers. "Instead of waiting decades to reach the top of the corporate leadership chain, I decided to find employment opportunities where I could become the boss quickly," Alan says.

Mentored by Dr. Stephen R. Covey

In 1971, Alan took an MBA class in organizational behavior taught by Dr. Stephen R. Covey. A rising authority in the field of leadership, Dr. Covey was an influential mentor for Alan. "I learned about empathy from his example and lectures," Alan says. "We became friends and continued to visit over the years."

Years later, Dr. Covey invited Alan and a dozen other former-students-turned-executives to attend a year-long private seminar. He taught them the principles that formed his world-changing book that would sell 25 million copies in forty languages: *The 7 Habits of Highly Effective People.*

"I learned from him to be proactive, begin with the end in mind, put first things first, think win-win, seek first to understand, then to be understood, synergize, and sharpen the saw," Alan says. "He would jokingly tell others I should give him the credit for my successes in life."

Dr. Covey founded Covey Leadership Center, which merged in 1997 with Franklin Quest to create FranklinCovey, a global leadership training company. Covey was recognized as one of *Time* magazine's twenty-five most influential Americans.

Graduating

Despite their happy student life, Alan was ready to move forward and make his place in the world. He was the first Hall grandchild to receive a master's degree. "I was so happy to graduate and start my career journey," Alan remembers. He'd talked it over with Jeannie several times, and they both wanted to stay in Utah. Despite opportunities in other states, leaving meant he'd be chained to a big company, and Alan wasn't interested in that prospect.

On graduation day in June 1972, Alan didn't know what the future held, but he felt sure his desire to follow a different path would pay off.

8

From Employee
to Employer

For any student or professor in the Hall Global Entrepreneurship Center at Weber State University, the name "Alan E. Hall" is synonymous with "entrepreneurship." However, the journey to successful business owner often means being an employee for someone else first. It doesn't always go right the first time, or the second, or third. In fact, it took several jobs—and failed start-up businesses—over a couple of decades before Alan found his winning business idea.

"I didn't have a roadmap. This wasn't a well-orchestrated career," Alan says. "It just sort of happened. What I learned in each job led me to be successful in the next opportunity. My vision was to find employment where I could be the leader quickly. I didn't have the patience to wait decades before becoming the president of a company."

By the time Alan graduated with his MBA and Jeannie had earned her master's degree in psychology, their $16,000 money cache from his golf bench advertising business had run out. Alan sent his résumé to some local companies. He wanted to learn a few more hands-on lessons in business, with a steady paycheck, before starting another venture on his own.

Hired, then laid off

He was hired for his first full-time job at In-Trade Limited, an import/export business located near Liberty Park on 7th East in Salt Lake City. He accepted an annual salary of $9,500 and sold imported ten-speed Japanese bicycles to dealers in the area. Since the new job was in Salt Lake, the Halls moved into an apartment complex called Creekside Circle in Murray. Even with a salary, the young family kept their wants and needs in check. "We were very careful with our money," Alan says. "We didn't have any debt and our living expenses were modest."

His boss, a successful entrepreneur, sent Alan around the state to sell bikes. Alan liked that there was only one other employee and that he had room to grow. Unfortunately, sales were declining as the ten-speed bicycle market was saturated and buyer demand decreased. Alan's boss tried to introduce new products to the market but ultimately had to lay off Alan just before Christmas in 1972.

"I was in a panic," Alan remembers. "We needed income to pay our rent, and at that time of year, people weren't hiring." Someone in their ward knew a carpet layer who needed help with an apartment complex project over the holidays. Humbled, Alan began to lay carpet until he found a new job.

"I survived it, but struggled emotionally and financially," Alan says. "It was devastating for me. I was so embarrassed. I'd been the president of my MBA class six months earlier, and now I was spending nights and days on my hands and knees laying carpet."

He learned that no matter what happened, he needed to find a way to provide for his family. "It would have been a mistake to wait to find something I was qualified to do, but cash was critical," Alan says. "I couldn't worry about my ego or reputation, not when I needed to pay the rent and get food on the table."

When his carpet-laying gig ended, Alan and Jeannie moved closer to their hometown, to a two-bedroom duplex on 4400 South in Roy, Utah. Alan's top resolution for the new year of 1973 was to find a job. They had Aaron, who was nearly two, and Jeannie was expecting their second baby, so the pressure was on for Alan to find income.

He applied at several places, including B-Mart Home Improve-
ment, a local carpet, lumber, paint, and supply retailer. Like a Home
Depot of its time, the chain had Idaho locations in Pocatello, Black-
foot, and Boise, and one in Ogden. Early in January, Alan travelled
to Pocatello, Idaho, to interview at company headquarters for an assistant manager position.

"It was wintertime and I was fearful of driving the car we'd bought,"
Alan recalls. He took the bus instead. "I stayed in a run-down hotel in
the heart of downtown Pocatello."

He was interviewed by the president of the company, who was
impressed with Alan's business acumen and knowledge of the lumber
business from his teenage years at Ogden Roofing and Supply. He
received a job offer and became the assistant store manager of the
Ogden store, located west of Wall Avenue on 36th and Pacific Avenue.
His starting salary was $12,000 a year, an increase from his last full-
time role.

"I was there to learn how to run the store. The goal was to train me
to be the store manager," Alan says. "What I quickly learned was that
the employees weren't culturally a good fit for me. Their lifestyles were
very different from mine. They liked to drink and party. I was focused
on rearing a family and living a righteous life."

Before he knew it, the store manager left and Alan was promoted.
"That was my philosophy—to be the boss as fast as I could," Alan says.
Every day, he arrived early to open the store and came back late at
night to lock up. He learned to manage a store that generated millions
of dollars in sales. He oversaw cash flow, profit and loss, advertising
contracts with the local newspaper, customer service, and employee
relations.

"It was a terrific job in terms of learning how to run a company, but
I didn't enjoy the demanding world of retail," Alan says. "Jeannie knew
I was miserable."

There were several downsides to his employment. Alan had to
work Sundays, and he hated missing church. He also didn't agree with
the policies of the company's corporate leaders. Within a year, he was
actively hunting for another job.

He'd heard about an opening at Weber State for the director of alumni relations. Alan applied and interviewed with the chairman of the alumni board, Paul Bott, and WSC vice president of community relations, Dean Hurst. "They both knew my family well, which definitely helped my application," Alan says. "The Hall name preceded me, as it has for most of my life. I was Joyce and Gene Hall's boy. I was Tracy Hall's nephew. I was Jeannie's husband. That helped my case tremendously."

Whether due to his name or his own merits, Weber State called and offered Alan the job.

Weber State alumni relations director

"I was ecstatic for that opportunity," Alan says. "I was given the chance to lead the university's alumni organization and empowered to take it to the next level."

In 1974, Alan began his position at Weber State as alumni relations director with a starting salary of $15,000. He was responsible for creating meaningful experiences for alumni and the local community. "I thrived on the variety of assignments and the joy of meeting new people on campus and in Ogden," Alan says. "I reported to Dean Hurst, who taught me new skills and lessons in leadership I continue to use today."

In this role, Alan worked closely with the other Weber State leaders. His service as alumni director spanned the administration of three university presidents: William P. Miller, Joseph L. Bishop, and Rodney H. Brady. He helped them plan alumni activities around the country, wherever Weber State held sporting events. "I'd set up a reception for Weber State alumni in Long Beach or Seattle or Colorado—wherever we were playing basketball and football games," he says.

Faculty, students, and alumni at Weber State liked Alan and adored his redheaded children, Aaron and Laura. "Jeannie brought them to campus for a picnic with me once in a while," Alan remembers. "We'd sit on the grass by the Lindquist pond and feed the ducks."

Alan learned how to execute tactical details, especially massive checklists for large-scale annual banquets. "I knew when things had to be prepared, implemented, printed, and when to mail invitations," Alan says. "I learned about executing critical minutiae, which was significant to my business success later in life."

The same type of detailed planning applied to fundraising, publishing the printed alumni newsletter, taking alumni on trips, and producing Alumni Community Theater (ACT) shows. "I was learning how to run an organization inside a large university," he remembers.

Alan's entrepreneurial drive spurred creative efforts to raise money for the university. For example, he participated in a special alumni fundraising campaign for the $11.3 million Dee Events Center. He organized a telethon and mailed out solicitations requesting donations from small donors. After "nearly two years of delay and frustration occasioned by legal matters and funding problems,"[1] officials broke ground for the massive 12,000-seat multi-purpose arena in March 1975. It was dedicated during Homecoming week in November 1977; Alan published the story of this grand success in the semiannual newspaper he produced.

Don Spainhower, Alan's former freshman basketball coach and the radio personality for Wildcat ballgames, asked him to help in the broadcast booth. He helped Mr. Spainhower host a football broadcast in Southern California, where he conducted pre-game interviews with the players. His assignment was to learn about their backgrounds, and then during the broadcast share with listeners interesting stories about each athlete. He did the same thing at a basketball game at Colorado State, but his favorite assignment was helping with the play-by-play of a BYU basketball game.

The regular BYU/KSL announcer, Paul James, was out of town and invited Don Spainhower to announce a BYU basketball game. Don agreed and invited Alan to join him for the broadcast. The game that night was a pre-season match-up between the All-Stars of Yugoslavia and a BYU team that featured a Croatian native, Krešimir Ćosić. "Don and I slaughtered the pronunciation of the foreign players' names, but it was a thrill for me to be courtside," Alan says.

Putting on a show with Alumni Community Theater

Alan also literally put alumni in the spotlight. Missing the fun of the stage from their college theater days, some Weber State alumni approached him about creating a community theater. Open to new ideas to engage the community, Alan committed to be the producer of Alumni Community Theater, or ACT.

The first ACT production was held in a 250-seat auditorium at the Union Station in Ogden. Thereafter, the organization hosted an annual production every year while Alan was the alumni director. He produced several dramas and a number of crowd-pleasing musicals, including *The Music Man* and *A Little Night Music*. He thoroughly enjoyed learning to produce live theater events, something he'd never done before.

Soon the audience outgrew Union Station. After evaluating various options, Alan decided the century-old Orpheum Theatre was a great possibility for ACT's new home. Originally built as a venue for national vaudeville touring companies, the theater could accommodate an audience of 1,750 people. In time, as Hollywood movies replaced vaudeville performances, theater management placed a large movie screen on the Orpheum stage. By the time Alan arrived on the scene, the theater had been closed for many years and was in disrepair.

Alan approached the Orpheum Theatre owners and asked if community volunteers could clean the theater and use it for ACT performances. A local news article in May 1977 featuring the history of the Orpheum Theatre stated that "the theatre was remodeled with new seats and the screen put on rollers so Weber State College could stage plays."[2] Manager Richard Gleams reported in the article that the stage curtain came from the New York City Radio City Music Hall in the 1920s, giving the theater a grand appearance similar to Peery's Egyptian Theater in Ogden. The ACT plays were the Orpheum Theater's final performances; it was demolished in 1983.

Every year during his time as alumni director, Alan attended the Association of American Colleges & Universities national conference. One year he was recognized on the grand stage with an award for alumni program fundraising. Another time, he received an award for organizing the Alumni Community Theater. "There was nothing like ACT in the country at that time," Alan recalls. "Getting national recognition led me to believe I could accomplish great things no matter where I worked."

Personal mid-life crisis

While he worked at Weber State, Alan carved out time for his start-up businesses in the evenings or Saturdays. "As much as I enjoyed my job, I was going through great internal struggles during my time at Weber," Alan says. "I wasn't totally fulfilled." He launched four failed businesses in those seven years. (See Chapter 9 for an in-depth look at those business ventures.) It was a bit of a mid-life crisis for Alan, who was unsure of the next steps on his career path. After working several years in higher education with decorated scholars, Alan considered pursuing a doctorate degree.

To explore advanced-degree options, Alan and Jeannie flew to California to meet with leaders of the Stanford Graduate School of Business. "After the meeting, I realized that being a professor wasn't for me," Alan says. "What I really wanted to be was the CEO of my own business." His idea of pursuing a PhD was set aside.

He and Jeannie prayerfully asked God for direction on how to provide for their family. They didn't know what lay ahead, but trusted He would provide guidance. "We always found God watched over us and blessed us, even during low points of our lives," Alan says.

By 1980, Alan had worked at Weber State for seven years. "I loved working there. They took good care of me, but my internal clock is set at seven years," Alan says. "It takes that amount of time for me to learn everything I need to know about an assignment. Once learned, I become bored with the job and feel a need to move on to new adventures."

This pattern of self-reinvention has repeated in Alan's life, often like clockwork at the seven-year mark.

President of Ballet West

"I knew a great deal about producing theater productions, so when I learned Ballet West was looking for a new president, I applied for the job. I felt I had something to offer," Alan says.

Dr. Quinn McKay, then president of Ballet West, told Alan about the opening. Years earlier, Dr. McKay had married Alan and Jeannie civilly during his tenure as dean of the business school at Weber State. With a new call to be an LDS mission president, Dr. McKay was leaving

Ballet West and suggested Alan look at filling his role as the president. Alan interviewed with the board of trustees and they offered him the job on the spot, with a starting salary of $25,000.

Alan wasn't sure it was the right move for him—he'd only seen one ballet as a child. Raising money for the arts, rather than education, was a whole new world for him. He told the trustees he needed to discuss it first with his wife. When he talked to Jeannie about the interview, they decided to ask God. "We knelt down by our bed and asked, 'Is this what we should do?'" Alan remembers. "The answer was, 'Go ahead and do it.'"

Alan called the chairman, Bill Jones, and accepted the position. If he'd known what he was getting into, Alan would have run the other direction. "It was good I learned as I went," he says. "It was an overwhelming role."

Alan was hired in May 1980, during the middle of Ballet West's twentieth anniversary. Not wanting to uproot the family, Alan drove from Roy to the Salt Lake City office every day for seven years—a sixty-mile roundtrip. "There was no FrontRunner train at the time, or I would have taken it," Alan says.

He worked on the second floor above the lobby of the Capitol Theatre, a landmark built in 1913 and known for its elegant turn-of-the-century architecture.[3] It had been renovated and reopened to the public two years earlier, and was recognized as a beautiful venue for performances and rehearsals. Under a "marvelous chandelier," Alan recalls, guests filled the theater's 1,559 seats.

In his role as president, from time to time Alan made brief introductory speeches prior to the opening of new ballet productions. Stepping in front of the red velvet stage curtain, he welcomed the crowd and thanked sponsors and large donors for their support. With the bright lights on him, it was his moment to shine, and he felt great pride being associated with the world-class organization.

Meeting Jacqueline Kennedy Onassis

Over the years of Alan's tenure at Ballet West, he took Jeannie to dozens of performances in the Capitol Theatre, and sometimes on trips to ballet performances in distant cities.

During Alan's first year at Ballet West, they traveled to watch the nation's most famous ballet company, American Ballet Theater (ABT). One of Ballet West's board members, Priscilla Stevens, a wealthy woman from New York City, was also on the board of ABT. She invited the Halls to come to the Big Apple and stay at her apartment, and she graciously provided them with tickets to see the ballet company perform.

"Jeannie and I had never been to New York City. This was beyond our imagination!" Alan says. "Her apartment was across the street from the Metropolitan Opera House."

As they were among celebrities and dignitaries, Alan wore his nicest black suit and Jeannie was in her Sunday best. They attended the opening night of *Swan Lake,* featuring the acclaimed Mikhail Baryshnikov, a Soviet-born dancer considered one of the greatest ballet dancers in history.

"We sat in the vast and magnificent Met auditorium gazing at the bejeweled surroundings, waiting for the performance to begin," Alan says. "We were spellbound with the beauty of *Swan Lake,* a ballet neither one of us had ever seen. Tchaikovsky's musical score was sublime, rich, and moving. Mikhail and Natalia Makarova were electrifying, he as Prince Siegfried and she as Princess Odette/Odile."

Alan and Jeannie were mesmerized with all they saw, heard, and felt. Their eyes filled with tears during the final scene of the ballet, overcome with the beauty before them.

After multiple standing ovations, Priscilla asked the Halls if they'd like to meet Mikhail Baryshnikov backstage.

"Really?" they asked incredulously.

They were led to a backstage door, where a guard monitored entry to meet Mr. Baryshnikov. Only those with special passes were admitted. Standing at the door was the most famous woman in the world, who also wanted to meet the famous dancer.

There stood the former First Lady, Jacqueline Kennedy Onassis.

She didn't have a pass, and for some reason the guard didn't recognize the female icon of America. But the Halls did. They suppressed squeals and didn't dare look at each other, for fear their star-struck surprise would be obvious.

Priscilla offered to escort Mrs. Onassis and her companion, along with the Halls, backstage.

Jackie got a few steps ahead of them. Jeannie elbowed Alan and whispered, "Look at her leg!"

He did, and saw there was a run in Jackie's nylons. "She's just a mortal like the rest of us," Jeannie whispered to Alan.

Jackie visited with Baryshnikov, as did Alan and Jeannie. They were quick to notice he seemed short in person, but also very muscular, as his grand jetés had demonstrated so magnificently during the performance.

Growing the Ballet West footprint

After seeing one of the world's finest ballet companies perform, Alan encouraged the Ballet West board to approve the creation of its own *Swan Lake* production. After obtaining permission, and with the support of Artistic Director Bruce Marks, Alan raised $500,000 for costumes and sets. With the production paid for, Ballet West performed the most famous ballet of all time in Salt Lake City and at the Kennedy Center in Washington, D.C., in front of cheering crowds.

As president and general manager of Ballet West, Alan reported to the board of trustees, which kept him on his toes. Alan served as an ex officio member of the board, meaning he attended meetings as the paid president. There were about thirty board members. Half were right-brained advocates for the arts who favored artistic expression and the artistic director's creative ideas. The other half were left-brained business professionals who were more concerned about the bottom line. They wanted to make sure the ballet was profitable. "At the board level there was a tug-of-war, where the trustees were for or against various initiatives," Alan says. "We had a split board that was rarely unanimously for me or for Bruce Marks."

Chairmen served on the Ballet West board for two years, and during Alan's tenure, he rubbed shoulders with former chairmen Bill Jones, Donald Holbrook, Steve Swindle, and Howard Jorgensen. "I worked with wonderful chairmen," Alan says. "They were outstanding leaders in the Salt Lake City community. I was blessed to be mentored by them. I was a young man and needed that coaching."

The chairmen tried to keep momentum going, but shied away from daring ideas for fundraising initiatives. Alan did his best to keep them happy, a constant struggle and lesson in not being able to please everyone. "I'd always talk with the business people and try to get their help, then try to curry favor of those who were interested in the arts," Alan says. "I learned that the very nature of boards means you're not going to make everybody happy."

Other notable board members included Elder James E. Faust, then a member of the Quorum of the Twelve Apostles, and Elder Ronald E. Poelman of the Quorum of the Seventy. "They were always of good counsel, and willing to help me," Alan says.

Working hard for the money

Raising money for Ballet West was a constant burden that monopolized most of Alan's waking hours. He worked with a budget of three million dollars a year, which covered expenses for new costumes, designs, sets, artist salaries, union wages, and orchestra expenses. Alan was responsible for raising more than one million dollars every year. "It was the first time in my life I'd done anything of that size and magnitude," Alan says. "I had to know every day how much money we had raised, what our ticket sales were, and what our expenses were against expected revenues."

Looking for ways to make dollars stretch further, Alan had to challenge the artistic director on costs. For example, toe shoes ran about $30 a pair, and each dancer wore them out after only one or two performances. Tutus were $250 each. A dancer's costume could cost several thousand dollars. "Since ticket sales only covered half of our expenses, we had to raise the other half," Alan says. "I was constantly asking wealthy people to help us."

Three big arts organizations in the Salt Lake City community competed for the same donor dollars: the Utah Opera, the Utah Symphony, and Ballet West. Alan found himself in a friendly but ongoing battle he felt he could never win. "I was always the junior kid in a competitive field of superior fundraisers," Alan says.

The Utah Opera fundraising efforts were led by famous opera star Glade Peterson. The Utah Symphony's campaign was led by president and chairman Wendell J. Ashton, publisher of the *Deseret News* and brother of an LDS apostle. "Wendell was all-powerful!" Alan says. "He was associating with all the men and women of wealth in the community. He was sixty years old with an extensive network, and I was thirty-five and a rookie. I couldn't match his wisdom or influence."

For example, Alan recalls taking prospective donors to lunch at the Alta Club, just kitty-corner from the Beehive House on the corner of State Street and South Temple. Across the room, he saw Wendell, working another donor. "He'd collect funds from them for the symphony," Alan says. "I was just trying to pick up crumbs he left on the table."

Alan found funding from four categories of sponsors: government, such as the National Endowment for the Arts and Utah State Legislature, corporations, individuals, and foundations, such as the Eccles Foundation and Bradshaw Foundation. When fundraising efforts fell short of the goal—and they often did—Walker Bank loaned money to Ballet West to cover a cash shortfall. "We had to have money to make payroll," Alan says. "Every week, I was on edge, thinking, *Are we going to make it? And where am I going to come up with money to pay our bills?*"

He focused on press relations as a way to build the organization's brand. At the time, Carole Mikita was beginning her career as an anchor and reporter for KSL-TV. "She helped us promote the ballet company. She did TV interviews with dancers and talked about exciting performances," Alan recalls.

As he excelled in raising funds for Ballet West over the course of his seven-year stint, Alan's salary increased. "Happily, I was making $60,000 a year, which was a reasonable salary," Alan says. "That sum provided our family with a bit of a surplus that we could use for trips or other needs."

Principal dancers and artistic principles

Artists at Ballet West had danced from the time they could walk. It had been their dream to perform on a professional stage, and at the time, Ballet West was one of the top five ballet companies in the United States. "All they knew was dance. Most of them didn't know how to drive a car," Alan says. "They were not street smart."

Alan admired the artists' hard work and talent. He saw behind the scenes of the grand stage, where the dancers would be suffering with blisters and muscle sprains. "I was thrilled to support their opportunity to dance," Alan says. "The artistry was first class."

Although the work was tense and unrelenting, Alan found joy and great pride in the performances of wonderful dancers. "I loved watching the handsome and beautiful principals and corps of the ballet as they danced to soaring music, in magnificent costumes amid remarkable sets. They were first-class artists and superb athletes," Alan recalls. "They spent many long hours in rehearsals learning to perfect their choreography, and it showed during live performances. I will always remember the great dancers during my time at the ballet: Bruce Caldwell, Stacey Swaner, Lee Provancha Day, Odette Millner, and Pamela Robinson. I watched them in awe as they danced in *Swan Lake*, *Sleeping Beauty*, *Giselle*, *Romeo and Juliet*, *The Nutcracker*, and *Carmina Burana*."

The company went to Aspen, Colorado, every summer for three weeks, where the artists rehearsed and prepared repertoire they performed the rest of the year in Salt Lake City. Ballet Aspen had a board of wealthy benefactors who financially supported Ballet West artists during the off-season summer.

Fundraising adventures for *Abdallah*

Early in 1985, Ballet West produced a lost ballet. Bruce Marks and his wife, Toni Lander, found a "long forgotten" 1855 ballet by August Bournonville, a Danish ballet master and choreographer. The ballet, *Abdallah*, was set in the Middle East. Bruce purchased Bournonville's own copy of the scenario, and together with Toni set out to "revive as much of the original choreography of *Abdallah* as possible."[4] They wanted to bring the little-known ballet to life in the modern age.

The board agreed to go forward with a world premiere of the unusual production, which Alan remembers having a theme similar to *Arabian Nights*. Financing such an ambitious and expensive production required Alan to reach outside his well-worn fundraising circles. Since the ballet was set in Basra, Iraq, Alan met with wealthy people with connections to the Middle East.

Utah Senator Orrin Hatch set up a meeting for Alan with Prince Bandar of Saudi Arabia, the ambassador to the United States. "He was a very distinguished and handsome gentleman," Alan recalls. "I went to his office and he greeted me warmly." Alan told him about the special ballet, and Prince Bandar agreed to donate. There was only one condition: that the U.S. government would provide Saudi Arabia with multiple AWACS aircraft, specially modified Boeing 707s with a long-range radar and surveillance system mounted on top. Alan shared the prince's request with Senator Hatch; only history knows what came of it.

Prince Bandar introduced Alan to Iraqi Ambassador Nizar Hamdoon, also in Washington, D.C. Alan remembers approaching the Iraqi Embassy and thinking it was an armed camp. Before entering the lobby of the embassy, guards searched him, finding a Ballet West gold-and-silver letter opener he'd brought as a gift for the ambassador.

"Their first impression was that I had come to assassinate the ambassador," Alan says.

Alan was led to a room, where a wall moved and opened a secret entry into Nizar's office. Later dubbed "a popular figure in the capital's diplomatic circles" by *The New York Times*,[5] Nizar had a powerful presence. Alan presented him with the letter opener and explained the reason for his visit. Although interested in the project, he told Alan he couldn't help fund the ballet. "He told me his government was fighting a war with Iran and all the country's money was focused on that problem, but he would ask other Iraqis to help me," Alan says.

Just before Alan departed from his office, Nizar handed him a gift. "As we stood to say goodbye, he gave me a fifteen-inch ceramic statue," Alan says. "He explained the person depicted was the ancient king Ur-Nammu, one of the greatest rulers in the history of Sumer, a region in Mesopotamia, now modern-day Iraq. Ur was the original home of biblical Abraham."

Years later, Alan thought the statue might make a good object lesson at church. "Before I even got it in the building, it broke!" he says. "Made me think it wasn't supposed to go inside the chapel."

Nizar definitely had connections to other Iraqis, and he sent eager Alan to meet with potential donors in California. When Alan parked his rental car at the designated hotel in San Diego, he had the eerie feeling he was being watched. He got out of the car, entered the plush lobby, and made his way to the designated guest room to meet with potential Iraqis donors. Alan carried a bag containing pink tutus and other pieces from *Abdallah*. "I thought that if I showed them costumes and part of the set design, they would give me a donation for the production," Alan says. "I was wrong."

He remembers walking into the room and seeing five Arabian men. "Pretty quickly, I could see this was going nowhere," Alan says. "These guys weren't interested in the ballet at all." They watched cagily as Alan pulled items out of his bag, as if expecting a machine gun. When Alan left, he was followed. He found out later they were a faction of Iraqi rebels. "I was clueless," Alan says. "What in the world was I doing? I could have been shot in that room!"

Another wealthy Arabian, Adnan Khashoggi, made a large financial commitment of several hundred thousand dollars for *Abdallah*. His pledge, however, was worthless, and hurt the ballet financially. Alan found out later he was an arms dealer who sold guns to rebel fighters in warring countries. Adnan not only promised money to Ballet West, but also to the Utah Symphony and LDS Hospital. "The hospital actually built a new wing in the name of his dad and then never received the contribution for its construction," Alan says. "He was dishonest with a lot of us, and we all suffered."

A couple's trip to the Kennedy Center

The fully funded *Abdallah* revival first debuted at the Capitol Theatre on February 20, 1985. A few months later, Alan and Jeannie, expecting their sixth child at the time, traveled to the Kennedy Center in Washington, D.C., for *Abdallah*'s East Coast premiere performance.

When they arrived at the Salt Lake airport for their Western Airlines flight, the Halls were surprised to be upgraded to first-class seats. They had purchased economy tickets, but someone in first class hadn't boarded the plane.

"All of a sudden, Senator Jake Garn, who'd been an astronaut aboard the space shuttle *Discovery*, stood next to me," Alan says. "He saw we were in his seats. Likely noticing that Jeannie was pregnant, the senator kindly insisted we stay where we were and he and his wife would sit in our economy-class seats."

The flight attendants and captain noted that Senator Garn was assigned to seat 3C. The crew was excited to have a celebrity on board their plane. "The flight crew didn't know what the senator looked like," Alan says. "So I pretended I was him."

The flight attendants asked questions like, "How's the Senate?" and Alan responded with a generic answer, "Things are going well!" At one point, another passenger asked, "How was your last flight into outer space?" and Alan answered, "It was fantastic!"

"What are you doing?" Jeannie whispered. "You're going to get in trouble!"

Throughout the flight, all the attendants and even the pilot visited the "senator." Despite the initial thrill of a tease, Alan was growing increasingly nervous. He finally decided he'd taken the story too far. He went back to Senator Garn and confessed. "He was bald as could be, and I had lots of hair. He was older, and I had just turned forty," Alan says. "We looked nothing alike."

When they landed in D.C., Alan admitted his impersonation to the first-class flight attendant, and asked her to tell the pilot. As the passengers began to disembark, Alan and Jeannie waited until Senator Garn made it to the front. "This is the real senator," Alan said, introducing him to the pilot and flight attendants. "Luckily for me, everybody had a good laugh."

The Halls stayed at the infamous Watergate Hotel, luxurious despite its scandal a decade earlier, and prepared for their evening with the stars. "There we were, two kids from little Roy, Utah, wearing a borrowed tux and ball gown," Alan says. "It was a thrilling time for us!"

Jeannie was eight months pregnant and worried her maternity church dress was not acceptable at such a posh event. She called a good friend who was married to a wealthy doctor and asked if she had a maternity formal gown. The kind friend supplied her with a beautiful gown and a pearl necklace to match.

Critically acclaimed

The East Coast premiere of *Abdallah* at Washington's Kennedy Center on May 1, 1985, received rave reviews from critics. "Delightful detail," hailed *The New York Times*. "Only a truly classical company, which is what Ballet West has become, could carry this feat off."[6]

Big stars of the stage and screen, dignitaries, and citizens of Denmark attended the premiere's gala, which "attracted an international group of critics and dancers, including a past and a future director of the Royal Danish Ballet—Flemming Flindt and Frank Andersen, respectively."[7] The evening was dedicated to Toni Lander, who was seriously ill and couldn't attend to see her own choreographic masterpiece.

At receptions before and after the ballet, Alan and Jeannie met a pregnant movie star, Jane Seymour, who came as a guest of Adnan Khashoggi. Jeannie was glad she wasn't the only expecting mother at the event. The beautiful English-American actress had co-starred with Christopher Reeve in the romantic film *Somewhere in Time* and had starred in the 1973 James Bond film, *Live and Let Die*.

Prince Bandar of Saudi Arabia, Nizar Hamdoon, and other Middle Eastern ambassadors made an appearance at the ballet in Washington, D.C. Senator Hatch and Senator Garn, whom Alan had impersonated on the flight, attended with the rest of the Utah delegation. "We were delighted to host so many famous and important people at *our* ballet," Alan says. "I was very proud to see Ballet West on a national stage."

Tension with the artistic director

One area in which Alan really needed wise advice was his working relationship with Artistic Director Bruce Marks. A New York City native, Bruce was a famous dancer and choreographer from American Ballet Theatre. Alan and Bruce had co-leadership responsibilities: "He reported to me for the financial side of the business, but not for the artistic side, which complicated life," Alan says.

Bruce had been with Ballet West since 1976, starting as co-director with Ballet West founder Willam Christensen. When Willam retired in 1978, Bruce was named artistic director. When Alan joined the team two years later, in 1980, an existing management team was already in place. "They were very loyal to Bruce Marks, not to me," Alan says. "I found myself in a challenging place, trying to get things done when people around me weren't in favor of what I was trying to do."

Often there were clashes between Alan, responsible for finances and fundraising, and Bruce, a "tireless advocate for the art form,"[8] who wanted grand-scale productions with little regard to cost.

"There was tension between us, and we both questioned each other's motives," Alan says. "Bruce wanted money growing on a tree, which he expected me to magically provide. He realized we couldn't do things without money. I believe there will always be tension between artists and management."

Bruce Marks was known as a superb male soloist for the Royal Danish Ballet and American Ballet Theatre in traditional productions, like *Sleeping Beauty* and *Swan Lake*. By the time he came to the company, he was tired of tradition. He wanted his creative signature on Ballet West performances, leaning more toward modern dance. His distinctive stamp was seen in the addition of new works to the company's repertoire from Bournonville and Balanchine, including nineteenth-century master works as well as modern dance classics.

Alan was more interested in achieving his revenue numbers through popular crowd-pleasers like *The Nutcracker*. "I had a great admiration for Bruce's talent, artistry, drive, and innovation. He had great passion to produce beautiful ballet," Alan says. "I still have the highest regard for him as a distinguished fellow, even if we had professional disagreements."

After five years of working together, Alan received sad news in May 1985: Bruce's wife, Toni Lander, had died of cancer at the age of 53. She had been the principal teacher for Ballet West and was an internationally known principal dancer with the American Ballet Theatre and London Festival Ballet. "She was a very sweet and wonderful woman," Alan says. "It was a loss for all of us."

Within time, Bruce formed a new relationship with a male friend. In today's world, his gay relationship would be accepted and even celebrated, but in the mid-1980s in one of the most conservative states in America, it was a different story.

"Had the media gotten wind of it, Marks' new relationship could have been detrimental to our funding efforts with conservative donors," Alan says.

On two occasions, Bruce and his partner had loud, public quarrels. One occurrence took place in the lobby of the Capitol Theatre and the other when Ballet West was in Aspen, Colorado.

It was a very tense time. Jeannie remembers how Bruce's outbursts stressed Alan, who frequently confided in her at home. "Bruce despised me and saw me as his enemy," Alan says. "Yet I'm sure he recognized the impact his behavior would have on the ballet in Salt Lake City."

In 1985, Ballet West invited John Hart, an English dancer, choreographer, and artistic director originally from South Africa, to stage three ballets created by Frederick Ashton, the famed English choreographer. Later that year, the board appointed Hart as the new artistic director for Ballet West.

Bruce Marks left Ballet West in late 1985 and staged *Abdallah* for the Royal Danish Ballet. He later became artistic director of the Boston Ballet.

John Hart invited recognized choreographers to join him on the artistic staff; Alan liked the talented team and enjoyed working with them. Having trained at the Royal Ballet School in London, John shared Alan's love for traditional ballet productions.

Appeasing donors, especially Mrs. Wallace

As CEO, there were many threads for Alan to weave in the tapestry of the arts. These included navigating the politics of the board, continually garnering sponsors, and appeasing dancer demands. "I had to be very diplomatic and discerning," Alan says. "It was part of the job to get things done."

Representing the ballet expanded Alan's connections to the rich and famous, larger-than-life personalities he'd never known before. He met frequently with people of great political stature and numerous titans of industry. "They were men and women of power and means, and I tried to look well groomed in my hundred-dollar suit from J. C. Penney," Alan says, smiling.

Appeasing donors was a full-time effort in itself. Some of them asked Alan to roll out a red carpet for them from the Second South lobby, along with literal trumpets to herald them in the building. "What egos!" Alan says. "Then we also had modest donors who didn't even want their names mentioned. There were a lot of people in between."

Then there was eighty-five-year-old Glenn Walker Wallace. She was tiny, perfectly groomed, and always wore lots of jewelry and precisely assembled outfits. She came from a long line of wealth. Mrs. Wallace co-founded the ballet, and two decades later, her opinion still held great weight on the board.

Born in 1898, Mrs. Wallace "studied piano, voice, and dance in Boston, which led to her lifelong interest in supporting music and ballet."[9] She was a sophisticated woman who lived in a mansion in the Walker Lane area of Holladay, Utah. "Her home was beyond imagination," Alan says. "It was rumored she slept in Marie Antoinette's bed!"

Her family owned Walker Bank, founded by four Walker brothers who had immigrated to Salt Lake City from England in 1852.[10] Since that time, Walker Bank had grown into a very large and powerful financial institution in the community. John Wallace, Mrs. Wallace's husband, had been the president and CEO of the bank.

In her golden years, Mrs. Wallace had ample time to make sure her beloved ballet remained first class. "She was a powerful influence across everything I did and had a commanding presence," Alan says. "She might as well have been Queen Elizabeth." As honorary life chairwoman and advisor to the board, her portrait still hangs on the second floor of the Capitol Theatre, where she's portrayed wearing a crown and sash.

Mrs. Wallace made an appointment to visit Alan almost every week, bringing unsolicited advice on how to do his job. Often, she'd tell him to do things the board hadn't approved, putting Alan in a bind. She had a habit of asserting her demands. One time she came to his office, looked down at his shoes, and blurted, "You should never wear brown shoes."

Despite Mrs. Wallace's imposing nature, Alan developed a fond relationship with her, and they regularly met during the entire seven

years he was at Ballet West. "We had great affection for each other.
She was a feisty grand-mère and I was like her grandson," Alan says.
"She introduced me to people of great wealth, and I went with her
to raise money for the ballet." In fact, her relentless fundraising efforts for the ballet continued even after her death. In Mrs. Wallace's
Deseret News obituary, the family requested Ballet West donations
in lieu of flowers.

Business lessons from Ballet West

The refiner's fire of Ballet West expanded Alan's capacity as a
businessman. "I worked diligently to make people happy by trying my
best to keep promises and commitments," Alan says. "I learned to not
give up on my principles."

He also learned to say "no," which went against the grain of his people-
pleasing nature. Although his business-minded focus exasperated some
people, Alan has maintained many good relationships with past and
present Ballet West employees and trustees over four decades.

"The difference today versus when I was a thirty-five-year-old leader
at the ballet is significant," Alan says. "I had no power base whatsoever,
no experience, no stature, no reputation or authority. Today, people will
listen to me, honor and respect me, but without that reputation back
then, it was challenging."

The fundraising quest weighed relentlessly on him. Somewhat in
desperation, it dawned on Alan there might be support for Ballet West
beyond the borders of Utah, since they were representing the western
region of the country.

He proposed a regional tour, visiting cities like Sacramento,
Phoenix, Boise, Albuquerque, and Denver. The idea was that Ballet
West could have "branches" in other cities, such as Ballet West Arizona
and Ballet West Idaho. Alan found several wealthy arts supporters in
those states who liked his plan, but it nonetheless failed. Those cities,
it turned out, also wanted their own ballet companies. Even in failure,
the experience of trying to build a regional presence was an important
lesson to guide Alan's future endeavors, like MarketStar's expansion
into Europe and Asia.

Teaching others to raise money

Alan's time at Ballet West served as a training ground for later professional opportunities. "My successes and failures at Ballet West prepared me well for the future," Alan says. "I believe it's important to take on interesting positions to gain new experiences and valuable life lessons. We learn so much by doing new things."

The Master of Fine Arts program at the University of Utah invited Alan to be an adjunct professor. Every year for seven years, he taught a class for one semester on the fundamentals of fundraising. He built a syllabus and curriculum and held the one-hour class at the Capitol Theatre. "A lot of my graduate students were planning to lead nonprofit organizations and needed to understand how to raise funds," Alan says. "Today, there are many people in Utah who came through that course and are doing what I taught them many years ago."

Alan's final act at Ballet West

When Alan came home at night, Jeannie could see he was often overwhelmingly stressed. "Maintaining emotional well-being was never easy in such a consuming role," Alan recalls. "Jeannie heard about my long days and never-ending challenges with money and people, and like a mother bear, she wanted to attack those who fought against me."

Alan eventually learned there was no job that could keep him happy forever. The pressure at Ballet West became too much, and he decided it was time for a change. He found himself in a persistent cycle of pleasing the board, managing donors, pushing back on the artistic director, and leading a partially supportive management team. Alan's seven-year clock ticked loudly. He needed a new opportunity.

Alan still had an interest in starting his own business. Since he'd lived and taught the fundamentals of the fundraising world, he considered starting a company to teach fundraising principles. He figured he could brand himself as a fundraising expert and be a top consultant for non-profit organizations. He even came up with a name: The Development Office. As he prepared to leave the ballet, he created a company logo, letterhead, and syllabus.

The Development Office, however, never got off the ground. Instead, Alan accepted his cousin David Hall's invitation to join him in a start-up opportunity, a fork in the road that drastically changed Alan's future for decades to come.

Entrepreneurship

During Alan's years as an employee, before he became president of Ballet West, he spent nights and weekends moonlighting as an entrepreneur. He couldn't ignore the nagging desire to be his own boss. He was motivated to turn his ideas into reality, so he funneled his spare time and money into his own businesses.

"For me, the thrill is in building an organization with a noble cause. I have always wanted to start and grow my own business," Alan says. "It's what I do. It's who I am."

An inherent challenge of entrepreneurship is the lack of a clear roadmap to success. He launched four businesses that failed, and lost money on each endeavor. Alan's ideas varied drastically. There was no single common thread through them except his contagious enthusiasm for their potential. He jumped not only from product to product, but across entire industries, searching for a profitable need in the marketplace.

Although he later had results to show for his efforts, those formative years of failure put tremendous financial strain on the young Hall family. Angel investors were unheard of at the time, so Alan and Jeannie bootstrapped his business projects. "I tried to start business ideas with our own personal and limited funds," says Alan. "Jeannie went to work to pay for my losses."

Jeannie was an exceptionally supportive spouse. "If we have to live in a tent, that's what we'll do, if that's what keeps you happy," she told Alan. Although the couple had lean years, losing at first $5,000, then $50,000, and finally using their home as collateral for a business bank loan, they worked hard, lived within their means, and always had faith that God would bless them.

His first business bust: the barnacle blaster

The first business idea Alan had while working at Weber State was certainly out of the box. Even though he didn't own a sea vessel or live near the ocean, Alan wanted to make waves in the ship industry. He knew barnacles adhered to the hulls of ships through a natural process called "biofouling." Barnacles on ships created considerable drag, slowing the vessel and increasing fuel costs. To give context, the United States Naval Academy estimated that biofouling creates enough hull-drag to increase the Navy's petroleum bill by about $250 million every year.[1]

To remove the encrusted barnacles, ships are periodically removed from the water. This inconvenient and expensive maintenance keeps boats sailing smoothly.

"I found a water system with a specialized pump," Alan says. "Instead of pulling the boat out of the water to scrape the barnacles, I planned to have a diver go under the ships using this high-pressure water system to remove the barnacles." It seemed promising—a way to help boat owners be more efficient and cost-effective.

After researching potential markets, Alan flew to California to obtain more information about potential customers. In San Diego, he presented his ideas to a boating industry expert. The man immediately told him it was a stupid plan. He explained that removing barnacles also removed paint from the ship, which would have to be taken out of the water to repaint the hull.

"He was right," Alan says. "I made marketing mistakes because I didn't know my customers well." Luckily, he hadn't spent a ton of money and the idea was nixed before making any substantial investment. As someone who'd lived most of his life in a landlocked state, he decided that ship cleaning was out of his range of experience. He still laughs about it: "Why would I know anything about barnacles when I live in Roy, Utah?"

His failed efforts were temporarily discouraging, but they didn't stop Alan from hunting for another problem to solve.

A bright idea: pedigreed bull semen

For his next idea, Alan stayed closer to home. He took a deep look at his own Weber County, searching for problems to solve. In 1978, there were nearly 800 farms covering more than 200,000 acres of Alan's home county, and the local agriculture industry was gaining momentum.[2] Within four years, there were more than 100 new farms in the same area. After taking a look at what farmers needed most, Alan decided to invest in a dairy bull.

Since the 1950s, U.S. farmers had used frozen bull semen to impregnate dairy cattle. That way, one hearty bull could sire hundreds of offspring, resulting in more milk-producing cows. Bulls who produce cows with high milk production are in demand. Or more accurately, their semen is in demand.

Semen-collection facilities like Reproduction Enterprises use innovative technology to collect, process, and freeze quality semen faster and more efficiently.[3] This is a booming business—The Associated Press reported that U.S. farmers spent $225 million on bull semen in 2005.[4]

With bull semen as their end product, Alan recruited three Weber State professors to invest in a bull. They pooled together $20,000— more than Alan's annual salary at the time—and selected a monstrous, pedigreed dairy Holstein bull from Pappy's Farm in Ogden named Stillaguamish Yakima Chief. Each investor put in about $5,000 to buy the bull.

The plan was to hire someone to collect the semen from Chief, then freeze the liquid in syringes to sell to farmers later. These syringes would be inserted into cows, leading to a new generation of strong milk producers. They set up lodging for their bull at a dairy farm, making ownership as hands-off as possible. Owning the bull (and the

pedigreed semen he produced) was sure to be a source of cash flow for
years to come.

Alas, misfortune struck before Alan and his co-investors could get
their bull-semen operation off the ground. One day, some teenagers
with guns shot their bull in the head and took off. "Next thing we knew,
the bull was dead and our money was gone," Alan says. "There were no
little cows to show for it."

Overnight, the entire venture was (figuratively and literally) shot.
There was no way to recoup their money. They couldn't have foreseen
or prevented such a misfortune. Now Alan had two business ideas fail
before he'd even made a penny.

Digging for diamonds

Alan's next business idea came while taking his kids to the dentist.
He knew dentists used drills with diamond burrs to grind down teeth;
what if he could produce those burrs with artificial diamonds?

Alan reached out to his famous professor uncle, Tracy Hall,
inventor of the man-made diamond. He figured he could buy tiny
diamond crystals from Tracy's company and put them on a little
steel shaft to create a diamond burr. He dreamed of reimagining and
dominating the dental drill industry with less-expensive and longer-
lasting diamond burrs.

Alan did his research, studying textbooks to learn how to chemically
attach diamonds to the steel. He set up a lab near the family's home,
close to the Ogden airport. Then he created a production line by hiring
a Weber State student to run the lab, and a team of neighborhood ladies
to inspect each of the assembled burrs. He believed in this product and
persuaded Jeannie to support the effort with $50,000 of their hard-
earned money.

All seemed favorable until he reached the essential step of selling
the product. Dentists liked the idea—but they wouldn't buy Alan's burrs.
Large dental suppliers held a monopoly over the market, offering every
tool, including dental drills, that dentists needed for their practice.
Dentists didn't want to offend their suppliers and lose needed inventory
by using Alan's burrs.

"I didn't know the market," says Alan. Despite an innovative solution to the problem of expensive diamond burrs, he hadn't thought to consult with his potential customers about the channel of distribution.

Eager to recoup losses, Alan racked his brain to find another potential need in the market. During this time, he served as a bishop in a young single adult ward, and all around him, students were getting married. Selling engagement rings to couples looking for diamonds seemed like an obvious and interesting pursuit. After a short period of time, he recognized he shouldn't be in the diamond ring business. "I didn't know much about the products," he admits.

Alan had been repeating the same painful business mistake over and over again, pursuing ideas where he really didn't know the market or industry. The barnacle buster and pedigreed bull semen both quickly faltered, and neither had cost Alan more than a few thousand dollars. The collapse of his diamond burr business, on the other hand, generated a huge loss—at least three years' wages at the time. Of these business failures, he comments, it was "foolishness followed by foolishness by foolishness."

This whole time, however, Jeannie's trust in Alan never wavered. "I gratefully give Jeannie credit for supporting my entrepreneurial journey," Alan says. "Any success I have had is due to my beloved wife. She never complained. Her basic belief was that I would somehow figure out how to build a successful business."

To bail them out of their financial pickle, Jeannie went to work at her father-in-law's pharmacy. She took their small children with her, and they played in a back room while she worked as a pharmacy technician. "She worked until the business debts were paid," Alan says. "We couldn't have made it without her many sacrifices."

New career trajectory with Netline

It wasn't long after the discouraging diamond incident that Alan was asked to be president of Ballet West. During that exhausting seven-year stretch, Alan took a break from entrepreneurial efforts. But eventually, Alan knew he had to move on. The Houston Ballet offered him a role as their CEO, but he turned it down. He wanted a new challenge.

One day while still at Ballet West, Alan got a call from his cousin, David Hall, who told him about his new company called Netline. He invited Alan to be the president, raise money, and help him run the business.

The timing was right, and it was an entrepreneurial quest Alan couldn't resist. He went straight from the classical tradition of Ballet West to tech start-up without missing a beat. Netline was immensely different from Ballet West, and Alan appreciated the change and the challenge.

It was an exciting time in the tech world. Alan had never even seen a computer before—they'd only been on the public market for a few years. His first day on the job, the secretary gave him training on how to run his IBM 286 computer. Alan remembers asking, "What do I do with it?" He didn't even know how to turn the computer on. Then the secretary showed him the WordPerfect DOS system, a whole new world in 1987.

For a year and a half, Alan drove the 160-mile round-trip from Roy to Provo. Luckily, it didn't happen every day. There were occasions, especially during the blustery winter months, when Alan called Jeannie and told her he wouldn't make it home. He'd stay overnight in a Provo apartment packed with six college students who had offered him a spare bedroom. He'd eat a microwaved meal, fall into bed, get up the next morning, and go back to work.

Despite the long hours, he enjoyed his job and learned something new every day. Alan's responsibility was selling David's new technology. This was a tall order. At the time, computers and printers were not connected. The computer would be in one room, with the printers connected by cables to a separate modem down the hall. It seems simple now, but Netline's innovative product made it possible to compute and print in the same room. David figured out how to send signals from computers to printers using copper wires within the walls of an office.

Alan traveled to expos and conventions to promote Netline. At a Las Vegas computer expo, COMDEX, Alan realized Netline was running into the same problem as his earlier ventures. Their product filled a valid need, but they didn't know how to sell it.

"We were burning through money," Alan remembers. "A lot of focus was on the engineers, who wanted every bell and whistle for a perfect product. That was a problem. Cash was spent on research and development and not on marketing and sales. I have since learned it is best to generate revenues with the first version of a product."

Today, as an adjunct business professor of entrepreneurship at Weber State, Alan teaches students the expensive lesson he learned at Netline: Talk to potential customers first before building a product. Learn about their needs and wants and create solutions to existing problems. Build a prototype and show it to potential buyers to see if the idea has merit, followed by an iterative process where designer and prospective client work together to develop the best solution.

This was not the scenario at Netline. Ray Noorda of Novell had invested several million dollars in Netline, but unfortunately had not seen an increase in the company's value or his investment. As a Hail Mary effort, Alan hired college students from BYU and sent them across the country to evangelize the Netline product in person. The problem was that retail stores for computer technology didn't yet exist, making it a challenge to find ideal dealers. At the end of a year and a half, out of funds and with no way of obtaining more, Netline closed its doors.

"Being involved with Netline was a pivotal experience for me," Alan says. "What I learned there became a fantastic introduction into the fast-growing world of computer technology. It happened unplanned, unanticipated—just out of the blue."

Netline's demise had been written on the wall, and Alan had seen firsthand the go-to-market mistakes that had contributed to the company's lack of growth and profitability. He began to wonder if there might be a better way to reach potential customers in a more agile, leaner, and less-expensive way. He also wondered if there were enough potential clients needing a better way.

As he read trade publications and computer magazines about scores of start-up tech companies launching new Windows applications on a weekly basis, Alan could see a compelling and fast-growing market opportunity. He also learned that every one of these fledgling companies desperately needed help in generating revenues. He had a solution for them. He convinced Jeannie he had finally landed on his best idea so far.

10

Basement Business

As Alan talked to potential Netline clients, he learned that computer hardware and software companies used a two-tier distribution model to generate revenues. A tech company sold its product to a distributor, who in turn sold the product to computer dealers, who then sold it to an individual or business. Two flaws in this model stood out quickly to Alan: One, dealers and their sales staffs rarely knew anything about the tech company's products, and two, distributors did not view dealer training as their responsibility.

As a result, dealers were not selling the new products. Every American small technology start-up had this same enormous problem, and Alan had a revolutionary solution for them.

His offer to potential clients was clear and simple: Alan's marketing and sales team would learn everything about the client's tech product, and they would visit every dealer across the country to train their sales staff on the product's features and benefits. Alan would charge the clients a modest fee for every training session. He promised these companies that once dealers knew about their products, they would begin to sell them.

Alan played with business name ideas and logo concepts and settled on "TempReps," which he registered with the State of Utah on June 13, 1988. He officially left Netline in August 1988 and started TempReps that September. His goal was to become the first full-service outsourced sales and marketing solutions company for tech products in the world.

First, he needed a customer.

"I was in my basement, calling companies like Intel, telling them I had this idea to help evangelize their products in stores around the country. They wanted nothing to do with me," Alan says.

With big companies turning him down, Alan decided to solicit smaller companies. With no email back then, his only options were calling or sending a letter. He called day and night, hoping to get a first bite.

In order to secure a client, he needed capital to pay his sales reps. Neither his parents nor his in-laws could help. Alan suggested to Jeannie that they use their house as collateral for a bank loan. With Alan's salary from Ballet West, the Halls could have upgraded their home like most of their peers. Instead, they had been frugal and retired their mortgage. They owned their home outright and had no other debts, including credit cards.

The loan was a real risk for a family with six kids at home. Yet even after his four failed business attempts, Jeannie believed in Alan's entrepreneurial spirit—enough to risk losing their house.

First Security Bank agreed to provide Alan with a business loan with his house as collateral. The branch manager, Mark Johnson, gave Alan the funds he needed to pay monthly expenses. Alan hoped his clients would generate the revenues to pay off the loan within twenty-four months. In the meantime, he watched his cash flow on a daily basis and kept Mr. Johnson posted on any shortfall issues.

"I tease people that had it failed, my family would have been living in a van down by the river, eating government cheese," Alan says with a grin, quoting Chris Farley's *Saturday Night Live* skit.

"I think Jeannie knew how scary this was. I was literally making sales calls to potential clients on Christmas Eve," Alan says. "I was driven to not let this thing die. There was no stopping me."

When Alan speaks to entrepreneurs now, he tells them, "You really have to know what it takes. There's no way around it. You just have to do it."

The fear of losing their home was a great motivator, but the strain took its toll. "I probably should have recognized the stress was killing me," Alan admits. "But I pressed on."

Heart angina at age forty-three

Stress truly was affecting Alan's health. Within a month of starting TempReps, in mid-October 1988, Alan had a recurrence of a severe heart angina attack he had experienced a few months earlier. According to the American Heart Association, angina is "chest pain or discomfort caused when your heart muscle doesn't get enough oxygen-rich blood. It may feel like pressure or squeezing in your chest . . . and usually happens because one or more of the coronary arteries is narrowed or blocked."[1]

In late July 1988, Alan was in Island Park with his family. "I felt this enormous pressure squeezing my throat," Alan says. "When I stopped walking it went away, but if I walked a few yards, the pressure returned."

He wasn't sure what was happening, but the terrifying sensation stopped him in his tracks. After a call to Alan's doctor, the family quickly returned home, an agonizing 250-mile road trip.

At the doctor's office, Alan struggled to walk on a treadmill. He was told his arteries were clogged, and in a few days, Alan was in a cardiac catheterization lab. The doctor performed an angioplasty, where they confirmed the diagnosis of a severe blockage in Alan's heart. The interventional cardiologist then inserted an inflated balloon within the coronary artery to push the plaque obstruction into the walls of the artery. Although the balloon pressure enlarged the opening in the artery, it did not remove the plaque.

"I remember that moment very well, lying on a cold table, sedated, covered with a sheet, shivering, watching the procedure," Alan says. "I thought, *I'm a mortal, and I might not make it off this table.*"

He thought about his wife and six kids at home. His oldest son, Aaron, was a teenager, but the rest of the children were still young. What would they do without their father?

"I could see the blockage on the screen and the doctor's attempt to place the balloon in the proper place," Alan says. "As he inflated the balloon, I felt my blood flowing again through the open artery." Although he'd been under tremendous stress, his heart troubles came as a surprise. Alan was only forty-three years old. Less than a month earlier, he had easily hiked Mount Ogden and Ben Lomond, mountain peaks just shy of 10,000 feet. Now he could barely walk.

A few months later, the same suffocating feeling attacked Alan's throat again. This time, Alan was with the family and a group of young boys at the Roy Recreation Complex swimming pool, celebrating Christian's seventh birthday. As he picked up each little boy and tossed them into the water, Alan felt terrific pain in his neck. Alan and Jeannie were horrified to think the balloon procedure had failed, but indeed it had. Within a few hours, Alan was in the catheterization lab again. This time, the balloon procedure worked for nearly two decades.

Heart disease continues to plague Alan. Over the last thirty years, he has been to the emergency room five times for angina attacks, and doctors have inserted several stents. After playing tennis one day in June 2017, he felt pain in his throat again. Jeannie took him to the emergency room and then to the catheterization lab. The doctor saw one artery had seventy percent blockage and couldn't be cleared with a stent. To slow the growth of plaque in his arteries, Alan began taking specialized heart drugs. "I hope to successfully manage my disease to ensure many more good years upon this earth!" he says.

The first three reps

In January 1989, after stressful months of heart pains and sales pitches, Alan landed his first contract with a little software company based in Vancouver, Canada. The $50,000 contract covered three reps to evangelize the client's product for a ninety-day term in Miami, New York, and Los Angeles.

Alan had worked with Netline's field reps the previous summer and approached three of them to work for TempReps. He hired Jeff Archuleta (who later had a singing son, David, of *American*

Idol fame) to cover the Miami territory, a female sales rep to cover
Los Angeles, and another young man to cover New York City. Alan
would pay them for every store visit and the manufacturer would
provide training.

The Canadian company sent a trainer to educate Alan's three
TempReps contractors on their product. "I also trained them to use the
local phone book to find computer dealers and to build a database," Alan
says. "I had a form they completed and sent back to me that reported
how many stores they had visited."

Alan trained his son Aaron and daughter Laura to call the stores
to verify the reps had shown up and trained the salespeople. "In terms
of how effective it was, based on the stores selling a client's product,
it wasn't that great," Alan remembers. "Once they were educated on
the technology, it still took a few months before the people in the store
knew how to intelligently talk about a new product."

Under constant financial pressure, Alan kept a tight hold on the
books. The money from the bank loan was mainly for paying his sales
people. He wasn't taking a personal salary. He paid his reps each week
but didn't give them per-diem allowances, nor did he cover their gas or
overnight stays.

He used part of the loan for travel to technology expos like
COMDEX in Las Vegas, so he could meet people in the tech industry
and secure new business. Alan's take-home salary for the first year of
the business was only $5,000. "We were living on food storage and
Jeannie's modest income," Alan says. "She did a great job managing
our personal expenses."

Previously working half time as a high school counselor, Jeannie
increased her work schedule so the family could have a little more
income and health insurance.

As the initial contract was coming to an end, Alan scrambled to
get another customer for his reps. He realized he needed to represent
four clients at the same time to make a profit. The first three paid for
operations, but the fourth client provided the profit.

Alan was constantly on the phone, attending trade shows, and
searching magazines in pursuit of the next client. "I recognized if this

company was really going to take off, this would be my life. Constant stress to sell," Alan says.

Selling these services was a slow process that required educating decision makers on the potential return for their investment. "But I did start to have success representing little companies that made products for Windows. They had very few funds for marketing their offerings, but they could pay TempReps our low-cost fee," Alan says.

As Alan worked to make traction on sales, he hired LuAnn Hammer, a friend in the neighborhood, to help with operations. She called to verify store visits. He also hired Julie Gottschalk as an assistant and Mark Britton to oversee payroll. They all worked full time in the Hall family basement. "We went to a hardware store and purchased a few cheap wooden desks," Alan says. "The employees entered the front door of our home and walked down to the basement. They saw my six kids running around, getting ready for school each day. There was no privacy for them or us."

The fledgling company focused on business fundamentals. "I was trying to get sales, we were recruiting new representatives, keeping track of our money, and calling stores for quality control," Alan says. "Every ninety days was a fire drill as we tried to close four new clients and find more sales reps. Every ninety days! It was unbelievable how much time and energy we all put in to launch a new tour."

Collecting in Canada

In March 1989, the first TempReps customer owed $50,000. "He wasn't paying our invoice. Not a dime," Alan says. "Right out of the chute, we were facing a financial emergency. It was a very tense time."

Alan's only way to contact the client was via phone calls, fax, or snail mail. He called repeatedly and left messages. "I was desperate: 'Come on! What's going on?' I'd say, but he wouldn't answer his phone," Alan says. "I finally decided to go to his office."

Alan consulted with Jeannie about the cheapest way to get to Canada. He decided to pay for a plane ticket to Seattle, then rent a car to drive to Vancouver, Canada. The unexpected travel expense hurt. "At the time I was agonizing over buying a $250 fax machine. These were really terrifying moments for us," Alan says.

He arrived at the client's office in Vancouver, ready to make a scene. "I told him I'd sit in his office until he gave me the money," Alan says. "I was very stern with him. We needed his payment to survive. My position was non-negotiable; I would not surrender. Without his check, our lives would have fallen apart and the business would have died. I could not disappoint Jeannie."

Coming back in the rental car to Seattle, there was a horrendous March storm, and it took Alan longer than expected to get to the airport. However, he had the check. "Looking back," Alan says, "there was a moment in my mind where I could see myself on the evening news on my way to jail, in handcuffs, for having strangled my client in his office."

Soon after the Vancouver trip, Alan experienced another crisis. He learned his rep based in New York City—whom he had been paying weekly—had been falsifying the store visits he'd reported. "As we called the stores he claimed he had visited, we quickly learned he had not visited any of them," Alan says. "He had stolen our client's money. I fired him immediately and notified the client."

Leaning on faith

Even during the rough first business years, with heart troubles, financial strain, and hard decisions, Alan knew he was being watched over. "We're never really left alone," Alan says. "God is always there to guide and protect us."

Alan and Jeannie leaned on their faith. "I prayed a lot. I prayed every night that my employees would be okay, that we would find new customers and that God would keep this thing going," Alan says. "And He did. At the same time, we were still trying to have a normal life raising our kids and serving in the Church. It was not easy."

Some wonder how Alan was led to start his company. He tells them he and Jeannie were prayerful about what to do. "God opens doors," Alan says. "Sometimes they're doors that seem strange to us—unanticipated doors—but He will lead us to opportunities He knows will benefit us."

Alan recognizes, looking back, that each step of his career led him to build TempReps. "My job at Weber State was a stepping stone, as was the ballet and Netline," he says. "Each of the opportunities led to the

THE LIFE AND TIMES OF ALAN E. HALL

next one. I believe God guides us on our unique and individual paths as men and women, as couples, and as families."

Ninety-day stress train, on repeat

Alan didn't see much of his kids during the start-up phase of TempReps. For the first couple of years, he was traveling across the country to talk to companies about the business model. He was constantly on the road reaching out to prospective clients. "I couldn't close a sale with just a phone call," Alan says. "It generally took multiple trips to prospects and conversations with numerous layers of company management before we landed a new client. It was exhausting work but the only way to keep TempReps growing."

Early TempReps clients included start-up companies who were creating products for Windows. There was a math product, a spell-checker, and a drawing tool. Most clients signed up for one tour that lasted ninety days and comprised 1,000 store visits in ten major American cities. The price tag was $100,000, about one-third the cost of a company's own full-time sales staff.

Alan found his clients wanted more coverage, so he increased his sales team from three temporary sales reps to ten. He recruited college students—usually from the computer science department—from Utah State, Weber, and BYU. Soon he was recruiting students from the colleges' business and marketing departments. Four clients trained them on their products at the Snowbird Ski Resort, in Salt Lake City, every ninety days. Students left school for a semester to work full time for TempReps.

Each of the ten reps was sent to cover a specific territory for ninety days. Alan gave them a list of stores to visit and the name of a Relief Society president in the area. "These good women helped them find temporary lodging," Alan says.

Alan felt very responsible for each rep, especially Jeff Farr from Ogden. He and his wife pulled up to Alan's house in a trailer with their two little babies, about to head to Texas. "The stress on me was unimaginable," Alan says. "I knew I was responsible for these young couples."

When he could, Alan visited his reps across the country. "I remember staying with my rep in Boston. He lived in a run-down apartment near Fenway Park, home of the Red Sox in Boston," Alan says. "I slept on the floor in his apartment and went with him the next day to visit computer stores."

For the next two years, every ninety days, the cycle continued with hiring and training ten new college-aged sales reps. The work was non-stop. In time, these temporary sales reps wanted full-time work, so Alan decided to change the business model. Going forward, he hired employees and guaranteed them regular annual work. Such a move was risky. It meant Alan had to have enough clients to keep his people working. Not wanting to disappoint his team, he doubled his efforts to secure new clients. "I felt a new level of pressure to perform for my people," Alan says. "I couldn't sleep at night knowing what I had to accomplish every day."

First big client

Luckily for Alan, after constant stress and a pittance of an income, he got his first big break. His team of ten reps had generated substantial revenues for Ami Pro, a TempReps client that had developed a word-processing program. "The president of Ami Pro was really, really happy with us and told me that," Alan says.

Lotus Corporation, a well-known spreadsheet company, acquired Ami Pro. "A few months after the acquisition, I received a phone call from the vice president of Lotus. He wanted to fly to Salt Lake City to see me about an opportunity," Alan says.

They met at a downtown hotel—Alan never had clients come to his "office" in the basement, for good reason. "He said to me, 'What you did for Ami Pro was remarkable and we'd like to engage TempReps to represent Lotus Corporation with a full-time team of reps,'" Alan remembers. "I was *thrilled*. This meant we had full-time work for our ten employees and a million-dollar contract."

In addition, the Lotus contract gave TempReps a measure of stability, national credibility, and legitimacy. With a major client under contract, TempReps enjoyed new fame and exposure. Alan started to receive calls from other large tech companies who wanted to learn more about his business model. "I will always be grateful to that Lotus leadership team that gave TempReps a chance," Alan says. "I will forever praise their names. Their public endorsement of a little company in Roy, Utah, was a turning point that led TempReps/ MarketStar into becoming a global business."

TempReps continued to represent a few start-ups and still had a few temporary employees for its other ninety-day engagements. With Lotus as their lead client, it was easier for Alan to approach bigger brands. In a matter of months, Alan signed a deal with Mitsubishi, a very large technology company that made laptops. In short order, TempReps grew to more than 100 full-time employees.

At the end of 1991, two years after signing an agreement for a bank loan, Alan and Jeannie were able to retire the debt. Their house was no longer at risk. "It was a very happy day for us to know that huge obligation was gone," Alan says. "Our hard work and sacrifice had paid off. We could breathe just a little bit easier."

In addition to paying off the loan, the Halls had enough money to buy a larger and more comfortable home. They'd been cramped for twenty years in a 1,052-square-foot house with six children and, for a time, seven full-time employees crammed in the basement. It was time for more space for the family and employees.

They paid $195,000 in cash for a 5,000-square-foot home in Roy, Utah, just a few blocks from the first home. Jeannie agreed to let the employees work in the basement once again. But this "basement business" wouldn't stay there for long.

In the Beginning

Gene & Joyce Hall – 1943

Betty & Hank Nowak – 1943

Alan – 1950

Jeannie – 1954

Alan Hall

1958

1963

1965

1975   1984

Family, Work, Community, Church

(Left to right) Christian, Aaron, Eric, Adam, and Alan, 1993

*With President Paul Thompson,
Weber State, 2000*

*The Mercato team: (left to right)
Tara Rosander, Aaron DeRose,
Greg Warnock, Alison Wistner,
and Joe Grover, 2013*

*Roy North Stake presidency: Dan
Emerson, Alan, and Chad Griffiths, 2009*

*Aaron, Adam, Christian,
Alan, and Eric, 1998*

*Weber State graduation with
President Charles Wight, 2016*

*Alan with Governor Gary Herbert
and his wife, Jeannette, 2010*

Family, Work, Community, Church

*Visiting with Jeff Bezos
of Amazon, 2012*

*With Desiree Cooper-Larsen,
Ogden rodeo director, 2015*

Coaching a girls basketball team, 2013

*With students of his entrepreneur
class at BYU Hawaii, 2012*

Some of the Hall Family men at the 2008 Masters Tournament

Jeannie Hall

Miss Weber State, 1968

With schoolgirls in Japan, 2000

Ogden High school counselor, 1998

Mormon Tabernacle Choir, 2008

*With Hadley Hall, Shelby West,
and Cole West, 2015*

*Fairy Godmother Jeannie with
Aubrey West, 2007*

Alan & Jeannie Hall

Wedding reception, 1969   *With Aaron at BYU, 1971*

Capitol Theatre, 1985   *Roy, 1987*

With President George W. Bush, 1999   *Westminster Abbey, 2006*

Alan & Jeannie Hall Family

Hall Family – 1987
Left to right: Laura, Christian, Alan, Jeannie, Aaron, Megan, Adam, and Eric

Hall Family – 2004
Left to right: Christian, Megan, Adam, Alan, Jeannie, Aaron, Laura, and Eric

Hall Family 2018

LEFT TO RIGHT:

Christian and Emily Hall; Adam and Annette Hall; Megan and Curtis Funk; Alan and Jeannie Hall; Kim and Aaron Hall; Laura and Matt West; Cami and Eric Hall

11

MarketStar Success

lan realized his TempReps team needed room to grow—
literally. In 1993, TempReps permanently moved out of
the Halls' home, ushering in a new era of professionalism.
"Jeannie was grateful we were out of her basement," Alan says. "She
finally had her home back!"

The shift to a new office, and later a new name, signified the
growth of Alan's biggest entrepreneurial success so far.

New office, new name

After exploring several options, Alan signed a lease at Ogden's
historic Old Post Office Building on Grant Avenue and 24th Street.
Built in the early 1900s, the three-story landmark boasts Corinthian
columns, marble halls, and wide-open spaces. The company flourished
for the next five years at that location.

By 1994, the company had also outgrown its name. Alan no longer
thought of the company as "temporary," since there were full-time
employees and a long-term contract with Lotus. In light of these significant
milestones, he and his managers changed the company name to Technology
Advancement Corporation (TAC) to describe their vision and direction.

TAC had three divisions: BlitzAmerica, IntroTech, and DataNow.[1] Under the TAC umbrella, the leadership team established two sub-brands to handle growing business across other industries and channels: Sports Advancement Company and ChannelMasters.

As the company grew rapidly, Alan felt ready to hire more personnel. Within two years of moving to the Old Post Office, the company had 415 full-time employees. His hiring managers added more marketing and sales professionals and managers to lead new client teams. "I couldn't personally manage all aspects of the business anymore, so I began to delegate the work to other leaders," Alan says. "The company was starting to have a larger organizational structure that required adding additional layers of management."

As more people were hired, TAC became one of the larger employers in the community. Many of the new employees were Weber State students who worked the afternoon and evening shifts. They were trained to staff trade shows, contact distributors, train end-users, provide technical support, assist retailers, and perform numerous marketing functions.

Finding the right people was a struggle. Managers hired employees as fast as they could, only to learn that many were not qualified for the position. Often within a few months, after hours of training and supervision, the company had to let them go. "It became clear to us that we needed to spend more time understanding a prospective employee's background," Alan says. "We learned that new hires needed to be more than just competent to be great employees at TAC."

He determined that an employer should consider seven attributes when hiring. Potential employees need to be: 1) capable of personal growth, 2) able to fit into the company culture, 3) happy with their compensation, 4) able to work well with others, 5) individuals with character and high standards, 6) committed to working long-term at the organization, and 7) competent to excel in their assigned duties.

Compiling these attributes and lessons in hiring, Alan wrote a book titled *The 7 C's of Hiring*, which focuses in depth on improving the hiring process. "I believe that by following the guiding principles of intelligent hiring, employers will be able to acquire the best talent and retain them for an extended period of time," he says. (See Appendix III for the *Forbes* article that explains these seven areas in more detail.)

To accelerate company growth, TAC's leadership focused on finding and engaging new clients. The plan was to expand the sales and marketing teams to promote services and contact prospective customers. To accomplish this goal, TAC invested money in new marketing materials, including a company website. New executives were added to the sales team. Each of these leaders oversaw a list of potential clients whom they contacted by phone, email, and personal visits at trade shows and company offices.

Thinking that their outsourced marketing and sales model would work in two other industries, TAC hired new executives with backgrounds in sporting goods and medical products. Their task was to determine if they might find and engage new clients. Within a year, company leaders determined that these "vertical markets"—companies that focus on meeting the needs of a specific industry—did not require TAC's capabilities. In time, TAC contracted with new companies in other industries that would use its services, such as Whirlpool and Motorola.

Businesses grow by offering new products and services, adding new verticals, and expanding into new geographies. It dawned on Alan that the TAC footprint could expand far beyond Ogden, Utah. With growth always on his mind, he decided to expand outside the United States. In short order, TAC began to hire employees in Canada.

Business betrayal

After moving into the Old Post Office Building, Alan experienced his first major business betrayal. He had an unmistakable spiritual warning the night before the incident, when he took Jeannie on a date to an evening theater performance at the University of Utah. "During the program, I had this overwhelming feeling of spiritual darkness, like the bells of hell ringing inside me," Alan remembers. "I didn't know what it was, but I recognized something really bad was about to happen."

The next morning, the chief financial officer, who had been with the company about six months, came into Alan's office with an ultimatum. "He wanted major ownership and control of the business. I recognized that was the moment I felt was coming, and I dismissed him on the spot," Alan says. "I wasn't willing to just hand over company ownership to him."

The last thing the CFO said before walking out the door was that he was starting a competing business. "Behind my back, he had gathered everything he needed to know about our clients and financials. He knew everything I knew about running the business," Alan says. "He secretly talked to employees about splitting off and building a company. It was about greed—that's how I saw it."

The former CFO recruited ten high-performing TAC employees, took the IBM client, and moved quickly to take other TAC customers. This left Alan in the awkward position of not knowing which remaining employees he could trust. "I had to figure out which employees were loyal and which ones weren't," Alan says.

Alan immediately called his lawyer to stop the damage and protect TAC's trade secrets and intellectual property. An Ogden judge allowed the company to compete against TAC as long as it did not use TAC's proprietary information. The competitor lasted eight years before closing in 2002.

"That period was deeply pivotal for me," Alan says, noting he's not a fan of confrontation. "I kept asking myself: Is this business worth it? Is it worth the hassle?"

Amidst the mental anguish, Alan pressed on, not to just save TAC, but to keep it growing. He wouldn't let this event or anything else stop him from driving forward. He knew his family and employees depended on him to maximize TAC's potential. He realized there was a higher purpose for building a company. For him, it was about creating employment for hundreds of people and paying them a marketable wage to support their families.

Culture based on five pillars

To provide his employees with a noble company culture, Alan established five guiding pillars. He decided the key principles should all be based on love, and in the following order: Love of God and a willingness to follow Him, love of one's self, love of family, love of fellow employees and customers, and love of community. These were the areas of life that mattered most to him. He believed his employees would agree with the notion that demonstrating love in every possible way would be a compelling work culture.

Declaring TAC's unique statement was a bold move. It was questioned frequently by executives at big companies. "There was always a struggle to balance 'our way' versus 'the big corporate way,'" Alan says. "When I would tell them about our company pillars, they would say, 'That's not our culture. Our culture is about making money, money, and more money.'"

Alan never backed down from this core philosophy. "We lost a few clients because of our culture. We also added new ones who understood we were committed to time-tested values." Over the last thirty years, thousands of employees have admired and treasured the company's philosophy of how to run a world-class business. Alan hears regularly from employees that they feel valued, appreciated, and grateful for the company's high standards.

Moving and incorporating

In 1997, TAC outgrew the Old Post Office Building after renting every available space in the building, filling the entire first level, and then starting to take over the upstairs floors. Alan looked in Ogden for another office space for his burgeoning team. Only blocks away, he found availability on the third floor of the distinctive blue-glass Thiokol building, located on Washington Boulevard and historic 25th Street. He signed a multiple-year lease.

"As Thiokol left in 1998, we leased another 50,000 square feet of office space and slowly occupied the remaining five floors," Alan says. The company has now been there for more than twenty years. It still remains the company's headquarters, although the organization has expanded to additional buildings in other cities.

The same year TAC headquarters moved, company leaders once again saw a need to change the name. They had landed business with several companies from other industries, and were representing businesses like Whirlpool, promoting washers and dryers, and taking cell phone manufacturers to market. Alan and others on the management team pondered what to call TAC going forward.

Funny phone call at work

Even though business was all consuming, Alan and Jeannie still found time now and then for a date. When Weber State University hosted a concert at the new Dee Events Center with Collin Raye, a big-name country singer, the university president invited Alan and Jeannie to sit with him, his wife, and other dignitaries. During the intermission, Alan got up to stretch his legs and wandered out to the main concourse.

"A young cowgirl who had been drinking came up to me," Alan says. "'Hello, can we visit?' she asked. I dismissed her and went back to my seat. I didn't realize the president and Jeannie had seen her with me."

The next morning at his office, Alan received a voice message from someone he believed to be the young cowgirl. "She asked when she could see me again and wanted to get to know me better. She gave me her phone number," Alan says. "That put me in a panic. Was she a stalker? How did she get my number?"

Alan was so disturbed by the message that he told the company attorney about it. Alan felt uneasy the rest of the day and told Jeannie about the call when he got home that evening.

She asked, "Well, what did she say? Did she leave a phone number or anything?"

Alan told her she did. Then Jeannie started talking in the cowgirl's voice and repeated exactly what was on the voicemail. It was Jeannie who had left the message!

"The funniest part was she left my own home phone number on the voicemail message and I didn't recognize it," Alan says.

Working with women

Alan enjoyed working with both male and female executives and preferred to keep his senior team gender-balanced. The women on the management team were actively involved in company leadership and empowered to accomplish their individual assignments. He characterizes them as hardworking, smart, dedicated, and loyal.

"I saw them as equal to the men in every way, and believed their compensation should reflect that," Alan says. "I valued their views and respected their opinions on business operations, policy, strategy, and corporate vision. I honored them for how they saw the world, in unique and different ways from men."

Alan recognized these women were also wives and mothers with many duties outside work, so he provided them with flex time. The women knew Alan supported a balanced-life policy. "They all had bright futures with the company, and beyond. As such, I encouraged their professional growth through education, additional work-related experiences, and entrepreneurship," Alan says. "I give credit to the great women who helped build a successful organization."

One caution on working with the opposite sex, he adds, is to recognize romantic temptations in the workplace for those who are married. Over the years, Alan saw how some employees made bad choices that eventually led to affairs—and tore families apart. "Problems with infidelity generally occur at work," Alan says. "It's a real reason behind many divorces. Be on guard at work. Remember to be loyal to your spouse. Don't do or say anything that you wouldn't want your spouse to know about."

1997 Entrepreneur of the Year

Business was booming. In 1996, Sony signed with TAC, the start of a two-decade relationship. In 1997, Hewlett-Packard signed its first partnership, using TAC's marketing services across multiple channels. The company attracted other global customers like IBM, Mitsubishi, and Intel.

"We were starting to engage very large brands," Alan says. "Over nearly ten years, we had been involved in the birth and growth of the computer industry. When I look back, our company knew more about what was going on in technology than anyone in the world."

Year by year, TAC's portfolio of clients and revenues grew exponentially; the company increased its annual revenue from $9.5 million in 1995 to $17.6 million in 1996. Such numbers attracted publicity. Ernst & Young, the multinational professional services firm, holds a national competition to honor entrepreneurs who achieve exceptional results. As CEO, Alan was handpicked to represent Utah in the competition as the 1997 Entrepreneur of the Year.[2]

Alan and Jeannie attended the national competition in Palm Springs, where they met leading entrepreneurs from forty-nine other states. Part of the competition included special dinners and educational seminars. With great interest, Alan attended an Ernst & Young session on how to sell a business. "Although we hadn't been in business for a long time, I wanted to understand what the future held," Alan says. Thanks to national publicity, Alan soon started receiving calls from venture capitalists, including Omnicom Group.

One night at dinner during the competition, Alan and Jeannie sat next to a young businessman named Jeff Bezos, who owned a company called Amazon.

"So Jeff, what do you do?" Alan asked.

"Well, I have a business that sells books online," Jeff answered.

Later, Alan told Jeannie, "That's a stupid idea. It won't work! People buy books from book stores."

Twenty-two years later, in 2019, Jeff Bezos' personal net worth topped $134 billion, and Amazon's market value exceeded $777 billion.[3]

When the Utah Technology Council invited Jeff Bezos to speak at the organization's annual banquet, Alan was the chairman of the board of trustees and the event's master of ceremonies. In front of a thousand guests, Alan shared with the crowd how he'd made a foolish forecast of Amazon's potential success. Mr. Bezos and the entire audience got a big laugh out of that.

Going global and a name change

Although Alan won an award for his growing business, expanding TAC's capabilities wasn't always pretty. There were definitely growing pains. "Companies like Intel, Microsoft, HP, and other big clients wanted us to have global coverage," Alan says. "We honored their exciting request by first analyzing how we might proceed. We soon learned that to do so required a lot of energy, time, and resources. It meant having to manage employees all over the world, in different time zones, speaking multiple foreign languages, with different cultures and traditions."

At the same time, after months of discussions, the company began a campaign to notify its clientele and the global computer industry that it had changed its name to MarketStar. For the third time, leadership spent substantial funds to brand the company and its vision for the future. "We felt the time was right to enlarge our scope and capabilities across global markets and industries," Alan says.

With new business cards in hand, Alan began his European expansion research by taking a trip to England. He asked Craig Bott, MarketStar vice president over strategy, to accompany him. They met with Tony Stratton, CEO of CPM, in Oxford, England, to learn about the marketplace. CPM, a global outsourced sales agency, was well established all over Europe. His hundreds of employees represented large consumer goods companies and they regularly visited thousands of retail stores across the continent.

In 1998, MarketStar partnered with CPM to establish a presence in Europe. Alan sent his son Aaron—accompanied by his wife, Kim, and baby daughter, Allie—to establish "MarketStar Europe," with headquarters in Oxford. Instead of sending Americans to Europe, Market-Star would hire local employees. Aaron spent a year learning the laws, regulations, and policies of hiring sales reps in England, France, and Germany. In time, Matt Roland Jones, a former employee of CPM, was hired to run MarketStar Europe.

Next, Alan set his sights on learning about Asia. MarketStar leaders established an office in Japan and hired a Japanese technology executive to manage MarketStar's operations in Tokyo. A Chinese executive was hired in Beijing to supervise MarketStar China's operations across his vast country. His first assignment was selling Motorola cell phones. "I made the mistake of thinking he knew nothing about selling phones," Alan says. "During a training session in Beijing, while I was teaching him and his team, he rudely interrupted me. He cried out, 'You don't need to tell us how to sell anything. We've been selling merchandise in China for 4,000 years!'"

His abruptness bothered Alan. He wanted to fire the employee on the spot, but instead Alan swallowed his pride and invited him to teach what he knew. They left the conference room and went into the heart of the city. His Chinese manager showed Alan street after street with rows of small retail stores selling thousands of cell phones.

"Obviously, the Chinese knew how to sell," Alan says. He flew home, satisfied that his manager and team could sell Motorola phones. "I wasn't surprised to learn that the MarketStar China team was performing well and exceeding all our expectations."

Next, they looked at expanding into Latin America. As a border country, Mexico was fairly easy access for MarketStar and American technology companies. Brazil and Argentina, due to their population sizes, also looked promising. Eventually, MarketStar put a group of reps in San José, Costa Rica; Mexico City, Mexico; and Buenos Aires, Argentina.

MarketStar's large tech clients were pleased with efforts to expand across the planet. Alan hoped, as did his senior team, that the company could surprise and delight its customers and still generate a profit. It took a few years to determine the outcome.

In addition to a presence abroad, clients also wanted MarketStar employees located closer to their headquarters. To meet their requests, MarketStar established offices in Raleigh, North Carolina, and in Atlanta, Georgia.

In the early 2000s, as some accounts grew larger, MarketStar leaders realized they needed to attract more sales and marketing talent. "We found hundreds of excellent new employees in the Salt Lake area," Alan says. "They filled several MarketStar buildings in Draper, Utah, which housed operations for Hewlett Packard, Intel, and Cisco."

Acquired by Omnicom

MarketStar's growth attracted the attention of Omnicom, a family of companies made up of ad agencies, public relations companies, and other media firms. When CPM was acquired by Omnicom, it opened a door for MarketStar. "Tony, our strategic partner in Europe, told Omnicom about us," Alan says. "The next thing I knew, Omnicom called and wanted to visit. Its goal was to acquire MarketStar and bring it into their group of companies."

After ten hard years of running the business as the sole owner, Alan was ready to sell MarketStar for the best price. They negotiated the terms of the purchase for several months, and Alan agreed to sell the business to Omnicom at the end of 1999. "Looking back, they gave us a fair value on the company. They bought forty-nine percent of the company initially, followed by the remaining fifty-one percent over the next few years," Alan says. "I agreed to remain as CEO for another seven years."

Alan didn't receive all his wealth from the Omnicom acquisition in one fell swoop. Instead, he received payments on a regular basis while he continued to work at the company.

As part of a publicly traded company, MarketStar reported to the parent company, Omnicom, on a quarterly basis. Omnicom leadership wanted MarketStar to continue its rapid growth and to increase its financial performance. Alan and his team were asked to double revenues and pre-tax profits annually. Such a lofty request added a new level of stress to an organization already under great pressure. "Fortunately for us," Alan reports, "MarketStar exceeded its financial growth numbers year after year. But it was all-consuming to make that happen!"

Aside from the challenges of growing the business, there were definite benefits to being on the Omnicom team. First, MarketStar's brand recognition increased significantly. "Being a part of the huge Omnicom brand gave us increased credibility and stature. We had become a part of the Madison Avenue advertising elite," Alan says. "We got acquainted with other Omnicom companies and their leaders. They were always willing to be our mentors and advisors."

The second big benefit of Omnicom was networking and training with the brightest executives in the business. Several times a year, Omnicom hosted senior management programs for CEOs at their headquarters in New York City or at locations in California. Alan attended fourteen of these meetings while he was the CEO. For two years, Alan attended a CEO leadership program sponsored by Omnicon at Babson College, a private business school in Wellesley, Massachusetts, that focuses on entrepreneurship education. Harvard Business School professors taught them the fundamentals of running high-growth companies.

Losing HP, gaining an honorary doctorate

Six months after Omnicom bought MarketStar, volcano-sized trouble erupted. While focused on a global footprint, Alan wasn't carefully watching his domestic operations. He had delegated day-to-day operations to several senior managers and assumed they were taking care of business. He was mistaken. In May 2000, MarketStar lost its largest client, Hewlett Packard.

A disagreement between a senior MarketStar leader and an HP manager had become so heated that the client decided to terminate the MarketStar contract and find another outsourced sales provider. All of this happened without Alan's involvement; he was notified by his CFO as he arrived at work early one morning.

He told Alan the HP contract was severed and they needed to let go 400 MarketStar employees. The news was devastating. Alan flew to Vancouver, Washington, to discuss the situation with several HP executives. He hoped he could change their minds and fix the soured relationship, but HP refused to consider his plea. He left Vancouver angry and deeply depressed. His next phone call was to Omnicom to report he had just lost HP—and a $25 million contract.

Two days after MarketStar lost the HP contract, Alan was awarded an honorary doctorate of humanities by Weber State University. "I don't even know how I got through the award ceremony. My heart was aching for my MarketStar people who had lost their jobs," Alan says. "One day had been a complete disaster, followed by a triumph. It was a week that truly mirrored the lows and highs of life."

With Omnicom questioning his leadership, Alan inserted himself back into supervising day-to-day operations at MarketStar. He had another high mountain to climb, his highest ever. He needed to fix a number of serious problems immediately. His first action was to fire the people who mismanaged the HP account. His second move was to ask his human resources department to help several hundred former employees find employment.

As he examined what had happened, he realized the leaders who had damaged the HP account had not represented MarketStar's corporate culture. Instead of honoring and respecting the client, they chose to berate and criticize the direction and policy of HP leadership. What they did was completely opposite and foreign to how MarketStar ran its business. Alan and his dedicated team went to work to right the ship. He was pleased with the employees who stayed on board, and gives them credit for working long hours to fix internal problems. He recognized and paid tribute to his sales team for finding and engaging new clients to replace lost revenues.

"Collectively, they saved MarketStar," Alan says. He learned monumental lessons from such a painful loss. "I learned you have to give people a level of trust, but you still have to follow up with them on their performance."

Eventually, Omnicom mandated an employee-engagement survey for more than 100 Omnicom companies. It helped identify strengths and weaknesses in company culture. It had two main measurements: employee morale and financial performance. There was a correlation between the two measurements: Omnicom found that if a company has happy, productive employees, revenues and profits will also be stellar. Managers who read the results of the employee survey could also see interpersonal problems between managers and workers and move to repair them. As MarketStar restored and enforced its cultural standards, revenues and morale increased. Omnicom recognized MarketStar, over many years, as one of its top-performing companies.

Establishing the Create brand

Ironically, sometimes MarketStar's success limited its growth. For example, by partnering with Intel, MarketStar was unable to represent Intel's competitors. To solve this complex problem, after several months of research and discussion, the MarketStar leadership team decided to build a separate business unit outside of Ogden.

Thus, in 2002, Create was formed as a separate company to engage with MarketStar's clients' competitors. Create had its own sales team, client managers, and field team. It also had its own database and reporting system to ensure confidentiality and data integrity. Create was not connected to MarketStar at all; it reported directly to Omnicom. Under this new brand, Create could legally and ethically work for LG, a competitor of Whirlpool, a MarketStar client. Create was headquartered in Colorado, and Aaron Hall managed the company for several years.

Another warning prompt

Wanting to grow their portfolio of companies, Omnicom invited a select handful of executives to find other brands for Omnicom to acquire. Alan was asked to participate in this unique initiative. "My assignment was to find great companies, learn about their reasons for success, and then recommend to Omnicom whether or not they should be purchased," Alan says. "An additional assignment for me was to supervise the company if it was acquired."

The first retail company Alan investigated offered in-store retail services. Their staff counted on-shelf products in stores and audited how they were presented. It seemed a perfect fit for Omnicom. Alan met with the president of the business in Las Vegas to discuss building a relationship.

"After our meeting, I saw him in the casino with friends that night, doing something I felt was wrong," Alan remembers. "As I watched him, I had this very strong impression that we should not do business with him."

Alan had felt that distinctive warning before, but this time he didn't follow it. Alan proceeded to recommend the company to Omnicom and shortly thereafter it was acquired. Alan was asked to supervise the newly acquired organization and be responsible for its performance. "Looking back, I wish I had heeded that warning," he says. "Working with that CEO was a daily hassle and the company underperformed for a whole host of reasons."

CEO succession

Eventually another leader became the face of MarketStar, but the succession plan took several years and three attempts. Alan wanted to remove himself from the day-to-day role of president so he could focus on the future of the company and his retirement. The first president he hired failed. The next, Chuck Duncan, was a banker by trade who had the right cultural fit. He performed well but left MarketStar to pursue other interests after a brief tenure. Alan considered hiring Dave Treadway, a leader at HP who managed the MarketStar relationship. "He really understood our business and what we were doing," Alan notes.

Alan was cautious in selecting a successor. After many discussions with Dave and Alan's senior team, Mr. Treadway was invited to be the president of MarketStar in 2003. In 2006, Alan became chairman of the company and Dave replaced him as CEO.

Alan had no regrets about letting someone else take his place as head of MarketStar. Dave arrived at the right moment—Alan's internal seven-year clock had sounded the alarm. "MarketStar gave me two or three of those time periods, and it worked because the challenges kept changing enough for me to still be interested," Alan says. "But there came a time when I was done. I was growing weary of it and needed a change. Plus, I had come to the end of my financial earn-out. I wasn't going to make any more money at MarketStar."

He didn't want a fancy farewell. "I just wanted to slip off into the dark on my horse," he says. "MarketStar was an important pinnacle in my life. It fulfilled my wildest dreams and has given Jeannie and me the financial resources to bless the lives of many more people."

MarketStar today

Alan's entrepreneurial persistence paid off. The company he launched in his humble basement in 1988 continues to this day to be a global outsourced marketing and sales juggernaut. MarketStar helps clients drive incremental revenues in their targeted small- and mid-size business space. It helps them grow more accounts and retain their loyal customers.

Nearly 20,000 employees from all over the world have worked for MarketStar during its first three decades. In September 2018, MarketStar celebrated its thirtieth anniversary. Considered the leader in "Sales as a Service,"[4] MarketStar teams manage more than 80,000 accounts and influence more than $6 billion in sales annually for its major clients.[5] They serve many of the world's leading and emerging technology and consumer brand companies such as Intel, HP, Microsoft, Google, Citrix, Pinterest, and AdRoll.

The company named Keith Titus, then president/chief operating officer of MarketStar, as the new president/chief executive officer, starting December 31, 2018. Titus replaced Dave Treadway, who chose to retire after fifteen years as CEO.

As for Alan's longstanding role at MarketStar, in 2019 he holds the titles of founder, past CEO, and former chairman. He continues to visit with the company's leadership upon request. "I will always be grateful to the wonderful employees who made MarketStar a world-class organization," Alan says. "In like manner, I wish to express my gratitude to the hundreds of clients who trusted us to serve them. I will never forget their kindness and support."

Alan wishes to specifically thank the following list of MarketStar employees, both past and present:

Dolores Atkinson, Dave Baugh, Crystalee Webb Beck, Craig Bott, Lois Bowden, Mark Britton, Jeff Farr, Marilyn Ferguson, Ted Finch, Dave Forsberg, Randy Gardner, Julie Gottschalk, Michelle Gunter, Maci Hakala, Aaron Hall, Adam Hall, Christian Hall, Eric Hall, LuAnn Hammer, Todd Handy, EJ Harris, Shelly Hart, Erin Housley, Craig Jarman, Mark Johnson, Jeff Jones, Mark Jones, Kim Kaleikini, Karen King, Jodie Nicotera Lee, Scott Lucas, Travis Malan, Catina Martinez, Ken Mayne, Sam Newey, Eva Oseguera, Gina Pinckney, Judy Shupe, Julie Simmons, Keith Titus, Angie Robinson Towns, Karen Tracy, David Treadway, Clain Udy, Debbie Wade, Lee Wells, Laura Hall West, Matt West, Amy Wilde, Rod Wilson, and Wendy Wilson.

12

Business Ventures Beyond MarketStar

A lan is known for his expertise in sales acceleration, growing businesses, and motivating others to execute the founder's vision. The following covers Alan's entrepreneurial ventures post-MarketStar as a founder, angel investor, managing director, technology advocate, adjunct professor, and spokesperson for growing economic power in Utah and beyond.

Utah Technology Council

"Coming from MarketStar, I realized the importance of supporting tech companies from start-ups to enterprises," Alan says. "Technology companies can be a powerful economic engine in a community, and I viewed the Utah Technology Council (UTC) as vital to the growth of the Utah economy."

A nonprofit organization with unique access to government, education, and community leaders, the Utah Technology Council identifies and moves forward important initiatives to strengthen Utah's technology sector.[1] For more than a decade, Alan was on the UTC board and executive committee, and then served from 2008–2013 as chairman. "It was an opportunity for me to be the voice for 5,000 Utah tech companies at the Utah Legislature and with the Governor's Office of Economic Development."

One of UTC's biggest economic events is its annual banquet. CEOs of statewide tech companies are invited to an exclusive dinner where the council honors Hall of Fame recipients and attendees hear from distinguished global technology executives on the future of technology. UTC has hosted luminaries from HP, Apple, Microsoft, Google, Amazon, and Cisco. These world-famous executives share their thoughts on future trends, opportunities, and potential challenges. In front of more than 1,000 guests, Alan emceed the banquet for many years. He was honored as the Trustee of the Year in 2006 and later inducted into the UTC's Hall of Fame in 2014.[2]

Grow Utah

In 2005, Alan and T. Craig Bott co-founded Grow Utah, a nonprofit dedicated to fostering entrepreneurship across Utah. "We launched this initiative as a way to pay it forward. As successful businessmen, we felt a need to help the next generation of entrepreneurs," Alan says. "Our vision was to create a robust entrepreneurial ecosystem in Utah that would foster entrepreneurial talent, drive innovation to solve market needs, connect entrepreneurs with community resources and support, and ensure there was funding for businesses of promise. Our focus has always been to connect start-up founders with valuable community resources through competitive business contests, experienced mentors, leadership conferences, and willing investors."

They have hosted competitions and rewarded winning companies with start-up capital for company growth. Alan personally invested in some of the winning businesses as an angel investor.

With Zions Bank as a major sponsor, Grow Utah has hosted competitions all over the state, from Logan to St. George. They set up programs to encourage community leaders to support local entrepreneurs by forming angel-investor clubs. They also invited local chambers of commerce and universities to lend a hand. In its fourteenth year of operation in 2019, hundreds of early-stage companies have flourished with the help of Grow Utah and its leadership team.

Grow America

Within three years, Alan proposed expanding the Grow Utah program. In 2008, he created Grow America to scale support for entrepreneurs across the United States. "A few years ago, we decided to give away one million dollars to successful early-stage companies, with the idea that they could create jobs, hire new people, and expand the local economy," Alan says. "Our actions are philanthropic. Our hope has been that our efforts inspire people to take the risk of starting and growing a new enterprise."

While Alan doesn't receive monetary rewards for being involved in Grow Utah or Grow America, he sees other benefits. He answers phone calls and reads letters and emails from people who thank him for the free programs that have made a difference in their lives.

World Trade Center Utah

Alan was a founding board member of World Trade Center Utah. WTC Utah is a licensed and certified member of the World Trade Centers Association, a network of more than 300 World Trade Centers in 100 countries. The mission of WTC Utah is to help Utah companies think, act, and succeed globally.[3]

Island Park Group of Companies

Island Park Group of Companies, LLC, is a personal investing entity focused on helping early-stage Utah technology companies. "The idea behind Island Park was a philanthropic way to help Utah companies start and grow businesses, which would hire people," Alan says. "We do get some return on our investment, but ninety percent of Island Park companies fail. It's really risky. I could gamble in Las Vegas and probably make more money than I do as an angel investor."

Island Park Group has been in operation since 2005, and since its start, it has made significant contributions to the Utah start-up economy.

"If you look at the way we've invested money, it's always been to put cash into companies that might provide us, one day, with a reasonable return on our investment," Alan says. Island Park has invested $30 million into start-up businesses that have created 7,000 jobs. Early on, Alan recognized he couldn't supervise all these businesses, so he asked David Norton, PhD, founder of Iomega, to run the day-to-day operations of Island Park Group.

Alan and David knew they needed manpower to find investment-worthy businesses. Using his university connections, Alan invited students in the Weber Entrepreneurial Association (WEA) at Weber State University to help with due diligence. Although they volunteered, the students didn't follow through. "I learned nobody wanted to work for free," Alan says. "So we established an endowment fund at WSU that provided scholarships for students who helped us analyze business opportunities."

Team in place, Island Park ran as a well-oiled machine. Alan taught students how to interview business leaders using a list of thirty qualifying questions. Students researched each company's management team, financials, products, marketing, and sales. They identified how much money the company needed to grow and how it would be spent. Once the students had the requested information, they brought David and Alan their report. "Many students told us these assignments were the best part of their education," Alan says. "We took them beyond theory and textbook readings to real-world experiences."

Alan is grateful for Erin Housley, Shannon Woodward, Debbie Wade, Brent Keller, Mark Hurst, and Alison Wistner. Each assisted him in finding, evaluating, and considering Island Park Group investment opportunities. Only a handful of the forty companies who received investments from Island Park have been profitable. In time, Alan hopes to receive a return on the invested capital that will make up for losses and then some. Jeannie's perspective is reassuring. She tells Alan, "You gave people jobs, you gave them opportunities, and you gave them the courage to try to live their dreams, even if they failed."

Mercato Partners

In 2006, Alan conceived the idea to start Mercato Partners when MarketStar helped Research in Motion (RIM) launch the Blackberry. Hundreds of MarketStar field employees helped RIM's sales skyrocket. "We had no ownership in RIM, but seeing their stock valuation climb, I realized if we'd been an investor, we would have made a lot of money," Alan says. "It dawned on me that if I were a venture capitalist, with what I know about marketing and sales, I could invest in early-stage technology companies, help them accelerate revenues, and then sell the enterprise for a huge profit."

To test this investing idea, Alan started with a $500,000 investment in a venture fund called vSpring Capital. He worked with venture capitalist Greg Warnock, who holds a PhD in entrepreneurship from the University of Utah. "Greg is exceptionally talented at investing," Alan says. "So when the time was right, I suggested to Greg that we start our own small fund."

In short order, Gazelle was formed to pilot the marriage of venture capital and marketing and sales expertise. With several million dollars in place, Greg invested in a few growing companies. Quickly, Alan and Greg learned their unique approach yielded a high return on investments.

In 2007, Alan proposed a full-fledged partnership with Greg. They formally combined Alan's deep expertise in channel sales, marketing strategy, and sales execution with Greg's data-driven, scholarly approach to investing. Together they co-founded Mercato Partners as a growth equity fund with a unique twist.

Early on, Alan and Greg needed investments from limited partners who believed in and understood their new model. The goal was to raise $52 million to establish Fund 1. Without proven experience, they initially struggled to secure money from large financial institutions. "We went to people we knew in Utah with high net worth and asked them to invest in our Fund 1. Fortunately, they were willing to roll the dice with us," Alan says. "Eventually, J.P. Morgan became an investor once it learned we had Skullcandy as one of our portfolio companies."

After nearly a hundred meetings with family, friends, and institutional investors, they achieved their Fund 1 goal. Alan put in money as an investor (or limited partner) and as a managing director of the fund.

At $52 million, Mercato's first fund was relatively small but had a great record with three public offerings (IPOs) and two acquisitions. Among them were Fusion-io, which makes devices that accelerate computer processing time; Skullcandy, a headphone and ear-bud manufacturer; and MediConnect Global, a company that offers secure retrieval of medical records. As of December 2017, Mercato Partners had returned to its investors nearly 3.5 times their money and has been recognized as one of the best-performing funds in America.

While their second fund of $135 million hasn't had any exit to date, several portfolio companies are positioned for future IPOs and mergers.

As managing director for several years at Mercato Partners, Alan was on the boards of four portfolio companies: Central Logic, Control4, CradlePoint, and Goal Zero. A large part of the fund's success has been Mercato's ability to find, engage, and invest in great companies with high-caliber leadership. In 2013, Alan left Mercato to consider other investment opportunities.

Alan enjoyed his association with Greg Warnock, Alison Wistner, Ken Krull, Aaron DeRose, Tara Rosander, and Joe Grover. "They were amazing team members," Alan says.

Plus550

Today (2019), Alan is part of a new venture initiative called Plus550. Five iconic Utah entrepreneurs—Rick Alden, Alan Hall, Josh James, Todd Pedersen, and Greg Warnock—launched a revolutionary new initiative to jump-start angel-level investing in Utah. They seek to return power to the entrepreneurs who've made Utah one of the fastest-growing high-tech, start-up regions in the country.[4]

Plus550 offers a simple process for entrepreneurs with normal deal terms and best venture practices and drives fair returns while positioning entrepreneurs for the greatest likelihood of long-term success.

Ever the entrepreneur

In his seventies, Alan still leads many innovative projects, from nonprofit causes to exciting business ideas. He can't help himself. He is always looking for new opportunities to invest in promising businesses.

"I love projects. The process of discovery and trying to determine if an idea is viable is exciting to me," Alan says. "I know from past experience that not all ventures are successful, but that doesn't bother me. For me, it's the thrill of the journey."

Alan is determined to pursue successful business ventures to fulfill his philanthropic passions. "I still want to make money in order to give it away," Alan says. "As long as I can personally bless the lives of people, I will not stop."

13

Giving Back

Motivations for Alan's philanthropic efforts stem from his childhood. Finances were a strain for his family, with his father often working two jobs to make ends meet. "My dad didn't make a lot of money while I was growing up.* I was lucky if I got a baseball for Christmas," Alan says.

He didn't wear the latest clothing styles like some of his peers at Ogden High, but teenage Alan had a caring home and a family who loved him, plus many wonderful friends. At the same time, his mother shared her abundance with others. She poured her energy and love into service projects for neighbors: delivering meals to new mothers, providing childcare, helping with funeral preparations, and much more. The community knew Joyce Hall was the one to call on for help.

"Because of that nurturing upbringing, making wealth for the sake of wealth isn't a driver for me," Alan says. "I enjoy making money and giving it away." Alan and Jeannie are well matched because neither wants

---

* After Alan left on his mission, his father continued working and became a successful and trusted pharmacist. Gene Hall received national recognition from Medicine Shoppe International, Inc., and at one point owned three pharmacies.

to use money for show. They believe, as the authors of *The Millionaire Next Door* put it, that money should not be used to build a supply of "wealth artifacts" to impress others.[1]

When Alan sold MarketStar in 2000, he divided his substantial earnings into three pots of money. One pot was for charitable giving, placed into a nonprofit organization, which they called the Alan and Jeanne Hall Foundation. The second was a sum for Alan and Jeannie's retirement. The third portion of money went toward Island Park Investments, Alan's vehicle for investing in other businesses.

"Giving is something we'll do until we can't anymore," Alan says. "When we see a need in the community, we are ready and willing to participate." Often the Halls are the lead donors in worthy causes, and then they invite others to help. They also believe giving back is about providing their time and talents, as well as other resources.

The Halls started their tradition of giving long before formalizing their well-funded foundation. They began making small contributions as a young married couple. As their wealth has grown, so has their capacity to fund philanthropic initiatives.

Establishing a family culture of giving

While Alan was serving as the bishop of the Weber State College 4th Ward, a young Hispanic ward member who had recently converted to the Church told Alan that his mother was dying of lupus. One of the counselors in the bishopric, Dr. Jeffrey Booth, treated the mother's illness, while the bishopric and their wives started planning ways to assist the suffering family. Besides caring for his gravely ill mother, the young man also felt responsibility for his seven siblings, ranging from three to seventeen years of age, and his under-employed alcoholic father. Even with the superb medical care donated by Dr. Booth, the young mother died a few weeks before Christmas.

The entire ward, students and leaders, worked together to raise funds and goods to help the family in their challenging circumstances. Although none of the bishopric members had extra personal wealth to give, they were not reluctant to ask others for money or donations of food, clothing, household goods, and toys for this bereaved family.

Donated items were often "gently used" and many articles had to be cleaned, mended, or refurbished. Jeannie took on the task of making sure all the gifts were presentable. Nothing was to be given to this family unless it was in like-new condition. Ward members wrapped all the toys and clothing on Family Home Evening nights or after church on Sundays, and raised enough funds to completely pay off the medical and mortuary bills.

On Christmas Eve, they filled two borrowed pickup trucks and numerous cars to capacity with boxes of food, toys, clothing, household products, and linens. They delivered the gifts to the family, who lived in a dilapidated rental house on 28th Street and Grant Avenue. Through the efforts of kind and loving ward members and their leaders, many of whom were struggling financially themselves, the family felt the Savior's love. Although they were still deeply grieving the loss of their mother and wife, the family felt comforted and uplifted. The hearts of the ward members, too, had been changed. That night, a Hall family tradition began, and has continued for more than forty years.

Since that first experience, the practice of helping families at Christmas has changed from receiving used items from extended family and friends; today, the Hall family uses their personal funds to supply the needs. Jeannie leads the efforts by finding three to five families in the community who are in dire need. She meets the mothers in their apartments, trailers, or motel rooms and tries to understand their needs. Then she arranges for the mothers to go shopping with her. The moms select school clothes, church attire, underwear, pajamas, and outdoor clothing, and a special toy or electronic device for each of their children. The moms don't see the total cost of the gifts, but are given gift receipts if items need to be exchanged. Then the Hall children and grandchildren take the items and wrap them for their assigned families, with the names of the children on each present. Gift cards and small things are purchased for the parent(s), and often rent or utility bills are paid. Jeannie gives an enormous amount of time each year to provide Christmas for multiple families.

On Christmas Eve, all the Hall family members put on Santa hats and deliver the packages to each dwelling. Either Alan or one of his sons dresses as Santa Claus. In the Hispanic homes, Santa speaks to the family in Spanish.

The Halls' oldest grandchild, Morgan West, loved the tradition and was sorry to miss it when she went on an LDS mission to Virginia. Alan and Jeannie surprised her by transferring funds to her account so she and her companion could provide Christmas to some needy families where she was serving. Each of the Hall children, now grown with children and resources of their own, also chooses a family or two to sponsor.

Challenges of helping others

Giving money away, surprisingly, is not always easy. "Some people feel entitled to charity. If we don't give them money, they're unhappy. Or they feel upset that we didn't give them more," Alan says. "So we think carefully about contributions and act intelligently. We've learned that charity requires understanding and patience."

He has learned that being charitable has its downside. "The moment some folks have a need, they rush over to ask for financial support," he says. "Sometimes we feel it's not appropriate to give money. Instead, we might buy diapers or formula, or help them find resources in the community." Jeannie is very familiar with community resources. In addition to giving gifts, she tries to help the adults and their children access appropriate services for their educational, medical, and housing needs.

Also, it can be painful to see these families' homes and conditions. Jeannie visited one of the Christmas families in a smoke-filled, filthy, inner-city motel room. The mom had four children, ranging from ages six to fourteen. Her current boyfriend lived with them, along with several pets. The kids were all sleeping on air mattresses on the floor. Their clothing was worn and dirty. "These kids are growing up thinking this is a normal life!" Alan says. "As much as we wish we could go in and save them, there are certain charitable intents that can only go so far." But as a family, they step up and do all they can.

The Halls donate because they feel it's their responsibility to share the abundance with which they've been blessed. They see it as their spiritual stewardship, "for unto whomsoever much is given, of him [or her] shall be much required."[2] Giving itself is reward enough for Alan and Jeannie, yet the organizations they give to may also want to recognize them in gratitude. It's a touchy subject, especially for Jeannie—she doesn't like the publicity. For example, when the Ogden-Weber Chamber of Commerce honored the Halls on the Wall of Fame in the Eccles Conference Center with a large framed photo of them, she felt uneasy about it. "Jeannie isn't comfortable with fanfare," Alan says.

Another troublesome aspect of giving is unwanted awards. For example, Weber State University commissioned a painting of Alan and Jeannie during his time as chairman of the board. "We didn't want them to do it, but they insisted, so we compromised," Alan says. Foregoing the pomp and circumstance of a public unveiling, Alan requested that the painting be "unveiled" in their home, without any applause. It now hangs on a wall in the university's business building.

Alan and Jeanne Hall Foundation

The Halls know they can't help everyone everywhere, so they focus on the people in the community where they live. They seek to improve the lives of low-income families in Weber County. Their foundation's theme is "no poor among us," chosen from a scripture describing the city of Enoch, where the people were of "one heart and one mind, and dwelt in righteousness; and there was no poor among them."[3]

Alan explains, "The Hall Foundation helps people who lack fundamental resources, including educational opportunities. We provide compassionate care for the afflicted, food for the hungry, and cultural experiences. Often the best way to help people is to partner with existing charitable organizations that serve those in need."

Giving back is a family affair, as the Hall children sit on the foundation board of trustees and share the vision of what their parents want to accomplish in the community. The board meets every February to assess and decide upon the grant recipients for that year. To be included in the evaluation process, organizations submit proposals on the foundation's website that indicate how much they need, who they will be serving and where, what results they expect, and how they will measure and periodically report the results.

Forming these partnerships requires relationship acumen. "Phi-
lathropy is like a business. We learn more about it all the time," Alan
says. "We are pleased to share which nonprofits have received contributions, but usually we don't share a dollar figure," Alan says. "We generally don't issue press releases about our gifts, although sometimes the
newspaper will print a story about a contribution."

In the last seventeen years, the Hall Foundation has given away
millions of dollars (cumulative) to many organizations, including:

• Ballet West

• Brigham Young University

• Brigham Young University—Hawaii

• Boys & Girls Clubs of Weber-Davis

• Catholic Community Services—Joyce Hansen Hall Food Bank

• Davis Technical College

• Intermountain Healthcare, McKay-Dee Hospital Foundation

• LDS Business College

• LDS Philanthropies

• Mentors International

• Midtown Community Health Center

• OFOAM (Ogden Friends of Acoustic Music)

• Ogden Nature Center

• Ogden Pioneer Days

• Ogden Rescue Mission

• Ogden School Foundation

• Ogden Symphony Ballet Association

- Ogden-Weber Technical College

- Prosperity 2020

- Red Cross of Northern Utah

- Hope Community Center, Roy City

- Lantern House (formally St. Anne's Center)

- The Church of Jesus Christ of Latter-day Saints

- Treehouse Children's Museum

- United Way of Northern Utah

- Utah Festival Opera & Musical Theatre

- University of Utah, KUED

- Weber Pathways

- Weber School Foundation

- Weber State University

- Your Community Connection

In many cases, Alan and Jeannie not only support worthy causes but also lead charitable efforts on behalf of the nonprofit entity. The following sections provide details about some of the Hall family's charitable efforts in each of the areas of focus for the community: educational opportunities, compassionate care to the afflicted, food to the hungry, and cultural experiences.

Educational opportunities
The Halls are dedicated advocates for education. Their love of learning and devotion to educating the next generation has changed the lives of thousands of Weber County residents, whether they are in elementary school, high school, or higher education. The following is a brief synopsis of educational campaigns Alan has led in the community.

Preserving Ogden High School

In 2007, Ogden School Foundation launched its capital campaign to restore the historic elements of Ogden High.[4] Although they had bond money for basic renovations, the school district leadership needed to raise $9 million more to restore the auditorium—during the height of an economic recession—to bring the school back to its 1937 glory. The district asked Alan, as a second-generation alumnus and well-known leader in the community, to get involved.

Alan led the effort as co-chairman with Rob White, and worked with Janis Vause, executive director of the Ogden School Foundation, and local influencers like Suzanne Lindquist, Rich Brewer, Karen Fairbanks, George Hall, and Carolyn Nebeker-Rasmussen. The committee met every week, identifying Ogden High School alumni and others who could donate to the cause. The campaign lasted for four years.

"It was a very hard time to raise money," Alan remembers. "People with wealth had lost half of it during the recession, but we persevered." Once the committee had raised $8.5 million, they hosted a celebration party with donors in the high school auditorium. They wanted to honor the many alumni and friends who had dug deep into their pockets to support the cause.

During the celebration, Alan announced the campaign was still short half a million dollars, and invited those in the audience to contribute the remaining sum. To the delight of everyone there, alumnus Spencer Eccles said he would give whatever amount was still needed.

The historic auditorium was perfectly restored to its original Art Deco design, perfectly renewed with gold leaf on its magnificent ceiling. The remarkable auditorium now had new plumbing, a new electrical system, a new roof, earthquake-proof walls, and 1,800 new seats. In 2013, once the high school renovation was completed, the school leadership and the project's leaders won a prestigious award from the National Trust for Historic Preservation.[5]

Alan visited the auditorium when it was being painted, and climbed the scaffolding to see the artists' beautiful work. He learned they were using the same brushes that had originally been used on the ceiling. The names of the original painters were preserved, in the same places where they had written their names seventy years earlier. "It's a glorious sight to be in that auditorium," Alan says. "When we think about Europe's magnificent architectural gems, I believe we shouldn't be so eager to raze our historic structures."

It takes a real community influencer to motivate such generosity. "Under Alan's adept leadership, the campaign was successful—which was something of a miracle, given the challenging economic times," says Janis Vause, executive director of the Ogden School Foundation, in an interview. "There is absolutely no quit in Alan Hall. He is a fierce, loyal, and passionate OHS Tiger, Class of '63. Because of him and the indefatigable efforts of others, Ogden still has the iconic, historic Ogden High School in our midst."

She continues, "Alan is an individual who approaches everything he does with a positive, winning attitude. He inspires all around him to serve others. His capacity to give of his time, resources, and energy is unprecedented. We are all blessed because Alan Hall lives in our community."

Prosperity 2020

Alan chaired Prosperity 2020, a nonprofit organization that seeks to make educational outcomes in Utah one of the best in America. "Sadly, our educational results in public education have fallen behind," Alan notes. "Utah was once in the top ten of all states for educational results, but now we are in the middle."

One of Prosperity 2020's goals included having volunteers read with kids in schools. Jeannie and Alan volunteered to read with a third grader at North Park Elementary, in Roy, Utah, for a school year. They found the assignment very fulfilling, and they saw a dramatic increase in their student's reading proficiency. Clearly, their efforts had made a difference.

Based upon this experience, Alan approached church leaders in Weber County and asked them to invite their members to be reading volunteers in the elementary schools in their neighborhoods. "Putting more money in education won't always solve the problem," he says. "We need scores of volunteers to contribute their time, talents, and energy to improve local education."

Alan spent three years working with the Utah Legislature and the governor to increase financial support for public education. He also met periodically with forty-one school district superintendents across the state to better understand their special needs. Sensing a need to help in his own community, Alan turned his attention to the local school district.

Roy Cone project

In 2014, Alan met with Gina Butters, principal of Roy High School, to help improve the school's low graduation rate. Between 2009 and 2014, the average graduation rate at Roy High School was seventy-one percent, leaving 150 students per year without a diploma.[6]

"For me, this was a case where my philanthropy, coupled with community advocacy, could make a big difference," Alan says. "I encouraged the principals and teachers from eight elementary schools and two junior highs that feed into Roy High to develop a plan and a budget to improve the graduation rate. With an action plan in hand, Jeannie and I donated $250,000 to the project and invited the Utah Legislature to match our gift."

The program had three initiatives. First, older successful students were assigned to tutor younger struggling students. Second, the school hired individuals as advocates to find failing students and encourage them to return to the classroom. Third, time was allowed within school hours for high school students to earn back credits for classes they had failed.

Combined together, these programs resulted in resounding success. In 2016, school officials estimated the graduation rate was about ninety-seven percent. Governor Gary Herbert visited Roy High School in 2016 to praise the outcomes of the program. Due to its overwhelming success, the Utah Legislature allocated funds to five other school districts that also needed assistance with graduation rates.

Weber State University

Few people "bleed purple" for Weber State University like Alan. He's been a public figure for the university and has helped grow Weber State for more than fifty years in a variety of roles, including student leader, alumni director, trustee, chairman of the National Advisory Council, chairman of the board of trustees, and adjunct professor.

The Halls are generous to Weber State University. Every year, they contribute funds for numerous scholarships and other important projects. In fact, each college on campus is a beneficiary of their financial support. Besides the College of Business & Economics, the colleges of Science, Education, Social and Behavioral Sciences, Health Professions, Arts and Humanities, and Engineering, Applied Science & Technology all receive significant Hall Foundation donations. In addition, Alan and Jeannie happily support Wildcat Athletics and the Center for Community Engaged Learning.

Brad Mortensen, selected as the new president of Weber State University in December 2018, met Alan in 2004. "At first I was intimidated by this successful, well-dressed, and accomplished businessman," Brad says, "but in no time at all, he became a true friend. Who else, with his wife, Jeannie, calls to sing 'Happy Birthday' in harmony on your birthday?"

From 2007 to 2016, Alan served on the Weber State University Board of Trustees. He was appointed by the governor to be the chairman for six years. During that time, Alan's top assignment was to work with the trustees, oversee the annual budget of $300 million, and support the presidents' initiatives—first President Ann Millner, then President Charles Wight. He met often with members of the Utah State Legislature to secure funding for the university. He attended groundbreakings and served as a public figure for the university, always wearing something purple to represent the Wildcats. Alan also wore his trustee robes to approximately eighteen graduation ceremonies, where more than 60,000 graduates received diplomas with his signature on them.

The term for a university trustee is an eight-year appointment, but President Wight petitioned Alan to stay one more year as the chairman of the board of trustees and as the chairman of the university's capital campaign, "Dream 125." The goal of the campaign was to raise $125 million for new buildings, additional scholarships, innovative programs, and special projects.

Alan was responsible for working with the press, deans, and various fundraising committees to reach the ambitious goal. "His leadership in the Dream 125 Campaign was amazing," says Brad in an interview. "He motivated a level of giving and achievement that exceeded our dreams, and he did this by leading with the example of his own philanthropy."

The campaign reached $164.3 million in donations,[7] with the Alan and Jeanne Hall Foundation as one of the lead donors. "Who spends hours and hours of unpaid service to your organization, only to then turn around and support it with millions of dollars?" asks Brad. "Alan Hall—and he's taught me to think big and reach for the best, to trust in the good of humanity, and foster a spirit of love of family, others, our community, and our God."

A singular capstone of the campaign was funding a new science facility. Inspired by designs of successful university science buildings around the country, the Tracy Hall Science Center (THSC) is a state-of-the-art facility with features that are ingenious and eco-friendly—not to mention aesthetically pleasing.[8]

The building was dedicated in the fall of 2016 and was a particularly meaningful event for the Hall family. University officials, donors, government leaders, and other distinguished guests attended a luncheon and ribbon-cutting ceremony to honor the legacy of H. Tracy Hall. Alan spoke at the ceremonial luncheon, along with his cousin David, Tracy's son. "It was a remarkable thing to have my family there and recognize my beloved uncle, who contributed so much to science with his discovery of the synthetic diamond," Alan says. "His name will be remembered forever at Weber State. It was a singular moment for me to be a part of his magnificent building."

The business department has also been a recipient of Alan's support. Established in 2013, the Hall Global Entrepreneurship Center offers a "wide range of opportunities to motivate, inspire, and provide unique resources to help students achieve their dream of starting a business, or increase their creativity and develop an entrepreneurial mindset."[9] Students can apply for seed funding, attend lectures, and learn from world-class faculty about entrepreneurship.

As a sales professional, Alan established the Alan E. Hall Center for Sales Excellence. Its focus is to promote and advance the art and science of professional selling and prepare students for future professional sales careers. The sales center combines academic insights with real-world industry experiences.

True to Weber State's global mission, Alan created an entrepreneurial program at Shanghai Normal University several years ago, where Chinese college students learn basic business principles of how to launch and grow businesses. Each year in May, Chinese students compete to win cash for the best start-up concept. Alan hopes that over time, the Weber State entrepreneurial program will be shared with foreign college students all over the planet.

To help local entrepreneurs, Alan partnered with Alex Lawrence, former university vice provost and full-time business faculty member, to establish Weber State Downtown at 2314 Washington Boulevard in Ogden. The renovated 18,000-square-foot building features a Wildcat Store selling university gear, Waldo's Café with drinks and snacks, and an Apple-authorized service center for computer repairs. The highlight of the building is the two floors of rentable workspace, meeting rooms, and open recreation areas that make up Startup Ogden, where start-up owners build their businesses.

"I have been with Alan in a large number of meetings—business meetings, philanthropic meetings, and personal meetings," says Alex in an interview. "He never changes. He's always cheerful, positive, encouraging, optimistic, and always willing to lead. Alan is the definition of selfless service, and his example is what has influenced me the most."

After his release from the chairman position, Alan took on a new role at Weber State: in the classroom. In 2017, he became an adjunct professor in the MBA program, teaching courses in sales management and entrepreneurship. It was a new experience to formalize his teachings into a syllabus. He brought in guest speakers to provide a boots-on-the-ground look at world-class business practices, with rave reviews from students. "The MBA-level sales class I took from Alan Hall was easily one of the most dynamic courses in the program," says Steve Tippets,

MBA student at Weber State University. "I learned how important it is to implement a successful sales plan to fuel a company's growth. Alan is an industry pioneer and visionary leader that made a lasting impact on my education and career."

Teaching is about giving back; Alan donates back to the university the money he earns from being on the adjunct staff. "I've always been a teacher at heart. I'm eager to share what I've learned with people," Alan says.

Alan's passion for education and innovation resonates far beyond Weber State—it benefits students, instructors, and university leadership throughout Utah. On the recommendation of Governor Gary Herbert and the approval of the Utah Legislature, Alan became a member of the Utah State Board of Regents, the supervisors of the Utah System of Higher Education, and will serve in this capacity until 2025.

According to May 2019 enrollment projections from the Utah System of Higher Education, Utah's public colleges and universities can expect to see more than 43,000 additional students over the next decade.[10] In their role as supervisors, Alan and the other regents govern the state's eight colleges and universities. "I look forward to working with the presidents of each institution. Working together, we can deliver a world-class curriculum at a competitive price to every student of higher education in Utah."

Compassionate care to the afflicted

The Halls support various organizations that promote health and provide services to those who can't afford medical care. Through helping the American Red Cross, United Way, and local health centers, they want all families in Weber County to have the medical and social service support they need.

Midtown Community Health Center

Midtown Community Health Center is a private, nonprofit group of eight clinics that provide quality, affordable healthcare services to community residents. The Ogden location, now located at 2240 Adams Avenue, was once in a rickety old building. "We gave them money and I chaired the fundraising effort to build a brand-new, larger facility," Alan says.

The center treats more than 26,000 patients a year with a mix of medical and dental visits.[11] Patients can access services with or without medical insurance. According to the Ogden *Standard-Examiner*, roughly two in three Midtown patients lack insurance.[12] "It's pretty amazing to walk in there and see all these moms and kids getting care for a small fee or for free," Alan says. "It's an incredible facility with caring medical providers."

Your Community Connection

Across the street from Midtown Community Health Center, at 2261 Adams Avenue, is the Your Community Connection Family Crisis Center (YYC). The YCC has served Northern Utah communities for more than seventy-two years. The agency provides services to victims of domestic violence, homelessness, rape, and sexual assault.

Alan and Jeannie led the fundraising effort to build a larger YCC facility to help those on the road to self-sufficiency. "The model's the same. We donate, then agree to help raise the money from other contributors," Alan says. "It's very gratifying to see how our efforts, combined with those of other supporters, affect families in a positive way," Alan says.

Food for the hungry

The Halls have learned to validate the true needs of organizations before they donate. "We investigate a charitable organization to learn if it is truly serving the community," Alan says.

Joyce Hansen Hall Food Bank

Ten years ago, the food bank facility run by Catholic Community Services of Northern Utah (CCS) was housed in a dilapidated building. It was almost a safety hazard, so Alan stepped in to chair its fundraising efforts.

The organization's plan was to turn Hopkins Elementary, a deserted school in west Ogden, into a food bank and offer other services as well. "I sat down with the leadership of the food bank and suggested we form a committee to solicit funds for a larger and safer facility," Alan says. "Our wonderful group raised $3 million, which gave the food bank team enough money to hire an architect and a construction company to remodel the old school," Alan says.

The Joyce Hansen Hall Food Bank is the largest food bank in Northern Utah and distributes more food than any other pantry in the state.[13] In addition to food distribution to more than 2,300 households each month, many of which are families with children, the facility offers Bridging the Gap, a mobile distribution at low-income elementary schools that gives students food to sustain them through weekends and holidays. They also sponsor the St. Martha's Baby Project, which equips low-income parents with infant layettes and case management. The Halls have continued to support CCS with yearly funds for community and family projects.

Leaders at CCS wanted to name the food bank after Alan and Jeannie, but the Halls preferred using Alan's mother's name. "My mom was a good example of charity, and this was a way to honor her memory," Alan says. "It pleases me to see her name on the building—the Catholic Community Services of Northern Utah Joyce Hansen Hall Food Bank."

As Alan visited the food bank, he saw a critical need for volunteers to sort food items, stack them in the pantry, and help with distribution. He reached out to the eighty stake presidents in Weber County and invited them to provide volunteers to assist with specific food bank assignments on a weekly rotating basis. Hundreds of service-minded citizens now spend a few hours each week over the course of a year to help with this noble cause.

"If members of The Church of Jesus Christ of Latter-day Saints are out of work and need food, their bishop takes care of them, but those who are not members don't get that assistance. We want to make sure everyone in the community has food," Alan says. "I love the fact that there are 2.9 million pounds of food provided to hungry citizens at the food bank throughout the year. Nobody in our community should go to bed on an empty stomach."

Cultural experiences

For decades, Alan and Jeannie have contributed to the arts. "Jeannie and I love the beauty and sublime qualities of the arts in Utah. We want to help others experience personal refinement through music, theater, dance, and visual art," Alan says. "It's very important to us to keep the arts alive for future generations."

After being the president of Ballet West and understanding the intricacies of fundraising, Alan knows how important it is for donors to promote the arts in a community. The Halls actively support musical and theatrical programs in Utah. Over the years, they have sponsored an annual opera or musical at Utah Festival Opera & Musical Theatre in Logan, the Tabernacle Choir Christmas concert, and the Ogden Symphony Ballet Association. They also enjoy supporting KUED at the University of Utah and its Masterpiece series, including *Downton Abby*, *Victoria*, *The Crown*, and *Poldark*. Most recently, they sponsored a new version of Ballet West's *Swan Lake*.

Ogden Pioneer Days

After a couple of years on the board of the Ogden Pioneer Heritage Foundation, Alan began his service as chairman in 2011. "It's fun to be the leader of the largest community event in Northern Utah and make sure the tradition continues for years to come," Alan says. "What I've tried to do is take our annual celebration to the next level."

Next level achieved. During Alan's watch, the rodeo has become financially stable by watching expenses, raising more money, and selling more tickets. The biggest fundraising accomplishment to date was bringing in $1.3 million from major donors to raze the old north grandstands and build a new structure. In addition, the Utah Jazz and Gail Miller donated 7,500 chair seats previously used at the Vivint Smart Home Arena. The green seats were placed on the north grandstands in 2018, creating a safe and beautiful place for rodeo fans.

"It's fabulous," said Craig Bielik, director of marketing for Ogden Pioneer Days, in a *Standard-Examiner* interview. "It changes the whole look of the arena. The green color matches nicely with the background and the trees. They're shiny and new."[14]

The Ogden Pioneer Days Rodeo draws more than 30,000 attendees each July, and the five nights of rodeo attracts close to 700 top rodeo athletes from around the United States.[15] With the help of a dedicated committee, an army of loyal volunteers, and a growing number of attendees, the rodeo has received national recognition in recent years. In 2015, 2016, 2017, and 2018, Ogden Pioneer Days Rodeo was ranked among the nation's five best large outdoor rodeos by the Professional Rodeo Cowboys Association. "This is a great honor for the organization, because rodeo participants (professional cowboys and cowgirls) vote on their favorite rodeo out of more than 800 PRCA-sanctioned rodeos," Alan says.

In August 2017, the Ogden Pioneer Days Committee received another special accolade. The organization was inducted into the ProRodeo Hall of Fame.[16] For many years, Alan has enjoyed associations with board members, including Dave Halverson, Desiree Cooper Larsen, Craig Bielik, and Jackie Belnap, an invaluable part-time employee. Even though he's not a cowboy, Alan knows the rush of the rodeo. Every year the committee kindly provides Alan with a horse to ride into the arena each night of the performance. So he wouldn't fall off his horse, Alan took riding lessons in Morgan, Utah, with horse trainer Jeff Wadman.[17] "It's exhilarating to work with wonderful community volunteers, world-class athletes, cowboys, and cowgirls who love this sport. It's their passion, their life, and I've developed a great appreciation for the people who enjoy the rodeo."

With his all-area pass, Alan gets up close during the rodeo performances each night. He loves to spend time by the chutes, getting the full experience of man versus beast. He sees the cowboys' hands twitch nervously, feels the dust kicked up by the bulls, and gets a sense of the true danger in the competition. To put 2,500 pounds of angry bull between your legs takes guts and gumption! "They give it their best every night they compete," Alan says. "I'm surprised by how many of them get broken bones or concussions from those bulls and bucking broncos—and then come back for more."

In 2017, Alan watched from the chutes as his father, Eugene Hall, was honored on Military Night in front of a cheering audience. Jeannie worked diligently behind the scenes with Rodeo Executive Board Member Desiree Cooper Larsen to surprise Alan with the special recognition for his father. Jeannie wrote the script for the rodeo announcer, Roger Mooney, which highlighted Gene's military service. Two granddaughters, Laura Hall West and Megan Hall Funk, escorted their ninety-six-year-old grandpa, a WWII Navy veteran, into the arena, where thousands of attendees honored his service to America. Completely surprised, Alan looked on with amazement.

The committee oversees not only the award-winning rodeo but also an entire month of activities and events for the community. These include the Horse and Hitch Parade, the Grand Parade, the Utah Cowboy and Western Heritage Museum's Hall of Fame induction ceremony, the Miss Rodeo Utah competition, Traces of the West art show, and the Trail to Pioneer Days horse project. "Things get really busy for Jeannie and me in July, attending all these events," Alan says. "We are honored and very pleased to be a part of this grand community celebration."

Philanthropic Leadership Award

The Utah Nonprofits Association recognized Alan and Jeannie with the Philanthropic Leadership Award on November 15, 2018.[18] This award recognizes outstanding individuals or couples who have been involved in philanthropy for a minimum of twenty years and have demonstrated an exceptional commitment in the community through direct involvement, financial support, and leadership.

A standing ovation welcomed the Halls to the Utah Philanthropy Day stage. Jeannie then spoke to nearly 1,000 banquet guests at the Salt Palace in downtown Salt Lake City. In her remarks, she humbly deflected praise, using her speech to recognize the work of those who do so much for Northern Utah communities. She expressed love for Alan and their family and thanked God, "who loves us, sacrificed for us, and has knit our hearts together in love." (See her full remarks in Appendix II.)

The awards program read, "As exceptional people of integrity, the Halls lead by the example of their generosity. This generosity extends beyond their financial support to include hands-on service for the missions they hold dear to their hearts. They are loving, caring people who are willing to give of their time and resources to make a difference in others' lives."

The gift that keeps giving

The Halls are grateful that their children and grandchildren are learning and living the principles of being wise stewards and are willing to share their resources with those in need. One memorable experience for Alan and Jeannie was when one of their children came to them and said, "There's a young woman at Weber State who's getting her degree in education, but she's handicapped. Mom and Dad, we need to buy her a special car that she can drive to school." Alan was so touched by his child's tender heart that the memory still makes him emotional.

Teaching the gift of giving is how Alan and Jeannie's legacy will continue. "In time, the Hall Foundation will be led by our posterity," Alan says. "We trust we have established a model of giving that they can endorse and follow for decades to come."

14

The Hall Family

Today, Alan and Jeannie have six children, six children-in-law, and a constantly growing roster of grandchildren—up to twenty as of September 2019. Each family member adds their own unique flavor to the Hall family buffet.

Raised in a humble home

All six of the Hall children were raised in the family's initial Roy home until 1992. Alan and Jeannie bought their first house in 1974, located at 1935 West 3875 South. It cost $28,000. "For us, it was a lot of money," Alan remembers. His father loaned Alan and Jeannie $5,000 to make a down payment, which they paid back over time.

With only 1,100 square feet and three bedrooms, it was tight for a growing family. "It was a very humble home, but we were comfortable and grateful to have a loving environment for our children," Alan says.

When they toured the house in 2016, the grown Hall children were surprised to see how small the home was. They couldn't believe there was just one bathroom upstairs and a three-quarter bath in the basement. They were surprised by the tiny kitchen, not much bigger than a ten-foot hallway, with appliances and cupboards on each side.

A frugal pair, Alan and Jeannie didn't buy any new furniture for two decades. They also didn't like the idea of being indebted to a mortgage, so they started doubling monthly house payments as Alan's salary increased. Amassing material things wasn't important to them. Their lives revolved around relationships—with each other, their children, extended family, neighbors, and ward members.

There were lots of children in the neighborhood, which made for a large Primary at church. Jeannie was called to be the Relief Society president while Alan was serving as the elders quorum president. They had four children ages seven and under when Alan was called as the bishop of the Weber State College 4th Ward, so Jeannie needed to be released from her time-consuming position. Family life was filled with many activities and was often challenging, but it was also lots of fun.

Although most of their time was spent locally, the family traveled to Disneyland on two occasions and looked forward to annual summer trips to the Nowak cabin in Island Park. When the children were young, Alan and Jeannie took them on camping trips and to college football games. He drove the boys from Roy to Provo every fall to see BYU football games.

Alan visited with his children on Sunday afternoons. "I sat with them one on one and invited them to tell me about their day and their life," he remembers.

Parenting styles

"Our kids are not really ours," Alan says. "They are God's children. They've been loaned to us until they become adults. For sure, parents have responsibility and are accountable to teach correct principles and guide their children. We've done our best to meet this noble obligation."

To understand how Alan and Jeannie raised their children requires a look at how they were raised themselves. The homes of the Halls and the Nowaks were different in many ways.

Jeannie came from a home of order and discipline. She was born in Houston, Texas, and the family moved five times before she was seven years old, primarily in the South. Southern customs and her father's military background in WWII led to an upbringing where manners were considered important. Jeannie and her sisters were taught to respect authority. For example, responding to a question from an adult was always, "Yes, Ma'am" or "No, Sir." One asked politely to be excused from the dinner table at the end of a meal.

Jeannie's parents were very supportive of their three girls. They happily paid for violin, piano, gymnastic, dance, swim, and voice lessons. They taught their daughters that they could do anything they wished to do. They attended all the girls' performances, mainly recitals. Henry and Betty treated each other with love and respect, and treated their daughters the same way.

The girls were also imbued with a sense of duty and discipline. Hard work, achievement, and obedience were highly rewarded. Jeannie's parents valued education as a way to succeed, and expressed approval of academic and other achievements. They expected her best behavior at all times, and she was a very obedient daughter—until she was nineteen, when Alan Hall came into her life and she converted to The Church of Jesus Christ of Latter-day Saints.

While Jeannie was raised with a firm set of expectations, Alan had much more freedom. His mother was loving and wanted him to play and experience life. Within the family rules, Joyce let Alan do whatever he pleased. His mother made his bed for him, cooked, cleaned, and took care of the rest of the children. Her whole life revolved around relationships and serving others. Alan's father played a minimal role in raising the children, for he was rarely home and often worked two jobs. This didn't bother Alan. He had plenty of validation from his mother, and an ever-growing group of friends. Enjoying such a long runway to chase after his childhood whims gave Alan a desire to give that same independence to his children.

When Alan and Jeannie started raising their own children, their paradigms of parenthood did not always mesh well. "Conflicts arose because of differences in our upbringing," Alan says. "We had biases based on how we were raised, and had to make compromises for the good of our relationship."

For the most part, Jeannie raised the Hall children. Alan was often gone at work, building businesses, or fulfilling church assignments. He didn't attend church in their home ward for eight years—other than to bless babies—due to his church assignments elsewhere. "I don't regret being away as much as I was," Alan says. "I needed to be the breadwinner and Jeannie was there to nurture, teach, and help our kids succeed in school."

Alan did his best to attend ballgames, recitals, and other momentous events for his kids. When he was at home, Alan's approach to parenting was different from Jeannie's. She expected the kids to get good grades, work hard, and help in the care and maintenance of their home and yard. When Alan was home, he was all about fun and leisure. "I think they had a good blend from both of us," Alan says.

The Hall children were taught to work and play hard. They participated in all sorts of lessons, church activities, and sports. All of them learned to help each other and perform indoor and outdoor tasks. It was wonderful for the whole family when Alan was home. His great sense of humor and love added joy to whatever activity they were doing.

The children were disciplined but never spanked. "We never punished them physically," Alan says. "At bedtime, on school nights, if Jeannie stood at the top of the stairs and threatened to 'come downstairs and beat them with a belt' because they wouldn't stop talking or giggling, the kids laughed even harder. They knew it would never happen."

Over the years, Alan and Jeannie became more aligned in their parental philosophy, but they still have different approaches. One day, their daughter Laura came over to the house with one of her daughters, who showed them a spaghetti-strap dress for prom that had a thigh-high slit up the leg. Alan's reaction was, "Don't you look pretty!" Jeannie's reaction was a little less enthusiastic.

Alan explains, "My answer was based upon a long-term vision. I would rather lose the battle and win the war. She doesn't wear temple garments yet, and she's a very righteous girl. I'm not going to condemn her for wearing something a bit immodest." Jeannie and Laura didn't condemn the girl either, but they did make a few modifications to the dress with her input.

Most parents and grandparents want to protect their kids from making poor choices. Alan sees mistakes differently. "It's Lucifer's plan to not let them experience any sin," Alan says. "Let them learn good from evil. We should allow one another to live life to its fullest. I believe we should teach them correct principles and let them govern themselves, as Joseph Smith said."

Even if a grandchild does something more serious, Alan says his reaction is the same. "They know when they've done something wrong. I don't need to point that out, " he says. "We should judge the actions of others carefully. I tend to look past the sin, knowing that deep inside there is a good person who has made a mistake. Most of the time, all of us will make the necessary corrections." Alan and Jeannie are totally aligned in this philosophy. They know that all of us make mistakes, which can be forgiven by repentance and the grace of the Savior's atonement.

The Hall children

The six children are all unique, with different personalities and talents, but one characteristic they all share is the desire to live the principles they have been taught. Alan and Jeannie are grateful for the choices each of their children has made, including their selection of spouses. They are especially thankful for the parents of their children-in-law, for nurturing and raising them in righteous homes.

Below is a short biography of each child, in birth order.

Aaron Tracy Hall

Aaron Tracy Hall was born on March 4, 1971, in Provo, Utah, while Alan and Jeannie were both pursuing their master's degrees. He surprised his parents with bright red hair. He also was a little jaundiced, so they called him "Golden Boy." Alan doesn't recall Aaron ever giving him any concerns, even when he was a young child. "He was always a very obedient fellow," he notes. He remembers little Aaron being strong-willed, smart, thoughtful, dependable, and loyal. "It was good for us to have the first child in our family set the standard of how all Halls should behave," Alan says.

As a young child, Aaron was reserved, sometimes quiet, but he grew into his personality as he got older. "His ability to breeze through school, with some guidance from Jeannie, likely helped his confidence.

I am sure he aced every test he took, from elementary school to high school and on through college," Alan says.

As he got older, Aaron participated in Scouting. Alan was his youth leader for a couple of years and helped him earn his Eagle Scout award. Alan and Aaron were home teaching partners, and they both have fond memories of monthly visits to Sister Ruth Hirschi.

Aaron was the first Hall child to have a driver's license. Alan and Jeannie owned an old 1965 Mustang, one they had used for many years as a second car. It was almost identical to the one Alan had driven when he was a Weber State student: azure blue with a white vinyl top. It was an undeniable beauty but remained parked by the side of the carport for many years. With torn upholstery, worn-thin carpet, and faded paint, it needed a total overhaul. By then Alan was driving a newer road-worthy car and Jeannie drove the "grocery-getter," a silver VW Vanagon that looked like a rectangular box on wheels but could carry the whole family and the groceries. Six months before Aaron's birthday, the Mustang disappeared, and they told the children they had sold it. In reality, Alan and Jeannie took the old 1965 car to be completely redone as a surprise for Aaron. Many of the Hall children drove that Mustang as teenagers, until it was retired and donated to the Weber County Sheriff's office as a D.A.R.E. (Drug Abuse Resistance Education) car.

Aaron was a kind teenager who showed genuine interest in others. Starting when he was in junior high school, the family sponsored three Navajo teenagers through the LDS Indian Student Placement Program.* Aaron took the lead in watching out for their Navajo siblings, even though one of them was older. Yolanda Benally shared a room with Laura and taught the family how to make Navajo fry bread. To this day, Navajo tacos are still one of the Halls' favorite meals.

"We tried to help them feel like part of the family," Alan says. "We took them with us to Disneyland and Hawaii, and those family vacations were great experiences for all of us. Although the Navajo

---

* From 1954 through the 1990s, the program helped LDS Native Americans receive a higher-quality education than they had access to on their reservation, by placing them with LDS families for a school year.[1]

children came from a different culture, they also became part of the Hall Family culture."

Kim Wade, a beautiful and vivacious blonde, came into Aaron's life at a back-to-school stomp at the beginning of their senior year. He recalls her dancing right by him. At the time, Kim was actually dating one of Aaron's friends, and Aaron was still seeing a girl in Ogden Valley. As the school year advanced, Aaron and Kim started dating. Kim took the lead for the first date, inviting Aaron to the dollar movie at the mall. (They went Dutch.) By the last semester of their senior year, they only had eyes for each other.

After graduating from Roy High School as a scholar athlete in 1989, lettering in football and track, Aaron attended one year at Weber State University and continued his great academic performance. When he turned nineteen, he accepted a mission call to Osorno, Chile. He was eventually called to be assistant to the mission president. "We were really proud of him—his Spanish was superb and he loved the people and the gospel," Alan says.

After writing Kim for two years during his mission, Aaron knew he wanted her to be his wife. He returned home in the spring of 1992 and they were married on December 28, 1993, in the Logan Temple.

Kim grew up in a loving family with three sisters and a brother. Her father was a mechanical engineer; her mother had a degree in business education and was a gifted pianist and musician. When the Halls met her, she was busy in extracurricular activities, especially the Roy High Royalaires drill team. "She was a very popular, pretty girl," Alan remembers. She graduated from Weber State with a degree in lifestyle management, with an emphasis in health and fitness.

A few days before Thanksgiving 2001, Kim's mother passed away suddenly from a brain aneurysm. It was a devastating time for the Wade family. More than a year passed before they were able to celebrate holidays without her. Kim took the lead and started family dinners again. "I believe her siblings look to her as a wonderful sister who has a healthy outlook on life," Alan says. "She is a loving and supportive wife and a wonderful mother. In her spare time, she is a triathlete and very competitive in her division."

Aaron graduated from Weber State as a top student in the professional sales department. While working part time at MarketStar and going to school, he quickly ascended in the ranks. "He was an outstanding employee who was admired by all who knew him," Alan says. "He didn't get any favors because he was my son. He had to earn his place. And he did."

After several years of leadership as the chief operating officer at MarketStar, Aaron completed an executive MBA program at the University of Utah on weekends. When he wasn't working or studying, he trained for Ironman triathlons. He's competed in a world championship in Florida and finished strong in numerous other Ironman events.

"He's just a remarkable individual," Alan says. Aaron served as a bishop in North Ogden. Recently, he and Kim completed three years as president and mission mom of the Texas Houston South Mission. He is a wonderful husband and father and a blessing to Alan and Jeannie.

Aaron and Kim are the proud parents of Allie Erin, Zachary Britton, Bode Alan, and Jessica Kate. Allie married Max Biegel on June 27, 2019, in the Salt Lake Temple.

Laura Michelle Hall West

Two years after Aaron's birth, Alan and Jeannie welcomed a little redheaded girl into their lives on April 30, 1973. "Aaron was a bit high-strung, but Laura was calm and peaceful," Alan recalls. "She had a sweet demeanor and helped Jeannie with everything, including her younger siblings."

As Laura grew, she liked to play with dolls, be with her friends, and dress up. She also enjoyed dancing. She studied ballet very seriously and auditioned for Ballet West's production of *The Nutcracker*, where she won the role of a Merliton doll. Alan attended Laura's dance recitals and show-and-tells. Looking back, Alan notes, "I was always there to be her dad in any way I could, but I guess I'd like to go back in time and have somebody counsel me on how to do a better job with daughters." (Laura disagrees: "I couldn't have had a better dad!")

Although other kids were drawn to her magnetic personality, Laura struggled with self-esteem in junior high. She was gifted with the same red hair and freckles as Aaron, but she struggled with her looks. She thought she wasn't attractive and that no boy would ever want to date her. Despite her self-criticism, she was very popular in school. She served as a class officer in eighth grade and was a student-body officer as a ninth grader.

In high school, Laura kept busy with friends and school activities. For several years, she channeled her energy into the Roy High School drill team, and served on the Seminary Council her senior year. She brought joy wherever she went. "Laura always took care of her little brothers and sister," Alan says. "She was very nurturing."

Jeannie inadvertently stepped in as a matchmaker to line Laura up with her husband-to-be, Matt West, before his mission. Matt's mother taught at Washington High School, a public, alternative school in Ogden where Jeannie was a counselor. One afternoon, as Jeannie was leaving for the day, she passed by Edna West's classroom. The door was open and a handsome young man was there, talking to Edna. She was so impressed with Edna's polite, handsome, all-American-looking son that she gave him the Halls' phone number. She invited him to come watch a basketball game during a tournament between his alma mater, Ben Lomond, and Roy High, where Laura would be performing with the Roy High drill team at halftime. By then, Laura had long outgrown her junior high insecurities and was a stunningly beautiful young woman. Their first date was the following week and they were steady companions from then on.

Laura graduated from Roy High and attended Weber State while Matt was on his mission to Estonia. She was invited to try out for the Miss Roy Pageant. With her beauty, poise, intelligence, and talent as a pianist, she won the title, and went on to represent Roy very well at the Miss Utah Scholarship Pageant. After Matt returned home and Laura had passed her title on to the next Miss Roy, they were married August 31, 1994, in the Salt Lake Temple. As newlyweds, they both attended WSU and worked. Laura was a part-time bookkeeper for Donna O. Kearney, owner of a make-up and hair studio. She learned many beauty tips, which she still uses and has passed on to her daughters. Laura earned her R.N. degree from Weber State University.

"Laura is a great soulmate for Matt, and has supported him in all his business activities and church assignments," Alan says. An active Church member, she has served as a ward and stake Primary president, ward Young Women's president, and in various other callings in the Primary and Relief Society.

Laura is a wonderful wife and mother. "Jeannie and I think of her as a celestial woman," says Alan. "She is always peaceful, uplifting, and loving."

Matt grew up in a single-parent home with his mother, older brother, and sister. The Halls love Matt as another son. He is kind, considerate, and works hard—the perfect "all-American boy" Jeannie saw more than 27 years ago. He is a loving husband and father and admired by many. He has served in many church capacities and was recently released as bishop of the Roy 18th Ward.

The West grandchildren are Morgan Michelle, Aubrey Maria, Shelby Jeanne, and Cole Matthew. "Morgan is the oldest Hall grandchild and served an LDS mission in Chesapeake, Virginia. She has set the model for the rest of the Hall grandchildren," Alan says. She was also the first Hall grandchild to marry—Morgan and Greyson Flint were married in the Ogden Temple on December 20, 2018.

Adam Henry Randall Hall

Even before Adam was born on April 9, 1976, he had a big presence. Just a week before his birth, a good friend had come to the Halls' front door and found Jeannie up on an eight-foot ladder, painting the entryway ceiling. As the friend gazed up at her, he said, "Sister Hall, you are the biggest pregnant lady I have ever seen." She laughed at the candid observation, and it's now a great family story.

When he was born, Adam weighed more than ten pounds. "He could practically walk when he was born," says Alan, laughing. "He was a big fellow!"

Like Laura, Adam was a peaceful baby. As Adam continued to grow, he was faithful, obedient, and well loved by everybody. Adam reminds Alan of his late brother Randy. All through elementary, junior high, and high school, Adam was well known and admired by his peers.

As Adam grew (he finished high school at 6'4"), he was a top student and fine athlete. He was the student-body president at Sand Ridge Junior High and a successful left-handed pitcher on the baseball team. When he was a high school senior, he became captain of the football and basketball teams. He also served for a year as the Roy High School Seminary president. By the time he graduated from Roy, he'd received two scholarships from Weber State: one to play football and one for academic excellence.

Four months into Adam's mission in Bahia, Brazil, Alan got a call. He was surprised to hear Adam's voice on the phone. He told his father, "Dad, I want to serve, but I have to come home." Adam had become ill with an E. coli infection after eating improperly cooked meat. He had nearly died in a filthy rural medical clinic, and the resulting illness threw him into a deep chemical depression. Alan was heartbroken to hear of Adam's pain. Because of the limited medical treatment available in Brazil, Adam returned home to get the help he needed to improve his health.

Back home in Roy, Utah, Adam struggled to make peace with what had happened. He had lived the life of an achiever and prepared himself for a mission for as long as he could remember. Having to come home early made him feel like a failure for the first time in his life. He suffered, thinking, *Why couldn't I do this? Why couldn't I finish my mission? Why did this happen to me?*

Hoping to help his son, Alan took Adam to visit Elder Marlin K. Jensen, a member of the Quorum of the Seventy. In his office in downtown Salt Lake City, Elder Jensen pulled out his scriptures and read aloud the story of the sons of Mosiah, who were missionaries. He showed Adam that some of the missionaries had faced insurmountable obstacles and challenges in declaring the gospel of Christ, through no fault of their own. Then he told Adam, "The length of a successful mission isn't defined by twenty-four months. A mission is defined by the effort spent serving your fellowmen with all your heart. Your mission was acceptable to the Lord."

With medication and reassurance, Adam returned to college and joined the football team. It wasn't long before he started bringing girls home. With the flurry of attractive young women around the house, Jeannie developed dating rules her boys knew by heart: both feet flat on the ground and keep your bodies upright.

After Adam dated numerous girls, a new young lady appeared in his life. Jeannie recalls the family's first introduction to Annette Berrett, the vivacious girl who is now Adam's wife: "She showed up on our porch and said she had come to say hello to Adam," she says. "She told me she had just washed her new car at the self-service station near our home... but she was dressed to kill, in a darling white summer frock. Her makeup and hair were perfect. She knew exactly what she was doing."

Adam wasn't home, but Jeannie invited Annette inside and called Adam at work. "There's a beautiful girl at our home who probably needs to go to lunch with a handsome guy," Jeannie told him. A little more than seven months later, on March 19, 1998, the couple married in the Salt Lake Temple. They were both still in college.

Annette grew up in Taylor, Utah, on a small farm with four sisters. Her dad worked at Hill Air Force Base and her mom was employed by the Weber School District. Annette was a senior class officer and a scholar-athlete at Weber High School. She attended Weber State, where she earned a degree in education, then taught PE, health, physiology, and anatomy at Weber High. "Annette's very pretty, and looked like one of the co-eds," Alan remembers with a smile. "She had to keep Adam's picture on her desk and flash her wedding ring so the high school boys knew she was married."

Annette has served as a Young Women's president, a gospel doctrine teacher, and in many other church capacities. She is a dedicated mother and a great supporter of her husband as he served as bishop of the Riverdale 8th Ward. She and Adam are now teaching teenagers in Sunday School.

Like the rest of the Hall boys, Adam worked at MarketStar through school. He graduated from Weber State with a bachelor's degree in professional sales and later earned an MBA from Regis University in Denver, Colorado. In addition to Adam's busy professional life and church service, he makes time to coach all their kids in sports. Their children are Avery Rose, Lily Belle, and Luke Berrett.

Eric Hansen Hall

The third Hall boy, Eric, joined the family on March 5, 1978. Eric is full of energy, vim, and vigor, and driven to succeed. In school, Eric was a good student and great athlete.

Listening and singing along to Broadway musicals like *Phantom of the Opera* and *Les Misérables* are favorite Hall family pastimes. When Eric was twelve, Alan took the family to see "Les Mis" in New York City. The family sat on the front row and Eric was mesmerized by the music conductor. Like the rest of the family, Eric knew each word of every song, but unlike his siblings, seeing the musical in person inspired his goal to develop singing skills.

"This talented son was not only handsome, he also had a magnificent singing voice," remembers Alan. Sometimes when the family heard him singing, they mistook his voice for the radio. In elementary and junior high school, Eric took the lead in several school musical productions. In high school, however, even though he auditioned and won the part of the lieutenant in *South Pacific,* the football coach would not let him participate in the musical. He used his talent in the choir and as a soloist for many school dances and often at church meetings.

During this time, Eric was still intensely involved in sports; by his senior year, he was the quarterback, field goal kicker, captain of the football team, and captain of the basketball team. "He'd also sing the national anthem before the ballgame started," Alan says. "He was multi-talented."

Like his brothers, Eric is a natural leader. He was always kind to everyone and had many friends. He also became president of the Roy High Seminary in high school. But unlike his strait-laced older brothers, Eric had a bit of a rebellious streak. During his senior year, Eric's chosen method of independence was growing out his hair—picture a high-school quarterback with long locks poking through the ear holes on either side of his helmet.

Eric received a full-ride double scholarship to Southern Utah University for football and academics. He was the kicker and backup quarterback at SUU; whether he went to class or not, though, is uncertain. When the family went to Cedar City to watch Eric's games, they found their son enjoying the good life, sharing banana cream pies from the local grocery store with his roommate, who was also a freshman football player.

From elementary school through college, Eric proved to be quite the magnet for attractive young ladies. "The girls were all over him," Alan remembers with amusement. By this time, Alan and Jeannie had a handle on how to manage hormonal teenage boys. The rules were simple: "Be home by 11:00 p.m., no more than three kisses, and keep the Lord's commandments."

After his first year at SUU, Eric served in the Chile Santiago West Mission. When he returned, he enrolled at Weber State and graduated in professional sales. With a degree in hand, he worked full time at MarketStar and nights at Ogden's famous Timbermine restaurant. The restaurant job proved to be very important—one of the female employees lined Eric up on a Valentine's Day blind date with Cami Elizabeth Jolley.

Cami is a lovely brunette with dark brown eyes, beautiful long brown hair, and a sweet personality. Her family lives in Pleasant View, Utah, where her father is a successful businessman and her mother is a personal-development consultant. Cami has two older sisters and two older brothers. She loved dance as a child, especially ballet; like Laura, she tried out for Ballet West's production of *The Nutcracker*. She auditioned three years in a row and was cast each year as a party girl because, she explains, "I didn't grow." She was a junior high cheerleader and graduated from Weber High, where she danced on the Warriorettes drill team and was a Sterling Scholar in family and consumer science. Cami graduated from WSU in 2005, with a degree in health promotion.

Eric is a superb golfer, so he arranged to give Cami an engagement ring on one of the highest holes at the Mount Ogden golf course. Her family and the Halls hid in the bushes, waiting for Eric to take a knee and pop the question. Everyone came out and cheered when he did. "Cami was such a find. We all like her so much," Alan says. "Her temperament is calm, mature, and elegant. She could be a princess."

Eric and Cami married in the Bountiful Temple on March 14, 2003, and began their family. They have four children: Corbin Eric, Bennett

Staley, Mya Elizabeth, and Anna Isabel. Eric is a successful medical-device sales manager. He has served in the elders quorum presidency in his ward, and is now the Young Men's president, where he has the added joy of working with his own sons. Cami is equally active, serving in the ward Primary presidency. Eric has a competitive edge. "He's the best golfer in our family," Alan notes. "When he plays, he lets his dad and brothers know he's going to beat them. Then he does."

Eric also has a reputation of serving and nurturing others. His brother-in-law, Matt West, recalls him being loving and kind to their oldest daughter, Morgan. When she faced serious medical issues as a little girl, he visited her often at Primary Children's Hospital in Salt Lake City.

Christian Alan Hall

On October 15, 1981, the fourth son joined Team Hall. "Christian is a remarkable young man. He's an amazing athlete and a superb student," Alan says. In elementary school, Christian was a gifted scholar-athlete and always one of the tallest in his class. He was a friend to everyone and well liked by his peers.

As with all his boys, Alan coached Christian until he was old enough to play on the junior high basketball team. In the sixth grade, he played for the Utah Heat in a competitive youth league. This great team won the Utah State championship and came in second to the national champion in 1994. Several of Christian's teammates went on to play Division I basketball at major universities.

Christian could dunk the ball when he was in seventh grade—it helped that he was already over six feet tall. He played well in other sports, starting as quarterback in football and pitcher in baseball. He was also the student-body president at Sand Ridge Junior High.

Christian loved to play the guitar. "He was a fine guitarist and entertained at assemblies with some of his friends. The students loved him! He was in love with Smashing Pumpkins, a popular rock group at the time," remembers Alan.

He was named one of the top basketball players in Utah when he was a sophomore at Roy High. However, by the end of his junior year, Christian was discouraged with basketball and football at Roy High, so he decided to transfer his senior year and play ball at Fremont High School. Although Alan thought Christian would still have been a basketball star at Roy, Alan and Jeannie supported his decision to change high schools. He played football and basketball and was a competitive high-jumper on the track team. It was amazing to watch him sail over the bar at over 6'5", his personal best. Looking back at that choice, Christian regrets leaving Roy High. However, he was a great student at Fremont and took several college classes at WSU during his senior year. By the time he graduated from Fremont, he had enough credits to be a sophomore at Weber State. His academic accomplishments also earned him a full scholarship, which he used throughout his entire bachelor's program.

One day during Christian's first year at Weber State, the Hall children gathered for a Hall Foundation board meeting. Christian looked at the foundation's financial statements. Halfway through the meeting, he raised his hand and blurted out, "Dad, I've just figured out how much I get. When am I going to get my money?"

His brothers and sisters burst out laughing. Alan replied gently, "Well, Christian, this money goes to help the needy. It's not for you." Thirty minutes later, Christian raised his hand again: "No Dad, really?"

A two-year LDS mission to the Peru Lima Central Mission gave Christian some perspective. "Working with poor members and non-members in Peru was a pivotal turning point for Christian," says Alan. "The mission experience matured him. He had an understanding that it was God's money and we were the stewards of it, not the owners," Alan says.

Back home, Christian returned to school and later graduated from Weber State in professional sales. After spending some time working at MarketStar, he found a job in medical sales, like his brothers. He also found a wife, the beautiful Emily Coleman. Alan recalls that after his mission, Christian had lots of girls chasing him, but one night he went on a blind date with Emily. Cami Hall, Eric's wife, knew Emily and had suggested to Christian that he take her on a date. It wasn't long before Emily and Christian were head over heels in love. "The next thing we knew, they were married in the Salt Lake Temple on August 18, 2004," recalls Alan.

Emily comes from the family that owns Coleman Knitting, a company that produces letterman sweaters and jackets and cheerleading uniforms. She too was a great student-athlete, lettering all three years at Weber High in both softball and volleyball. She attended Weber State, graduating in 2004 in professional sales. She worked for more than six years in the pharmaceutical industry. "She is a lovely, tenderhearted, kind person," Alan says.

Although Emily is a diminutive 5'4" and Christian towers over her at 6'5", she can hold her own when they ski and golf together. "She is a great mother and supports her husband in all his church callings," Alan says. "They are creating a wonderful home for their family."

Despite struggles with infertility, Christian and Emily are proud parents of four children. Both Hadley and Benson Christian were conceived through the miracle of in vitro fertilization. Emily was nineteen weeks pregnant with their third child, Nixon Coleman, when they lost him to a devastating miscarriage on October 29, 2016. He was about the size of a man's hand. "He was already a perfect, beautiful human being. His hands and feet, although very tiny, were remarkably formed," Alan says. "He looked like a tiny doll with his eyes closed. Holding this little precious grandson was a very tender moment for me."

Christian asked Alan to join him and Dick Coleman, Emily's father, to give Nixon a name and a blessing. The three priesthood holders sat on a couch in the hospital room and lovingly held the baby's lifeless body. Emily, her mother, Kathy, and Jeannie closed their eyes in reverent prayer. "Tears flowed as Christian, using the priesthood, announced that his second son would be named Nixon Coleman Hall," Alan says. "The Spirit of the Lord filled the room with heavenly love and peace as Christian pleaded with God that he and Emily would, at a future time and place, be reunited with their beloved son. I have no doubt that the desires of their hearts will come to pass."

On the same day little Nixon was born, his cousin Cole West was playing quarterback and defense on his little-league football team. Cole's team won the mini-bowl championship that morning. Several days later at Nixon's graveside service, eleven-year-old Cole wrote Nixon's name

on the special game ball that he had earned as the MVP. He presented
this precious gift to Christian and Emily. "They wept for the love they
have for Cole and Nixon," Alan says. "This moment reflected how
bonded these cousins are and how much they love each other."

The safe and happy arrival of Davis Nixon Hall, on November 11,
2018, has again brought joy and delight to Christian and Emily. Davis is
Alan and Jeannie's twentieth grandchild.

Christian has served as a counselor in the bishopric and is currently
the executive secretary in his ward. Emily has participated in leadership
and teaching positions in all the auxiliaries. The past three years she has
led the activity days for the girls in Primary. Christian and Emily teach
and nurture their own children in the gospel of Jesus Christ, always
looking to the day when they will be an eternal family with little Nixon.

Megan Jeanne Hall Funk

Megan is the youngest Hall child, a deeply desired miracle baby.
Nearly four months into Jeannie's pregnancy with Megan, she suffered
a massive hemorrhage at home. Having had two miscarriages earlier
in their marriage, she was well aware of the signs. Heartbroken and
devastated by the loss, Jeannie went to the doctor the next day. When
he performed an ultrasound test, however, he heard a strong heartbeat.
Unbeknownst to Jeannie and the doctor, she had been carrying twins.
She had lost one of them, but thankfully the other baby was healthy.

Her pregnancy continued uneventfully, and five months later, on
May 29, 1985, Megan Jeanne was born. The whole family was delighted—
Laura was thrilled to finally have a little sister—and the baby quickly
became the princess of the house. Loved and adored by her siblings and
parents, Megan never lacked for attention or care. "It was fun watching
her grow and develop," Alan recalls. "She was a beautiful little girl, with
big blue eyes and long blond hair. Even after she cut a big chunk of her
hair off when she found some scissors at about four years old, she was
darling!"

At North Park Elementary, Megan became the last Hall child to
complete kindergarten through sixth grade. Alan remembers her being
very popular and well liked by her peers. She was also talented and

witty. A 298

loving child, Megan was a chatterbox, outgoing and playful. "She mirrors my personality," Alan says.

Megan took dance and gymnastics lessons and excelled at both. Alan also continued his coaching career with Megan and her team-mates in basketball. He quickly learned that girls were different from boys. He couldn't slap them on their bums when they returned to the court and had to give coaching tips carefully so they wouldn't burst into tears. He recruited Jolyn Emerson, the mother of a team member, as an assistant coach.

As she grew, Megan enjoyed a love for music, singing, and dancing. In junior high, she joined the cheerleading squad, a sport she continued to participate in for all three years at Roy High. Megan has always had a tender heart and a desire to serve others. In junior high, she received a special award for reaching out to students who struggled academically or socially, or who just needed a friend. In her senior year, she received a $2,000 scholarship from the Ogden Rotary Club for "Service Above Self." She also excelled academically.

Although Megan has fought anxiety, depression, and trichotillo-mania over the years, she's triumphed over many challenges. She has used the power of exercise to help fight her battles. For many years she has been a Les Mills certified instructor in several fitness programs. Witty and vivacious, Megan is a wonderful teacher, and the students love her.

She graduated from Weber State with a degree in elementary education and later earned a master's degree in school counseling from the University of Phoenix. She taught second and third grade for seven years, full time and part time. Her part-time teaching worked well when she taught morning classes at the Ogden Athletic Club. She worked temporarily as an elementary school counselor before the birth of her own precious daughter, Gia Jeanne Funk, who was born April 2, 2018.

Megan knew Curtis Funk in high school, but fell in love with him after his mission when they were both in college. "God could not have given Megan a better spouse," Alan says. "Curtis is a remarkable husband and family member. He loves Megan and Gia and supports them both in everything they do."

Curtis comes from a wonderful family with two older brothers and an older sister. Like Megan, he's the baby of the family. His parents recently returned from serving as LDS senior missionaries in Knoxville, Tennessee. Curtis was born in Ogden, but moved from Roy to California at the age of three. In first and second grades, he won awards for perfect attendance. He returned to Roy in third grade. In sixth grade he received the Hope of America Award, but from junior high on, it was hard to keep Curtis in the classroom. He was gifted in many areas, always curious, and loved to explore and learn new things. He just didn't care for sitting in class.

In high school, Curtis played keyboard in a four-member band. They won the Northern Utah Battle of the Bands and were allowed the honor of recording one of their songs in the John Lennon Tour Bus. Somehow, even though he seldom went to school, he managed to pass enough classes and make up enough attendance credits to graduate from Roy High and Seminary. He even performed at the high school graduation ceremony, playing piano and singing an original song he had composed for the class of 2003. He left for an LDS mission to the West Indies after graduation and was a devoted missionary and assistant to the president. After he returned home, Curtis attended WSU and completed the professional sales program.

Megan and Curtis began dating after his mission. They were creative, fun, and had a great time together. Curtis impressed the family with his piano skills, especially while lying on his back on the piano bench, with his head underneath the piano. He played the piano and sang to Megan on her birthday. Curtis and Megan became engaged after skydiving over Ogden, Utah. He landed first, and once she was down and cleared from her parachute, Curtis asked her to marry him in front of the entire Hall and Funk families.

While dating, they decided to read *The Book of Mormon* together every night before parting and finish it by their wedding on August 22, 2007, in the Salt Lake Temple. Curtis discovered that by marrying Megan, he also acquired her twenty-year-old cat, Tigerlilli. They have since added Franky, a golden retriever; Walter, a goldendoodle; and a white cat named Morty, who has the distinction of having one blue eye and one green. Megan has adopted every stray animal she could find throughout her life, and Curtis loves them too.

Curtis bought his first business, FuneralRecording.com, from his older brother, Jim. It offers online funeral webcasting and recording services, allowing family members to attend services from anywhere in the world. Then came Tukios, an innovative video-creation software now used by thousands of funeral homes around the world. (*Tukios* is a Swahili word for "event.") "He's intelligent, a visionary, and a fantastic entrepreneur," Alan says. "My boys tease me that Curtis is the most beloved of them all because he's the only entrepreneur."

Megan and Curtis love to travel and have been on many Hall family trips. They have also visited New Zealand, England, Fiji, and Alaska.

Megan takes it upon herself to keep her dad in check. While Alan is usually the leader asking people tough questions, Megan regularly pulls him aside to make sure he's behaving himself. Megan tells him, "You've got wealth and you've got power, so I'm going to ask you every time I see you: You're not fooling around with anyone, are you Dad?" To which he sometimes replies with a teasing grin, "Only with your mother."

Megan and Curtis continue to serve as leaders and teachers in the Church in numerous assignments. Currently, Curtis is in the elders quorum presidency and Megan works with the Young Women. For every one of Alan and Jeannie's children and their spouses, their greatest priority is to teach their families about Heavenly Father and our Savior, Jesus Christ.

Sunday dinners

As each child has grown up, married, and brought new members to the Hall family, traditions have grown more bountiful—and boisterous. Sunday dinner is one of the family's finest and fondest traditions. "I have lots of friends whose kids are scattered all over the world," Alan says. "They hardly see their grandkids. Fortunately, all our children live within fifteen minutes of our home. We consider ourselves very blessed to have our children and grandchildren living so close. We get to see each other often."

Every other Sunday afternoon, the whole family assembles for a family dinner. Around 2012, Alan and Jeannie expanded their home to accommodate a growing family. Hall children, in-laws, grandchildren, and frequently visiting friends and guests gather in the Hall home for an exciting evening of lively conversation. It's easy to see that the group enjoys each other's company. They all let loose and tease each other. "We'll talk about anything and everything. Nothing is off the table," Alan says, "yet there's still harmony."

While the grown-ups laugh and poke fun at each other, grand-children play downstairs in the Hall Playhouse, which Alan and Jeannie designed to be a haven of happy memories. Framed with stained-glass windows Alan and Jeannie designed and made themselves, the room is filled with costumes, props, and a stage with a purple velvet curtain—a symbol of Alan and Jeannie's love for the performing arts.

Jeannie often plans the meals, but all the women in the family help prepare the food. When dinner is complete, the men of the family clean the dishes, continuing a tradition Alan started as a newlywed. When the Nowaks came over for dinner early in Alan and Jeannie's marriage, younger Alan, looking to impress his in-laws, was quick to wash the dishes. Knowing their dad had never washed the dishes any other time, the kids now laugh at Alan's contrived service.

After dinner, the grandchildren often perform on the stage in Alan and Jeannie's basement. Adults sometimes join them as they dance and sing songs, usually little tunes made up on the fly. The whole family shares a love of music and theater. Alan and Jeannie began taking their children to see Broadway musicals when they were young, starting with *Les Misérables*. They continue the tradition today as they take each grandchild to New York City for a Broadway tour after they turn eight. "I want them to see *Wicked, Phantom of the Opera*, or whatever's on Broadway," Alan says. "I am excited to introduce them to the arts and to establish a personal memory with them that they will never forget."

Shared traditions like Sunday dinner and trips bond the family.

"That's the way we've done it for many years. Wonderful activities have brought us together as fond friends," Alan says. "They would die for each other. A sense of family has been deeply instilled in them."

On being grandparents

As grandparents, Alan and Jeannie are humbled and filled with joy by the examples their children set with their individual families. "It is interesting to me to see how our love and affection grows from our children to their spouses and then to our grandchildren. It seems that love and caring have no bounds or limits," Alan says. "Surely God is the quintessential example of this principle."

In their Roy home, Jeannie keeps their walk-in pantry stocked with treats on shelves that the grandchildren can easily reach. Alan and Jeannie love supporting them in their activities; their schedules are often filled with ballgames, dance and singing recitals, piano performances, show-and-tells, and even lunch at elementary schools. "We love attending every event we can," Alan says.

The Hall cousins see each other at sleepovers, family dinners, and on annual trips together. "That friendship will last in many ways for most of their lives," Alan says. "We are all blessed that their parents have taught them to love each other."

He's also impressed with how his grandchildren make thoughtful choices. When his granddaughter Morgan came to him about a big decision at the end of her junior year, he shared his thoughts. He wanted her to make the call, but gave her his opinion on the pros and cons. Morgan prayed about her options and decided not to be a high school cheerleader her senior year. She had cheered for three years in junior high and high school, so it was hard to give up. The Lord immediately ratified the results of that decision when she was called to serve on the Roy High Seminary Council. She continued to be an active, engaged, happy student in all her classes, influencing others for good. She had a great senior year. "I admired her maturity and the process she followed to make a thoughtful decision," Alan says.

He realizes that at some point, some of his posterity may make choices that lead them astray. "I anticipate at some point that a few of them will be wild," Alan half teases. "Even if they misbehave, I won't stop loving them. I trust the Lord will help them find their way back."

Rejoicing in posterity

When he thinks about his family, Alan is reminded of the words he has heard many times in the temple about having joy and rejoicing in posterity. "Each family member brings me joy as I watch them happily serve one another and those around them," he says. "I rejoice that they willingly love the Savior and are faithful in keeping His commandments. What more could I hope for from my wonderful family? I am at peace knowing they are righteous souls blessed by God."

15

Spirituality and Serving in The Church of Jesus Christ of Latter-day Saints

Throughout Alan's life, sacred spiritual experiences have taught him truths beyond what the mortal eye can see or hear. These lessons of the Spirit have built Alan's personal convictions of the salvation that comes through the reality of a living God, His Son, Jesus Christ, and The Church of Jesus Christ of Latter-day Saints.

For more than forty years, Alan has served in leadership positions both in the workplace and in places of worship.

"I became a successful business leader by being a well-schooled and thoughtful church leader," he observes. The trajectory of leadership in Alan's church associations parallels his work success. At the same time, lessons learned in his journey from employee to employer have influenced the way Alan serves in the Church.

Most of all, spiritual experiences have taught Alan how to love people. From working with the youth to presiding twice as a bishop and as a stake president, Alan has sought to see others as God sees them, and to love them wholeheartedly. The following outlines Alan's church service, starting after his mission until present day (2019).

Back to his home ward

After serving as a full-time missionary for two years in Central America, Alan returned to his family ward, where he taught Sunday School to teenagers.

In his junior year at Weber State, Alan was set apart as vice president in the Weber State LDS Student Association (LDSSA), the student leadership organization of the Weber State Institute of Religion. "I was assigned to help plan and implement firesides, dances, and multiple social activities," Alan says.

Peace Corps, married student ward, and Murray, Utah

The young Hall couple did not attend church while living in the jungle during their Peace Corps year, because Itajuípe did not have an LDS branch. However, they attended a Sacrament meeting on the two occasions they traveled to Rio de Janeiro. Sunday in their jungle home consisted of reading aloud *Jesus the Christ* by the apostle James E. Talmage.

After returning to the United States, they became members of the BYU 1st Ward, where they served in various church callings. Alan was a counselor in the elders quorum presidency and Jeannie was a Relief Society teacher. When they graduated from BYU, they lived for six months in an apartment complex in Murray, Utah. They attended a family ward and taught Sunday School classes.

Special dream as elders quorum president

When they moved to Roy, the Halls lived in a small duplex and attended the Roy 12th Ward, where they served in church auxiliaries. Jeannie was the ward librarian and Alan served as the Young Men's president from 1973–1974. When they bought their first home, they moved into the Roy 6th Ward. Jeannie served as a youth Sunday School teacher, a Relief Society and Primary teacher, and a Young Women's leader. She also served as the Relief Society president, and Alan served for three years as the elders quorum president.

During this time, Alan longed for a deeper relationship with God. "I had a testimony of the restored gospel after serving a mission, but wanted to know more," Alan says. "I decided to repent of every sin so I could have a closer relationship with my Heavenly Father."

Alan made a conscious effort to be spiritually aligned. He read *The Book of Mormon*, relating the scriptures to himself as a young father and husband, often finding helpful insights. "One night, after going to bed, I had a powerful and magnificent dream about the Savior."

Alan treasures what he saw and felt in that dream. "I saw the Savior and His divine light, a glorious light, an illumination beyond imagination," he remembers tenderly. "I also felt His love. It was a sublime feeling of intense affection, utmost pleasure, and absolute joy. If I could have died at that moment, I would have willingly left mortality to be in that supernal environment."

This special dream became his spiritual anchor and foundation. "I learned in that moment, in a very personal way, that the Son of God lives and loves us," Alan says. "I had been given a gift of sure knowledge about the Savior and Redeemer of the world. I had moved from having faith that God exists to knowing it for a fact."

Counselor and bishop in a student stake

Alan's church experiences have been guided by other intersecting points in his life. For example, his position at the university led to unexpected church callings. In February 1978, Alan had been working as alumni director at Weber State, then a four-year institution, for about four years. "I was working closely with the president of the college, alumni, and the athletic director, who happened to be a counselor in the Weber State College Stake," Alan says. "One day I got a call to see the stake president of the college stake, who invited me to be a high counselor."

Four months later, when Alan was thirty-three, the stake president called him to be bishop of the Weber State College 4th Ward. He was ordained and set apart in June 1978, with Paul Checketts and Richard Blake as his original counselors; Jeff Booth and Jerry Pacheco later served as his counselors. John Cardon, Wayne Rollins, and David

Maxwell served as clerks. Bishop Hall wasn't much older than the ward members, who were college students between the ages of eighteen and twenty-eight.

"Many of the students were going to or coming home from missions," Alan says. "I often gave them priesthood blessings and shared with them the principles of a happy and prosperous life."

The bishopric grew close to the young men and women they served. They hosted activities, camping trips, and frequent parties. The bishopric members, including the Halls, often invited ward members to their homes for family home evening. "We had Aaron, Laura, Adam, and Eric at the time, and my kids loved all the attention they received from these wonderful college students. Even though our home was humble, the activities were filled with love and enthusiasm," Alan remembers.

Sometimes Alan dealt with serious situations, such as when a ward member broke covenants. He presided at disciplinary councils for a few ward members, helping them repent and return to living righteously. "We only lost one soul—a young man who declared he was gay and couldn't reconcile his feelings with the Church," Alan says. "But most people went through the repentance process and returned to full fellowship."

Weber State College Stake presidency

Alan served as a bishop in the student ward for five years, and in 1983 was called to serve as the second counselor in the Weber State College Stake presidency. He was pleased to assist Fred Baker, the stake president who kindly taught Alan more about church government. Three years later, Alan returned to his home ward, after an absence of eight years.

On one occasion, Alan and Jeannie hosted Elder James E. Faust, who was a member of the Quorum of the Twelve Apostles, and his wife, Ruth, for dinner. The Fausts had come to Ogden to attend a Ballet West performance.

"How long have you been away from your home ward?" Elder Faust asked Alan.

"Eight years," Alan replied.

"That's way too long. Your children are growing up without ever seeing you at church," Elder Faust said.

Elder Faust was right. During the eight years Alan served in the college stake, Aaron grew from a seven-year-old into a teenager on the verge of driving and dating. Alan realized how his kids were affected when they took a family trip to Colorado for a few weeks with Ballet West. Jeannie was getting the kids ready to attend a local Aspen ward on a Sunday morning when eight-year-old Eric looked at his dad, who was putting on a tie, and asked Jeannie, "Where will Dad go to church?"

"I realized at that moment that it had been a long time since I had sat with my children in Sacrament meeting in our home ward," Alan says.

Frank conversations with young men

In 1986, Alan returned to the Hall family's Roy 6th Ward and was soon called to be the Young Men's president, giving him built-in time with Aaron and his teenage friends. Alan focused on two things: helping them become Eagle Scouts and teaching them to be morally pure.

Although being an Eagle Scout had not been emphasized in Alan's teenage years, the program gained traction for the next generation. Seeking to help the young men in his ward achieve the rank of Eagle, Alan led an effort to encourage and support several young men to obtain the skills and knowledge they needed to earn the required merit badges. After a year of coaching, four young men in the ward, including Aaron, earned their Eagles.

Alan also gave the young men something he never received at their age—a frank conversation about sex. One Sunday, he taught the priests a lesson on the sensitive topic that they would never forget.

"I was very direct with them and used localized language they would understand, words they'd hear at Roy High," Alan says. "As I spoke, their heads were down. None of them wanted to look at me."

Why was this so important to Alan? "I believe we should discuss the matter in a careful and honest way. Sex is part of life, and these kids deserved to have it explained to them in a clear and positive manner," Alan says. "I talked to them about how procreation is a gift and they need to be aware of their passions and control them."

Teenaged Aaron felt embarrassed at the time, but years later, as Bishop Hall, he would give the same lesson to the teenage priests in his ward.

A painful but tender experience

In the early days of TempReps, Alan sent an employee to work in Texas. The man had a wife and young children, and going on outings with the whole family was often—as many parents of small children can attest—a logistical challenge. One hot summer day, they returned from an outing and were gathering children, toys, diaper bags, and strollers. The man thought his wife had taken in their sleeping toddler, while she thought he had. It was not until several hours later that they realized she was still in the car, and by the time they ran outside, the little girl was dead.

Horrified and grief-stricken, the father called Alan. "It was such a tragedy for the grieving couple," Alan says, remembering the sorrow he felt during that conversation. "The police wanted to arrest the father for child abuse, and they had no money for a funeral or attorney."

Alan and Jeannie paid for the funeral, and within a year, Alan received a call from the employee's wife. She'd been mourning the death of her little girl when the deceased daughter appeared to her. "I was in my bedroom this morning reading the scriptures when our baby appeared to me," the mother said. "She said to me, 'Mom, I'm okay. Don't mourn for me anymore. I am happy and fine,' and then she left."

The daughter appeared as a full-grown woman who looked like her mother, but as a spirit. Since that time, the mother has written a book about the spiritual encounter.

"Not many have such a divine experience," Alan says. "It taught me that life really does go on after death. It was a powerful moment for me."

Priesthood power on a pioneer trek

After years of serving in the ward Young Men's organization, Alan had a series of stake callings. He was the stake Sunday School president for two years, from 1988 to 2000. He was then called by President Nolan Karras to be a stake high counselor and then to be his second counselor in the Roy Utah North Stake presidency. During this assignment, Alan had a significant spiritual experience on a pioneer trek with the youth in the stake.

Alan led approximately 150 youth and their leaders on a four-day pioneer trek in the mountains near Evanston, Wyoming. Jeannie and Megan were with them. One hot summer afternoon in July, after stopping to eat lunch on a flat, treeless hilltop, a powerful thunderstorm approached the group.

"We could see numerous lightning bolts coming through the clouds hitting the ground," Alan says. "It dawned on me that I had scores of people in harm's way. We were like lightning rods on the top of that hill as the furor of the storm rapidly approached us."

He took quick action and asked the group to kneel down with him to plead with God to protect them from the threatening storm.

"However, as I started to pray, I was prompted to use my priesthood power to command the elements to move away from us," Alan says. "I had never used my priesthood in such a dramatic way, and definitely not in front of many witnesses."

Having faith that God would agree with his action, Alan commanded the winds, clouds, and lightning to depart. Then they all witnessed a miracle. "The kids and leaders watched in amazement as the thunderstorm split in two and half of it went to the right and another portion of it moved to the left," Alan says. "It was a singular moment I'll never forget. All of us who were there that day will always remember how the power of God saved our lives."

Bishop of the Roy 11th Ward

In 2003, Stake President Thomas Jensen extended a call to Alan to serve as bishop of the Roy 11th Ward. The call surprised Alan, and he only had a short period of time to find counselors. He prayed and was divinely directed to visit Mark Oyler. "I had heard his name and went to his house, under the pretense of merely saying hello. We visited for thirty minutes and I knew he should be my first counselor." A friend, Jim Davidson, was called as second counselor. Terry Heslop was asked to continue as ward clerk and June Balaich was invited to be the executive secretary.

"The highlight for me as the bishop was being imbued with a special love for the people in my ward," Alan says. "I developed this deep affection for everyone, no matter their status or worthiness."

Bishop Hall led the congregation in many important ways. He was the presiding high priest, responsible for the temporal and spiritual welfare of approximately 500 people. He managed welfare efforts and decided how to use fast offerings to bless people in need. He presided over the Aaronic Priesthood quorums and oversaw youth programs for young men and women. He was also ultimately responsible for proper records and providing Church headquarters with accurate member information. He was a judge in Israel, responsible for determining if ward members were living the gospel worthily. If they were, he would sign off on priesthood advancements and temple recommends.

He served his ward members with love and unrelenting service. During his nearly six years as bishop, Alan officiated at approximately fifty weddings and twenty-five funerals. He remembers visiting the hospital often to see ward members who were injured or ill and holding a special ward fast for a sister who was dying of cancer. As the father of the ward, his congregants all became like family members to him.

A surprise new calling

In March 2009, Tom Jensen was released from his calling as stake president after nine years of service. On a Saturday afternoon, Elders Robert H. Garff and Spencer J. Condie of the Quorum of the Seventy interviewed twenty brethren in the stake, looking for the new stake president. They invited Alan to be interviewed.

Soon after the interview, Alan remembers conducting a funeral for a deceased sister in his ward. "Following the service, Elder Condie called me to once again meet with him, and asked me to bring my wife," Alan says. "I figured I might be a counselor."

Elder Condie told Alan that the Lord wanted him to be the next stake president of the Roy Utah North Stake. "I accepted the call and felt very honored and blessed to be invited to lead the stake family," Alan says. "I was then asked to quickly recommend counselors."

With only a short amount of time to act, Alan asked God for the names of two brethren. As he did, they came quickly to his mind. He was inspired to recommend that Dan Emerson and Chad Griffith be invited to serve with him as first and second counselors, respectively. They too accepted the assignment. On Sunday morning at the Ogden Tabernacle, the members of the stake sustained Alan, Dan, and Chad. Mark Oyler, June Balaich, Kevin Merrill, and Richie Kinmont also served with President Hall in the Roy Utah North Stake.

Following the conference session, the visiting General Authority invited the new stake presidency, along with their wives and families, to a room where he set them apart. "He placed his hands on my head and gave me the priesthood keys to manage the stake," Alan says. "I felt those powers come into my body. It made me shake and brought tears to my eyes. It was a real, physical thing. I knew the Lord expected me to be a good shepherd for the 3,000 members of our stake."

Lessons on calling leaders

Many of the lessons Alan has learned running a business translate into running a large church organization, and vice versa. Delegation is an important and critical skill. "In both arenas, I deal with multiple issues, more than I can implement alone, so I have become a skilled delegator," Alan says. "I just set apart a new bishop and gave him the priesthood keys of administration. With direction from the Lord, he can manage the affairs of the ward by delegating certain tasks to his counselors and to the other leaders on the Ward Council. I also use the same principles of effective delegation as the stake president."

Alan seeks God's help in every decision he makes. During his nine and a half years as stake president, Alan worked with many stake and ward leaders. Professional résumés hold no bearing when considering someone for church leadership positions; the only qualifications are worthiness and willingness.

"One time I interviewed six men as potential candidates to be a bishop," Alan says. "Out of those six men, any one of them could have been the bishop. All of them were worthy and capable. It was up to me to determine who the Lord wanted. God has established a pattern for

making decisions, as a guide. He asks us to do our homework on an
issue and to make a careful decision. Then He invites us to bring our
decision to Him for ratification. Following a prayer, if we feel peace,
we've made the right choice. If we feel doubt or confusion, the decision
was wrong."

Alan has learned to lead others by setting high expectations. He
received great satisfaction from seeing his stake members progress and
grow closer to the Savior. Each year, Alan and his counselors met to establish a spiritual theme with related goals for the members of the stake
to pursue. "We asked our members to come unto Christ and follow
Him," Alan says. "We explained this can happen as they read daily from
the scriptures, minister to one another, proclaim the restored gospel,
make and keep sacred covenants, keep all the commandments, pray
daily, and attend the temple often."

Presiding from the pulpit

President Hall led countless church meetings, including eighteen
stake conferences and fifty-four ward conferences. He was known for
his informal, ad-lib style at the pulpit. "I talked to the congregation as
beloved friends, and I invited the Spirit of the Lord to tell me what to
say," Alan says. "I rarely prepare a written speech. I prefer to let God
inspire my thoughts and words. Having the faith to wait at the pulpit
for the talk to arrive takes courage. Happily, the Lord has never let
me down."

At a stake conference in August 2017, Alan hosted Elder Kim B.
Clark, former dean of the Harvard Business School, past president of
BYU–Idaho, and commissioner of the Church Educational System,
who complimented President Hall on his approach to leading the Roy
Utah North Stake. "Surely, there is no other stake president on earth like
you," he said.

Other visiting general authorities who presided at a Roy Utah North
Stake conference were Elder Carl B. Cook, Elder Enrique R. Falabella,
Elder M. Russell Ballard, Elder Lynn L. Summerhays, Elder Christoffel
Golden, Jr., and Elder Steven M. Petersen.

Spiritual prompting during the Sacrament

As stake president, Alan often helped families in heart-wrenching situations. At one point, for example, he met with a sorrowful wife. Her husband, a war veteran, had unexpectedly left her. They went to bed one night, and in the morning, without any warning, she found his wedding ring on his pillow.

"He had five kids, with a daughter leaving on a mission," Alan says. "Their situation gnawed at me." Alan went to the ward Sacrament meeting where the man attended church. He met with the bishop and learned that the man suffered from post-traumatic stress disorder.

During the Sacrament, Alan thought of this troubled man and his sweet family. As he sang the hymn "I Stand All Amazed," he had a spiritual experience. "I've taken the Sacrament thousands of times, but this time it was different," Alan says. "From the top of my head to the bottom of my feet, I started to buzz. I began to have an overwhelming love for this man. I started to weep, and couldn't stop crying."

Throughout the service, Alan communed with the Spirit. "I was burning with a spiritual fever," Alan says. "The Lord let me know I needed to find this brother, wrap my arms around him, tell him I love him and that the Savior loves him too. The Spirit told me to give him a priesthood blessing."

For the next month, Alan kept praying for the man to return home. When he finally did come back to his family, Alan was overjoyed and anxious to visit with him. He went to their house and embraced this troubled veteran. When Alan told the man and his wife of his experience during the Sacrament, the couple began to weep. "I then placed my hands on his head and blessed him by the power of God that he might find peace and joy," Alan says.

Loving effort to shepherd lost souls

According to Alan, conducting a disciplinary council is one of the most spiritual moments a stake president has. "It's a time when we need to be very close to God," Alan says. "It's a time when we need His guidance, especially as we consider the eternal soul of a person."

He calls these meetings a "loving effort" to help people confess their sins and successfully go through the process of repentance. The goal is bringing them to Christ and helping them return to a path of righteousness.

Before the councils, President Hall would gather information by talking to involved parties. "Based upon what we learned, we would decide what discipline best fit the circumstances. We would then take our decision to the Lord in prayer," Alan says. "We would say, 'Heavenly Father, we've made a decision and we now ask Thee to ratify our decision.' Once God revealed His will on the matter, we would inform the member."

Restoration of priesthood and temple blessings

When set apart as a stake president, Alan was given priesthood keys from the First Presidency to restore priesthood and temple ordinances that were lost due to transgressions to those who sincerely repent and return to live the gospel. Upon receiving written authorization from the First Presidency, a stake president can, using his priesthood power, reinstate these special eternal blessings upon a member of his stake. Over the course of his tenure, Alan was instrumental in helping several individuals come back to Christ.

Alan's recollection of a remarkable experience

On March 14, 2018, I received a surprise phone call that I will never forget. When my phone rang, I looked at the number of the caller and didn't recognize it. I answered anyway.

"Hello," said a pleasant voice. "Is this President Hall?"

"Yes," I responded. "How can I be of service to you?"

"President Hall, I am President Dallin Oaks' secretary," the woman said. "He asked me to see if you might have a few minutes to speak with him."

I paused briefly to gather my thoughts, as I could feel my heart rate increase. I was about to speak with one of the most highly accomplished and powerful persons I knew, and I became a bit tense and nervous. My mind filled with a range of bizarre questions. Why would the first counselor in the First Presidency of The Church of Jesus Christ of Latter-day Saints want to speak with me? Had I done something wrong? Was he calling me to repentance? What could he want to discuss with me?

For many years, I have known of Dallin H. Oaks as a distinguished scholar, attorney, well-respected judge, university leader, and beloved General Authority of the Church. He was the president of BYU when Jeannie and I graduated with our masters' degrees in 1972. He had graduated from the University of Chicago Law School and had clerked for Chief Justice Earl Warren of the U.S. Supreme Court. He practiced law for a season and was a law professor at his alma mater prior to his tenure at BYU. I knew that before his calling as an apostle in 1984 he had been a justice of the Utah Supreme Court, and that he had been the national chairman of Public Broadcasting Services (PBS) for many years.

On a few occasions, Jeannie and I had briefly spoken with President Oaks at special receptions right before the Tabernacle Choir Christmas concerts. He was there on behalf of the Church and as a past chairman of PBS to greet and thank the supporters of PBS and the Choir. The instant we shook his hand, we knew who he was. We had, of course, seen his face and heard his powerful voice scores of time when he had spoken at General Conference.

Collecting my composure, I told his secretary I was free to speak with him.

A short pause, and then I heard President Oaks' familiar and cheerful voice.

"Hello President Hall, how are you?" he said. "I understand you are conducting stake conference this weekend. May I attend your meetings?"

Somewhat surprised with his request, but also relieved it wasn't something else, I said, "Yes, of course."

"I've been praying to learn from the Lord where I should go to church this weekend, and your name and your stake came to mind," he said. "Would you please send me at your earliest convenience the agendas of your stake conference meetings? Oh, and by the way, President, please don't tell anyone I am coming, except your wife and your counselors." As we finished our brief conversation, we agreed to speak again the next day.

As I ended the call, Jeannie said, "Please tell me everything!" What I shared with her was only the tip of the iceberg regarding her involvement. It was a treasured moment of great excitement for us: We were going to host a member of the First Presidency in our stake and home.

As planned, President Oaks and I spoke again the next day. We reviewed the agendas for the Saturday night and Sunday morning sessions of stake conference. We discussed the speakers and their assigned topics and the hymns the congregation and stake choir would sing.

He was comfortable with our plans and said he would like to speak at each meeting. He told me his wife, Kristen, would be with him on Sunday, and asked if they could join us for lunch on Sunday at our home. He told me to invite my counselors and clerks and their wives to the lunch, along with the entire Hall family.

Within a few minutes of this call, a fellow from Church security called me to schedule a trip to our stake building on Friday to evaluate the premises.

"Hey Jeannie girl, guess what?" I told my wife. "Can you organize a fabulous luncheon next Sunday around noon? We'll be hosting a few guests at our home."

Within minutes, she went to work planning a very special meal for about fourteen very important people. She quickly called President Oaks' secretary to learn what he and Sister Oaks liked to eat. His bodyguard told Jeannie that President Oaks loved chocolate milk, especially the TruMoo brand.

Over the course of nine years as stake president, I had conducted stake conference meetings seventeen times. All of them had been special and memorable occasions, but the one on March 17-18, 2018, would surpass them all.

I arrived at the stake center at 4:30 p.m. on Saturday, March 17, and anxiously waited to welcome President Oaks. My nervous counselors and clerks joined me. We were well prepared and ready for any change of plans. Fortunately, it was a beautiful spring evening; rain, wind, or cold temperatures would not be an issue. We watched with excitement as President Oaks arrived with his bodyguard at 5 p.m.

I opened his door. He stepped out of the car, called out hello to us all, and gave me a bear hug. I can vividly remember his warm and happy smile and the love we all immediately felt flowing from him.

Once in the building, we met for a few minutes in the High Council room. Jeannie and the counselors' wives had prepared some refreshments for him to enjoy prior to the meeting and to eat on his way home. He took a moment to visit with Jeannie and each of my counselors, clerks, and their spouses and to express his joy in being with us. In the meantime, the adults in our stake were filling the several hundred seats in the chapel and cultural hall for the meeting that would start at 6 p.m.

I will never forget the looks on the faces of the great people in our stake when they saw President Oaks walk into the chapel. He began to move through the crowd, shaking everyone's hands and offering a kind word to each person. The excitement in the room was palpable. Those who had been seated stood on their feet.

"Look who's here!" they whispered to each another in astonishment. I could see people sending text messages and taking pictures with their cell phones.

As the meeting started and the stake choir sang, we all sensed a feeling of joy fill the chapel. Those who offered prayers, sang, and spoke during the meeting rose to the occasion. Though anxious, they gave their very best effort. President Oaks was the concluding speaker that evening. He had everyone's focused attention as he spoke about the Savior and His gospel plan for happiness. As the meeting ended, President Oaks shook as many hands as he could as he left the chapel for his home.

I knew word would spread that President Oaks would be back at 10 a.m. Sunday, and I worried whether we would have enough chairs to accommodate a larger crowd. Latecomers would have to sit in an overflow classroom to hear the speakers.

Sunday morning we were once again at the stake center waiting for President Oaks' arrival. We were thrilled that his lovely wife, Kristen, had joined him. She wore a beautiful jacket and skirt and President Oaks looked handsome in a navy blue suit.

Nearly an hour before conference started, the building was full of people. Every chair in every room was occupied. Our agenda moved forward as planned, with the meeting starting at 10 a.m. As before, President Oaks shook as many hands as he could before the program started, with his wife by his side.

Sitting on the stand next to President Oaks was a thrill for me. I spoke just before President Oaks, who was the concluding speaker. Once again, he spoke with the Spirit of God and bore witness of the living Savior, our Redeemer. He testified of the truthfulness of The Book of Mormon and affirmed that the restoration of the Lord's church continues today via revelation. He testified that we are God's children, that He loves us, and that He is constantly there for us.

We who were there those two days may not remember what the speakers said, but we will never forget the joy we felt being in President Oaks' presence.

My story ends with a luncheon at our home with President and Sister Oaks right after the conference. Around our dining room table were the Oaks, my two counselors and their wives, my two clerks and their wives, a watchful bodyguard, and Jeannie and me.

Knowing my wife well, I was sure Jeannie had stayed up all night to make sure everything was ready and perfect for this grand occasion. We enjoyed visiting with the Oaks for almost two hours. They shared wonderful stories with us about their lives and we all laughed together. I will long treasure a wonderful photo of all of us—it's one of my favorite pictures.

Soon our children, their spouses, and their children arrived at our home. President and Sister Oaks lovingly spoke to each of them and took pictures with them, and it was a very special experience for all.

As we said goodbye that memorable day, Jeannie and I felt that God had sent the Oaks to us, our stake, and our family as a special gift of love. It was a tender mercy that we will always cherish and happily share with family and friends forever.

Ending a chapter as a stake president

With the exception of the lifelong appointment as apostles and prophets, assigned positions change in The Church of Jesus Christ of Latter-day Saints. After nearly a decade of service, Alan was notified of his upcoming release as stake president.

Prior to the stake conference in September 2018, Alan and Jeannie took cinnamon rolls to his final High Council meeting and thanked them for their unwavering support and dedication.

"We knew we'd only get a few minutes to speak in stake conference, so in August we arranged a forty-minute 'farewell speaking tour' to talk to the great people in each of the six wards," Alan says. "We wanted the opportunity to express our love and affection to everyone."

Elder Clayton Weatherford, the visiting General Authority, oversaw the release and succession in the stake presidency. On September 9, 2018, President Hall was released from his calling with a vote of thanks from hundreds of stake members.

Alan and Jeannie received the following letter of thanks the next day, showing the lasting impact they made in their stake:

> *Dear President and Sister Hall,*
>
> *How do you thank two people for not only changing your life for the better, but also for elevating and being part of your family? A simple "thank you" does not seem sufficient.*
>
> *You have given years (really your whole lives) of unconditional love and inspirational leadership. You have given amazing talks and blessings to make us a stake family. You have made everyone part of your own family by sharing them through talks with us. I will never forget the times you left us with a special blessing from our stake president.*
>
> *Thank you for the privilege and wonderful opportunity you gave me to work and learn from you both while serving as the stake Relief Society president.* I cherish that time and could write volumes on the things I learned.*
>
> *You have both lifted our stake to a new level. Only the Lord knows how hugely you have freely given of your time, talents and money too.*
>
> *Thank you so much for so many things that have blessed our lives! President and Sister Hall, though your mantle may change, our love and respect for you from our whole family and our whole stake . . . NEVER will!*
>
> *With much love,*
> *Fred and Helen Thompson*

---

*Jeannie served as Helen's counselor for seven years.

Member missionary in China

Alan has had many opportunities to share the gospel he loves with people around the world. He recalls a trip to China, when he was unexpectedly asked about Jesus Christ. "I went over as chairman of the Weber State University Board of Trustees to our sister university for an entrepreneur competition we started," Alan says. "When the students from Shanghai Normal University took us on a tour, we saw a Buddhist temple and I asked about their religion."

One student took Alan aside where no one could hear them. She asked him to tell her about Jesus. At the time, proselytizing about Christianity was forbidden, which the Halls learned while attending an LDS Sacrament service, filled with tourists and ex-patriots. In one of the pews was a Chinese official, making sure Latter-day Saints didn't try to convert any native Chinese.

"You want me to tell you about Jesus?" Alan replied gently. "I could go to jail if I do."

As Alan looked at this curious student, he felt compassion. He gave a quick discussion about the Savior and the restoration of the gospel. Then she asked Alan to share the same information with her classmate. When the brief conversation ended, the first student asked him, "Why don't you tell all Chinese people about this?"

Alan referred her to www.lds.org, where she could learn more information.

"I think there's pent-up demand among Chinese youth about religion, God, and their divine identity," Alan says. "They are God's children and eager to know about the Lord and His church."

The children of several Chinese government leaders have joined the Church and attend BYU in Hawaii and Provo. The parents are Communist Party leaders who have testimonies of the restored gospel and have read *The Book of Mormon*. "I believe the time will come when they too will be baptized," Alan says.

"You have until eighty-five to figure it out"

Alan has learned that it takes most people many years before fully committing to following the Savior with exactness. He jokingly tells people they have until they're eighty-five years old to change. In fact, Alan once had an eighty-five-year-old man meet with him to obtain a temple recommend.

"My daughter suggested I get my life in order," the brother told him. "So here I am."

He had grown up in an active religious home, but when he served in World War II, he did many things he regretted. He wasn't faithful to his wife and never attended church again. Even worse, he'd spent decades selfishly seeking carnal pleasures, ignoring the needs of others.

"I'm here now, fully repentant and ready to be faithful," he said with tears in his eyes. President Hall gave him a temple recommend, and the man was later sealed to his wife, who had passed away earlier. He died shortly thereafter.

Before he died, he asked Alan, "Won't the Lord be unhappy that I did no good at all for sixty-five years of my life?"

"The Lord's atonement covers everybody. No one is left out," Alan responded. "He'll be happy that you repented of your sins and moved on."

Temple work for Henry and Betty Nowak

Jeannie's parents passed away, never having embraced the gospel during their lives. "They could never get over that Jeannie had joined the Church, but they recognized that she had blossomed being a member," Alan says. "They couldn't deny it."

"I had a dream one night that her deceased father came to me and said, 'Why didn't you teach me the gospel?'" Alan says. "And I thought to myself, *We tried.*"

When the Hall and Nowak family members performed the temple work for Henry and Betty, Alan felt that Henry had accepted the gospel. In the Bountiful Temple, Jeannie and her sister Michelle were sealed to their parents and became part of an eternal family.

Alan's testimony of the gospel of Jesus Christ

Alan shares what he's learned and the testimony he cherishes:

"Over the course of my life, I have gained a clear witness that there is a God in heaven and that I am one of His many sons. I have also come to understand that Jesus Christ is my Savior and Redeemer and through His atonement I may enjoy eternal life. I also recognize that by having made and kept sacred covenants, I can qualify as an heir to God's heavenly kingdom.

Most importantly, I know that I will live again with my beloved wife and my growing posterity. Because of my beliefs and knowledge, I have strived to live righteously. In doing so, I have been richly blessed from my youth until the present time.

My faith has increased and become sure knowledge based upon several profound spiritual experiences. For example, a few years ago, while Jeannie and I were discussing the role of the prophet Joseph Smith, I began to have a powerful feeling overcome me. It started at the top of my head and slowly moved through me until it reached my feet. I felt a glowing warmth encompass me that lasted for several minutes. In short order, it became clear that God was telling me Joseph was indeed His prophet of the Restoration and any contrary thoughts should be dismissed.

In sum, the depth of my conversion has resulted from hundreds and hundreds of small tender mercies, when the Holy Ghost has spoken to my heart and mind. On some occasions, I was warned of danger; at other times I was comforted and given hope or courage. Most of the time, a divine message was to assist another person in need, someone who God knew I could help. All in all, these occurrences have built a solid and unshakeable foundation of spirituality that is an anchor to my soul."

CHAPTER

16

World Travels

It's no surprise that Alan and Jeannie are drawn to adventure—
after all, they started their married life with a year in the faraway
Brazilian jungle. As they added young children to the family,
however, they set aside traveling abroad in favor of simple, affordable
family vacations nearby. As their family and financial capacity grew,
they continued to check off the Hall Family travel bucket list with
experiences around the globe.

Today, Alan and Jeannie have few expenses. Their house was paid
off decades ago, and they don't have children living at home. While they
could buy collections of fancy cars or private planes, Alan and Jeannie
have little interest in grandiose luxuries. Instead of buying things that
wear out and lose value, the Halls prefer to spend their money helping
others and creating experiences with those they love most.

"Most of the money we make, I'd say ninety percent of it, we donate
to bless the lives of those in need," Alan says. "We also set aside a portion
for fun family trips that build memories."

Camping trips

Alan remembers one of their first camping trips as a young family. "We took little Aaron up Cottonwood Canyon," he says. "Jeannie and I both knew how to camp. It was fun to build a fire, and have a small tent, sleeping bags, and flashlights."

As their children grew older, Alan and Jeannie started taking summer camping trips to Christmas Meadows, a beautiful wooded area in the Uintah Mountains. They would set up a large tent, and sometimes they invited other families to join them. "There was a lot of preparation for a camping trip and a lot of cleaning afterwards," Alan says. "We were always on guard, making sure the kids didn't drown in the river or get injured in the forest. But we always seemed to have fun."

The family traveled in a silver VW Vanagon nicknamed "Bertha" that had two seats up front and plenty of bench seats in the back. When the Hall boys were teenagers, they started calling the van "the Silver Bullet"—until Jeannie found out that was lingo for a can of Coors Light beer. The Vanagon's nickname went back to "Bertha."

Island Park cabin

As a young family, they looked forward to their tradition of staying at the Nowak family cabin on Bill's Island in Island Park, Idaho. It wasn't winterized, so they only went in the summer. For five or six days, the growing family filled the snug 800-square-foot cabin, claiming sleeping spots in the loft and living room. Surrounded by the great outdoors, the kids had space to be free and rambunctious.

They practiced target shooting behind the cabin with a BB gun. One summer, a friend of the boys taught them how to shoot chipmunks with the gun. After killing them, the boys cut off their tails, which they hung on the clothesline. When a neighbor reported their crime, Jeannie was horrified. "We had a little chat and the boys went back to shooting pop cans on a log," Jeannie says.

The cabin was a few hundred yards from Island Park Reservoir's stunning blue water. Alan taught his kids to waterski and fish behind the Nowaks' boat, *Betty Boop*. They sometimes rode bikes around the island and roughhoused while Jeannie prepared meals. They would often play games at night, laughing at inside jokes and teasing each other. "Those were cherished times, bonding times," Alan says. "Summers were really fun."

Sometimes they took day trips to nearby sites. The family hiked in Yellowstone and saw shows at the Playmill Theatre in West Yellowstone, where college students acted in summer performances. They rode trail horses at Harriman State Park. Alan and Jeannie took the children to Mesa Falls and Big Springs, too. "I think the kids loved those beautiful locations," Alan says.

Whenever the family was in Island Park on a Sunday, they joined the local LDS congregation. About 300 members of the Church lived in Island Park year-round, so the thousands of summer visitors overloaded the two church buildings—a regular-sized facility and a large A-frame building. To accommodate large summer crowds, the bishopric modified Sunday services from a three-hour block to a one-hour session. Some Sundays there were three one-hour Sacrament meetings, with more than 2,500 in attendance.

Upgrading the Island Park cabin

In time, trips to the grandparents' cabin came to an end. The Nowaks donated their cabin to the McKay-Dee Hospital Foundation. In about 1996, Alan and Jeannie bought their own cabin to keep the family's Island Park tradition alive. In line with their debt-free philosophy, Alan and Jeannie paid cash for a 3,400-square-foot cabin on the shores of the reservoir. They decorated each of the four bedrooms with a different outdoor Western theme: fishing, hunting, Native American, and cowboy.

"We finally had a winterized cabin and could snowmobile in January," Alan says. "We loved that place. It was a great fit for our family, but in time we outgrew it," Alan notes. As their kids married and brought their spouses to cabin getaways, the family needed more space.

They didn't need to wait long for the perfect vacation dwelling that could accommodate the whole family. In 2003, the Halls bought a beautiful home on the water. They named the new homestead "Bello Monte" (Portuguese for "beautiful mountain"), and it became a haven for Hall gatherings.

"It's one of the best places on earth," Alan says, "and after almost fifty years, we're still keeping the Island Park tradition alive, going summer and winter." The Halls enjoy being together over the Fourth of July and during the Christmas holiday, and often invite extended family members to join them during the rest of the year.

Business travel

As a couple, Alan and Jeannie have enjoyed many business travel perks. For fourteen years, their trips were courtesy of Alan's employers. For example, when Alan was the director of alumni at Weber State, he helped host alumni in places like Mexico, Hawaii, and on a Caribbean cruise. Ballet West sent them on business trips to places like New York City, Boston, and Washington, D.C.

When Alan became his own employer, he traveled the globe representing his company. "MarketStar afforded me the opportunity to do a lot of traveling," Alan says. "Because of business, I visited many places in the world where we had employees. They showed me what was important to them in their locations." He flew to places like Australia, China, Japan, England, France, and South America to meet with strategic partners and employees.

When he could, he took Jeannie with him. "I liked to tie business with personal travel as much as possible," Alan says. "We visited many wonderful places across the earth." In some cases, trips abroad were short, since they always had duties back home. It was too costly to bring their kids along (and they didn't mind getaways for two), so Alan and Jeannie would leave them home with a college-age sitter.

Abroad for America's unforgettable tragedy, 9/11

In September 2001, Alan was excited to take Jeannie and sixteen-year-old Megan with him on a business trip to Europe. He had planned meetings with Tony Stratton, a fellow Omnicom executive, and MarketStar employees in London and Paris. His meetings with Tony were scheduled for September 9 and 10 in England.

Early on September 11, 2001, Alan, Jeannie, and Megan took a train via the Channel Tunnel (the "Chunnel") from England to France.

Upon arriving in Paris, they made their way to the Louvre Hotel, a magnificent building in the heart of the City of Lights. As they unpacked in their hotel room, they saw a startling story on CNN. "In shock, we watched the first plane hit one of the Twin Towers," Alan says. "Within a few minutes, we saw the second plane hit another tower."

In a world where news travels quickly, a ripple effect erupted across the globe. The hotel staff notified the Halls that the hotel was on lockdown. All guests were required to stay inside. "The whole city of Paris was closed. Soon we saw troops monitoring the streets through our hotel window," Alan says. "It was terrifying to be so far away from home. We didn't know what was happening in the rest of America or how it would affect our lives."

Jeannie wept, terrified for her family, and called their five children back home so they knew their parents and sister were safe.

After several hours, the restless Halls couldn't sit still any longer. "We decided to leave the hotel when it was dark and walk the empty streets," Alan remembers. "We quietly headed toward the Eiffel Tower. There were military guards everywhere with machine guns. They told us to return to the hotel, so we did."

Plans to visit their niece Jessie Coon, who was serving an LDS mission near Paris, had to be scrapped. All missionaries in France were advised to stay in their apartments.

"As the crisis continued, we wondered how we would return home. Airports in the United States were all closed, halting international travel indefinitely," Alan recalls. "Then we were told we could catch our flight to Italy from the Charles de Gaulle Airport, and hopefully make our Delta flight back to New York City."

The Halls arrived safely in Venice. Men with machine guns marched in the streets, and museums were shut down. Public areas were abandoned. "It looked like an armed camp," Alan says. "People were in a panic, and so were we. How would we make it home?"

They decided that since they were there, they might as well see a couple of other Italian cities. They took a train to Florence. After a few days there, they took another train to Rome, where flights to the United States were finally available.

Almost a week after the terrorist attack in New York, they boarded the first flight scheduled from Rome back to the United States. The Halls vividly remember the captain announcing to the flight full of people that nothing would stop them from landing safely at the JFK airport. After several hours in the air, they neared the American coastline. "Tension in the cabin was palpable," Alan says. "Passengers and the flight crew were nervous. We could see U.S. Air Force fighter jets out the windows, escorting our plane into the New York area."

The pilot flew around Manhattan as he approached the runway. "We could see columns of thick, black smoke still rising from the destruction below," Alan says. "Our hearts sank as we as thought of the loss of so many lives. When we landed, passengers cheered and wept as the pilot declared, 'Welcome home to America, the land of the free and home of the brave.'"

Annual family trips

When Omnicom acquired MarketStar, Alan and Jeannie celebrated by taking their children to Hawaii. Since then, the Hall clan has returned to the Aloha State several times. "Maui is our favorite island," Alan says. "We enjoy the people, golf, tennis, running, snorkeling, and fun luau parties at night. It's a great place for kids of all ages."

Since that first big trip, travel has become nearly an annual family tradition. At Christmas, Alan and Jeannie announce where the family will travel the following year. Sometimes the parents choose the location; other years the kids decide where they'd like to go. Jeannie works with one of their sons to manage the trip. They plan the itinerary, book the tickets, and arrange transportation and lodging. "Jeannie and the kids do all the management and logistics," Alan says. "All I do is get on the bus. No heavy lifting for me!"

Traveling with such a large group can sometimes be challenging with strong personalities, but the Halls make it work. "Everybody behaves and gets along well. We have a really good time together," Alan says. "We compromise on this and that, and overall look forward to those trips."

Over time, they've found efficient ways to travel with such a large group. For example, the thirty-three Halls prefer traveling on a rented bus. "This way, we can party on the road together and don't have to manage several different cars," Alan says. "We also like all-inclusive resorts for families, where all the meals are included in the price of the resort."

The Halls enjoy the sand, sun, and (most of all) on-resort restaurants. With a group that large, finding a place to eat that fits everyone's tastes can be a challenge—but resort restaurants give them options within easy reach.

Cancún hurricane

Alan, Jeannie, and a few of the Hall children speak Spanish, so Mexico is a frequent destination. They like to interact with locals on these trips. For example, the Halls attend church no matter where they travel. In Cancún, the Hall clan doubled the size of the congregation in a tiny LDS branch. They sat in a humid meeting room with no air conditioning and sang hymns with the local Saints. "The whole service was in Spanish and we happened to be there on Fast Sunday, so several of us bore our testimonies," Alan says. "Some were in English, some in Spanish."

A memorable trip was when Hurricane Emily hit their resort in Cancún. Jeannie's parents, Alan's dad, and the entire Hall clan were with them on this occasion. "The resort staff asked us to leave our hotel rooms and gather in a wind-protected restaurant until the storm passed," Alan says. "Leaving the restaurant wasn't allowed, so we slept on the floor by the salad bar."

The Category 4 storm hit with all its fury, and the wind howled all night long. "We'd never been in a hurricane, and the experience was frightening," Alan remembers. "We were only a hundred yards from the beach and the high ocean waves were moving closer." The Hall family prayed they would be protected, and played games to keep their minds busy.

When they were cleared to leave the restaurant the next morning, they were grateful they had survived the storm. Fallen palm trees and uprooted plants covered the beach and resort landscape. The coral reef near the hotel had protected them from the crashing waves. Their cell phones didn't work because violent winds had knocked down communication towers. "It was a mess," Alan recalls. "We learned what happens in the middle of a disaster, and how helpless it feels to have limited resources." Within a few days, the Halls were able to fly home from Cancún.

Cruises

Other trips have been less traumatic and much more enjoyable. The Hall family loves cruises, and sometimes they invite family friends and other special guests to travel with them. They have cruised the routes east and west of the Caribbean, seeing places like St. Thomas and Jamaica. Son-in-law Curtis Funk served an LDS mission to the Caribbean and he enjoyed introducing the Hall clan to the beautiful people of those islands.

Other destinations

The Hall gang has traveled together to Costa Rica, Jamaica, Boston, San Diego, Disneyland in Anaheim, and Disney World in Orlando. New York City is a special family favorite. Sometimes Alan and Jeannie plan special trips for family members. In 2016, they took some of the Hall women (daughters, daughters-in-law, and a granddaughter) to see the Miss America Pageant in Atlantic City, New Jersey, and Broadway shows in New York City.

"We've never been anywhere we didn't enjoy," Alan says. "I guess everywhere is our favorite." Being a Peace Corps volunteer opened their eyes to travel beyond typical tourism. When the family goes to a new country, they see famous sights but also make time to mingle with the locals and learn about their lives.

Alan and Jeanne continue to learn new languages, which adds depth to their experience as travelers. In 2019, Alan is learning French and Italian, in addition to the Spanish and Portuguese he already knows. How does he make time for learning languages? He uses an app on his phone every day that teaches him new vocabulary. "I see myself as a global citizen, and learning new languages helps me to communicate with interesting people we meet on our journeys," he says.

South America

The Halls have seen many countries in South America. In addition to Alan's mission in Guatemala and El Salvador and the duo's Peace Corps experience in Brazil, Alan and Jeannie traveled to pick up their sons Aaron and Eric in Chile and Christian in Peru after they completed their LDS missions. Traveling from Machu Picchu to the Amazon River to the Andes Mountains, Alan and Jeannie had the wonderful experiences of not only being with their sons again, but also exploring the lands where they served.

Asia

Alan and Jeannie have been to Asia, where they met wonderful new friends. They visited the Great Wall, the Forbidden City in Beijing, and the glories of Shanghai. Their trip to China was on behalf of Weber State to visit the faculty and students of Shanghai Normal University. Alan helped launch and fund an entrepreneurial program at the school, where the organization holds an annual student entrepreneur competition the first week of May.

Some travel experiences haven't gone as planned, like one trip to Japan. Alan and Jeannie traveled to Tokyo with a MarketStar employee, Floyd Mori, an American of Japanese ancestry, and his wife. One day, Alan ate an Asian pear that upset his stomach. On the same day, Floyd's wife had her purse stolen. They had planned to attend a session at the Tokyo Temple together that night. With Alan sick and Mrs. Mori without her temple recommend, Jeannie and Floyd went to the temple together while their spouses stayed at the hotel.

Jeannie was the only Caucasian in the temple that night. With blond hair and standing more than six inches taller than the rest of the patrons, she really stuck out in the crowd. "The Spirit was strong and it was a glorious opportunity to be there," Jeannie says. "The four of us also attended a Japanese ward on Sunday when the Primary children presented their Sacrament program. It was so delightful to see their beautiful faces and hear familiar songs, all sung in Japanese. The Lord's church is truly for all His children."

Europe

Alan and Jeannie have toured many European countries, some several times, including Spain, Poland, Italy, England, France, Switzerland, Austria, and Germany. "Our travel bucket list is important to Jeannie and me," Alan says. "We want to see the world before we die."

Because of Jeannie's Polish heritage, they traveled to see the land of her ancestors. On one train, Alan saw a little girl with red hair and freckles sitting across the aisle. He told her she was his long-lost daughter and showed her a picture of the red-haired, freckled Hall children. She smiled.

Another Polish young woman took them on a tour of Auschwitz. After the tour, she told them she was recently married and had a little child. Although she and her husband worked, the young couple lived with her parents because they didn't have enough money for an apartment. "My first thought was to start Grow Poland and to encourage local companies to provide people with better-paying jobs," Alan says. "Our love for Poland was magnified because of that trip."

They also love Italy, a country they've toured extensively. They invited a sister from their ward on one trip, because she had a daughter who was finishing her mission in Sicily. "Jeannie and I suggested we go together to meet her daughter and tour the southern region of this magnificent country," Alan says. "She agreed, and Jeannie, Megan, and I accompanied her to Italy."

Traveling actors

"Going to England several times has also been a highlight for us," Alan says. "I love England." Between 2011 and 2012, Alan and Jeannie helped sponsor a PBS television documentary directed by Lee Groberg. The film was called *Fires of Faith: The Coming Forth of the King James Bible*.[1] Covering subjects from the international politics of the day to the king's runaway libido, the film used a scholarly perspective with a goal to accurately tell the story of the King James Bible for its 400th anniversary in 2011. The film debuted that year on BYU-TV and was broadcast across the nation on PBS stations.

Alan and Jeannie accepted the invitation to be extras in the film. They invited friends Mark and Jill Hurst to join them on the trip. They flew to England, where they spent time on sets inside a picturesque castle in the beautiful English countryside. Along with the film crew and professional British actors, an Oxford professor was on location to verify historical accuracy.

"We enjoyed every minute of the filming. We were dressed in costumes of the 1600s and marveled at the rooms in the castle," Alan says. "I remember being in a spacious room with the actors who portrayed King Henry VIII and Catherine of Aragon." During their England visit, Alan and Jeannie wondered about their own English ancestors. "Were they farmers? Did they work for the king? They lived in England during the reign of Henry the VIII."

After a positive response to *Fires of Faith,* Mr. Groberg approached the Halls about sponsoring another documentary called *First Freedom: The Fight for Religious Liberty,* a ninety-minute documentary that examines how the American Founding Fathers codified freedom of conscience for the first time.[2] The production includes reenactments of colonial days, key expert commentary, and the Founding Fathers' own words. The film depicts God's divine role in the formation of the United States.

Again, the Halls were asked to be extras. They flew to Philadelphia, where they worked from midnight to 6:00 a.m. during non-visitor hours at Independence Hall. "As extras, we dressed like the people of colonial times and visited with the actors portraying George Washington, Benjamin Franklin, and Thomas Jefferson," Alan recalls.

After the scenes in Philadelphia were completed, the Halls traveled to Williamsburg, Virginia, for the next filming session. The producer surprised Alan with a speaking part in the documentary. "Be ready in thirty minutes," he said, handing over lines for Alan to memorize.

Impromptu actor Alan played the role of a British judge. He quickly dressed in a judicial wig and robe, visited the make-up trailer, and found his place in the same courthouse where the depicted events actually took place. In his scene, Alan played a judge of the English Crown who sentenced a Baptist minister to jail because he had preached to the people of Williamsburg.

"That was my Brad Pitt moment, and I'm still hoping for an award," Alan teases. "Every once in a while, the show is aired on PBS and I see my part. I'd love to do it again!"

The Halls still make regular donations to KUED and BYU television to support family-friendly television. They contributed to the production of *Downton Abbey* in its final year, and enjoy sponsoring high-quality historical productions with interesting themes and messages.

Future trips

The Halls look forward to visiting countries and continents they haven't seen before. "Maybe Tahiti," Alan says with a grin. "I've seen about every state in the United States, but there are still more places we'd like to see in the U.S. and Canada."

That includes their home state. "We need to see more of Utah and its world-famous landscape," Alan explains. "We've been to Moab, Zion, and Bryce Canyon, and now plan to visit the other great national parks in the Beehive State."

The Halls also are planning service-oriented trips. The Hall Foundation has sponsored Weber State students who travel abroad to participate in service projects. Alan and Jeannie want to do something similar with their own grandchildren. "We'd like to find a third-world village where we can perhaps build a women's center, a school, or a library—something that has a lasting impact on the community," Alan says. "We hope our future family trips have elements of both service and pleasure."

17

Influence of Music

From his dad's Spanish records to the rock and roll of the '50s and '60s, from the Beatles to Broadway, and from classical opera to boot-scooting country, music has played a starring role in the scenes of Alan's life. "Music is always in my ears or on my mind," Alan says. "I am grateful for the positive impact it has had on me."

A musical childhood

Alan's lifelong enthusiasm for music started young, with lyrics in another language. His dad originally taught himself Spanish to teach it to junior high students, but then used it often to communicate with Hispanic customers in the pharmacy. To enlarge his Spanish vocabulary, Eugene frequently played records of Nat King Cole and other artists singing famous Spanish songs. These melodies were Alan's first recollections of music at home. "I learned all these Spanish songs as a child, listening to my dad play his favorite Latin tunes," Alan says.

Joyce took Alan to see *The Nutcracker* ballet when he was a boy. It was his first exposure to the performing arts, and he was thrilled to hear the music. "I don't remember the dancing per se, but the music was sublime to me," Alan says. After that, Joyce had him take violin lessons, followed by classes in social dance. "I didn't do well in either," he says. "I was more interested in sports."

Alan's family owned a "hi-fi," the 1950s household term for "high fidelity" record player. The hi-fi of Alan's generation replaced the phonograph of his parents' generation. Eugene and Joyce bought Alan a small transistor radio with an antenna wire he could attach to the screen of his bedroom window. As a teenager, he listened at night to the local radio station, KLO. "I loved listening to the popular rock-and-roll tunes sung by the Everly Brothers, Elvis Presley, Fats Domino, the Beach Boys, and the Lettermen," Alan says. "I'd fall asleep to the sweet sounds of the great musical artists of the '50s and '60s."

Television added to Alan's fascination with music and dancing. "American Bandstand," hosted by Dick Clark starting in 1956, featured teenagers dancing to Top-40 tunes. When Alan got home from school each afternoon, he turned on the TV to watch kids in Philadelphia dancing to rock-and-roll hits. "The girls were pretty and the guys were handsome. They all knew how to dance the Twist, the Pony, the Watusi, and the Jerk," Alan remembers.

Alan's parents' generation grew up listening to the soft love songs and ballads of big-name crooners like Bing Crosby and Frank Sinatra. In the 1930s and '40s, big bands with the orchestral sounds of Glenn Miller, Benny Goodman, and Artie Shaw were all the rage. "Elvis Presley set the new standard for my generation with a musical style that upset the older generation," Alan remembers. It wasn't just his lyrics that caught attention—it was also his hip thrusts. One Sunday night, the Hall family watched the number-one program on television, *The Ed Sullivan Show*, and saw the king of rock and roll perform his song "Don't Be Cruel" in a loud plaid jacket. The camera censored him by staying above his waist. Eugene and Joyce were appalled with his lyrics and gyrations, as were other parents.

Sock-hopping through school

As Alan grew older, his music choices continued to veer to the popular songs. "Music was a major factor in my youth," he says. "To be accepted by my peers, I needed to be able to talk about the current hits of the day."

Popularity also required the ability to dance. At Alan's school, children attended "sock hops," where everyone went to the gym, took their shoes off, and wiggled to the sweet sounds of the latest hit tune. As an elementary school kid, Alan was clueless about how to move his feet, so the sister of a classmate taught him how to do "the Twist" by assigning him a chair for a partner. "She taught me how to roll my hips and swing my legs and arms to the beat of the music," Alan remembers.

Although he still doesn't consider himself a good dancer, he recalls with fondness the excitement and joy of dancing with the cute girls on the gym floor.

During Alan's high school years, a British boy band took the world by storm—the Beatles had arrived. The night they were scheduled to perform "I Want to Hold Your Hand" on *The Ed Sullivan Show*, Alan begged his parents to let him stay home from Sacrament meeting to watch it.

In high school, Alan also was introduced to musicals. He remembers seeing *West Side Story* in a movie theater for the first time. A beautiful actress, Natalie Wood, played Maria. "The music was soaring, magical, and resounding," remembers Alan. "I loved every note. It was glorious to me. I bought the album of *West Side Story* and listened to it over and over."

From Broadway to the next genre

When Alan returned from his mission in 1966, rock and roll had evolved into a rebellious movement. The country was deep in the throes of the Vietnam War and music challenged the establishment, with protest songs taking up airspace on the radio.

Alan was still a big fan of Broadway music, so when a professional touring company of *Camelot* came to a stage in Bountiful, Utah, Alan took a date to see it. Actually, he took several dates. "I think I took six girls at different times to that show!" remembers Alan. "I got tickets to see it again and again."

Jeannie took Alan's passion for Broadway musicals and expanded it to include a love for classical music. She introduced him to the glorious sounds of Beethoven, Mozart, Handel, Schubert, Chopin, Bach, Verdi, and Puccini. As Alan took on the role of president of Ballet West, his exposure expanded to the music of ballet and composers like Adam, Tchaikovsky, Prokofiev, and Copland. Classical music, including opera, affects Alan in ways that the music of his youth does not. "The beat of rock and roll moved my feet," Alan says, "but great classical music stirs my soul. Each note is divine and magnificently beautiful."

Songs of faith

Music in church was also very important in Alan's young life. In Sunday School, Alan learned to sing from the church hymnbook. "I think sacred music brings people together," Alan says. "Church music is meant to do that. We're all singing the same words and there's a spirit that flows over us."

"Spiritual music can touch us in ways that nothing else can," Alan says. "I've seen and felt this happen over and over in my life, and realize music has the power to influence us for good."

Although Alan introduced Jeannie to the restored gospel of Jesus Christ, Jeannie exposed Alan to a whole new layer of church music. A member of the Mormon Tabernacle Choir* for six years, Jeannie inspired a new love for the hymns Alan had sung since his youth. "I treasure the hymns of Zion and marvel at the inspiring arrangements of Mack Wilberg, the music director," Alan says. "There is a sublime spiritual power that flows from the choir's voices that lifts my heart with each and every rendition." Alan traveled with Jeannie and the choir on several U.S. tours and will always remember watching their performances.

Enjoying music, everywhere and all the time

Today, music is an ever-present part of Alan's life. "I'll listen to music when I'm in the car, when I take a shower, when I'm out in the yard working. I have it on all the time," he says. On a recent flight, he listened to an entire ABBA album, one foot thumping along at 30,000 feet.

Alan's taste in music is diverse and expansive. "One day, I'll be listening to Elvis, the next day I'm listening to the Tabernacle Choir," he says. If he hears a new tune he likes, Alan goes to iTunes and downloads

---

*Now called "The Tabernacle Choir at Temple Square"

it so he can listen on the go. He has filled his iPhone with a wide variety of music, including "Love Remains" from country music singer Collin Raye, spiritual hymns like "The Morning Breaks," and a soundtrack from the Broadway musical *Cats*.

"I'm always listening," Alan says, smiling. "When Jeannie and I drive somewhere, we'll listen to *Evita* or Adele. We both love music." For Jeannie's sixtieth birthday party, Alan surprised her by inviting friends and family to a private concert at the Snow Basin Lodge.

While recordings are great, there's something transformative about performances in person. Alan has attended many Broadway performances over his lifetime. *Les Misérables* is his all-time favorite, followed by *Wicked, Phantom of the Opera, The Lion King, Evita, Jersey Boys, Hairspray, Mamma Mia*, and *Cats*. He saw *South Pacific* at the Metropolitan Opera House with a full orchestra. "It was magnificent. I wept," he says. "The two leads were so incredible, I saw it three times."

According to Alan, you're never too old to enjoy music. At age seventy-two, Alan signed up for piano lessons. "I look forward to the day when I can play the tunes I truly enjoy," he says.

The Sound of Music tour

When Alan and Jeannie traveled to Austria in 2015, they went on a tour to see the sites in *The Sound of Music*. They saw where the real-life von Trapp family was intertwined with Salzburg's history. Every year, 2.5 million tourists visit the landmarks of the singing family.[1] They saw the Pegasus Fountain, where the dance scene with Maria (Julie Andrews) and the children was filmed. They saw the Schloss Leopoldskron, the famous house where the movie-version family lived. They saw Nonnberg Abbey and St. Gilgen, where the opening scene of the Hollywood film captured the hearts of America with song.

Movies aren't always accurate, and the tour gave Alan and Jeannie a behind-the-scenes taste of reality. "The closing scene where the family is hiking to safety was actually in a place where they would have hiked right back into Nazi territory," Alan says. Interestingly enough, the story of the von Trapps is not popular among the locals. "They aren't interested in *The Sound of Music*," Alan says. "But I sure love the sound of music."

18

Philosophy of an Abundant Life

The well-rounded life of Alan E. Hall has been built decision by decision. He could not always foresee where his choices would take him. In fact, much of his life has unfolded as a divinely orchestrated surprise.

Ten-year-old Alan—the boy who played the bugle in the Pioneer Days parade—never imagined he'd someday be chairman of the Ogden Pioneer Heritage Foundation. Twelve-year-old Alan—the boy who saw his first ballet with his mother—never guessed he would later be president of Ballet West, attending premieres with movie stars.

Two decisions have been a constant compass in his life: the choice to succeed and the choice to build the kingdom of God. Alan has not let barriers hold him back from those goals. Those decisions have rewarded him and his family in every imaginable way. How can others replicate his success? By understanding Alan's philosophy of an abundant life, which is anchored in basic beliefs about God, family, community, money, and service.

Granted, some of Alan's advantages are unique, but he lives by universal truths that anyone, anywhere, of any age, race, or gender can apply.

Standing on strong shoulders: the Hall family name

Alan did not grow up in a wealthy family, but he was born to rich advantages, thanks to his strong family name. "My family name has carried me for most of my life," he says. "Except for two times, my job opportunities were due to my family name and my parents' influence."

He's right. The owner who hired Alan for his first job at Ogden Roofing and Supply knew his parents. His mother's uncle, Elmer Ward, manager of Defense Depot Ogden, helped him secure a job as a forklift driver. His mission president, who called him as an assistant, knew his uncle Tracy. Although his name didn't carry any weight in the Peace Corps, Professor Tracy Hall may have influenced Alan's admission to BYU's MBA program. He was a shoo-in as the Weber State alumni director with his family name, and then became president at Ballet West through a leader who knew the Hall family. His cousin, David Hall, invited him to join Netline, which led to the idea for MarketStar. Line upon line, all these opportunities came from standing on the shoulders of strong pioneer families, the Halls and Hansens.

"Scripturally, when the Lord asks us to honor our parents, I think it's because He wants us to recognize they give us splendid opportunities to succeed in life," Alan says. "We should be forever thankful for their personal sacrifices, wise guidance, and unceasing support."

Reaping the benefits of a strong family name means a long-term commitment to a community. "We could have lived anywhere, but we chose to make our home in Roy, Utah, where after forty-six years, the Hall name is valued," Alan says.

Alan and Jeannie raised their children in Weber County where they could thrive and prosper in a smaller ecosystem, giving them more opportunities to rise to the top. "Jeannie's always said it was better for us to be at Weber State than at the University of Utah or BYU," Alan says. "That's because we know the people, it's a smaller community, and we have had so many opportunities here. We love the Y and the U, but Weber State is home for us."

A family heritage of kindness and hard work has influenced how the Hall children were raised. "We've always told our children, 'You carry the Hall name. Please honor it and behave accordingly,'" Alan says.

As each child entered the public school system, the solid reputation of their older siblings preceded them. Teachers expected each Hall child to be a good student and a leader among their peers. That same expectation continues today for Hall grandchildren. "Jeannie and I hope that they too will honor their parents by being noble family members in every aspect of their lives," Alan says.

Raising children while building wealth

Long before Alan achieved financial independence, he learned a life-changing lesson on parenting from a well-known philanthropist. Alan invited a donor who had made a significant contribution to a new Ballet West production to attend a special dinner at the Alta Club prior to the opening night of the new ballet.

The elderly donor's adult children attended. They were dressed to impress, but did not behave appropriately. They drank so much alcohol they became boisterous, to the point that they lost all inhibitions. "One son who lost consciousness rested his head on a plate of mashed potatoes," Alan remembers. "It was very embarrassing to his aging father."

He leaned over to Alan and whispered, "My wealth has destroyed my children. I have enabled their terrible lifestyle. If I could do it over again, I would be a postal clerk and my children would have no money." He added for emphasis, "Don't forget what I just told you."

"I took heed," Alan says. "I listened."

Alan and Jeannie followed the donor's advice as they raised their children. They didn't want them to grow up with a sense of entitlement. They chose to raise their children in a blue-collar, middle-class community where friends and neighbors are hard-working, self-reliant people.

Ultimately, the simple yet powerful decision of where to live protected the Hall children from being spoiled. For example, the Hall kids grew up driving an old used car and wouldn't have considered asking for a brand-new car when they got their driver's licenses. Instead, the Hall children drove Alan's 1965 Ford Mustang, which they refurbished periodically to keep it running properly. In 2010, it was donated to the Weber County Sheriff's office to be used as a D.A.R.E. car.

"As for receiving college degrees, Jeannie and I felt our kids should pay for their education," Alan says. "We chose not to provide them with money to attend school. They had to obtain the needed funds from wages earned at work or via scholarships."

With their own financial security in place after Omnicom's acquisition of MarketStar, Alan and Jeannie were in a position to give their children a small but important financial boost. They wanted to do so in a way that would help, not harm. They decided to assist each married couple with a modest down payment to help them secure a mortgage to purchase their first home.

By solidifying their own monetary situation, Alan and Jeannie have been able to give abundantly to others. They are guided by three simple rules:

1. Always give full credit and glory to God.
2. Focus your time, talents, and energy on building the kingdom of God.
3. Work to make sure there are "no poor among us."

Investing in the pillars of the community

Alan splits his time between many equally important interests. "I've always thought I should learn about every aspect of life. This includes the not-for-profit world, the profit world, the Chambers of Commerce, education, health care—all pillars that make up our community," Alan says. "Doing so has given me a well-rounded look at how the world works."

Establishing influence on boards has been a way to give back. Alan has been deliberate about aligning with nonprofit and for-profit organizations that espouse values that match the personal beliefs that he and Jeannie share. They've focused on the needs of families where they can make a significant difference for good as lead donors and solicitors of funds. "Jeannie and I are pleased to help agencies that serve the poor: poor in wealth, poor in health, poor in spirit, poor in education, and poor in culture," Alan says.

Lessons from seven decades of leadership

Leading others requires self-mastery. Alan has learned he's better able to lead when he makes time to care for his body, mind, and spirit. "When we do things that hurt our body, we lose the ability to be creative, ponder, think, and develop," Alan says. "The creative mind is open to everybody, and it's so fulfilling and satisfying."

Spiritual motivations drive Alan to work on entrepreneurial projects. He's drawn to an inner call to creativity. "God is the ultimate Creator and we should be creators in as many ways as possible," he says. "I see entrepreneurs as creators. Building a business is great preparation for godhood. It's very fulfilling to take an idea and grow it into a meaningful enterprise."

At any given time, Alan is working on a list of about ten projects, ranging from fundraising to business to church activities. How does he keep up with it all? His secret is working with talented people. To make an impact at the level Alan has achieved, he has mastered the art of motivating and managing people. "Everywhere I've gone, I've been honored to work with great people," Alan says. "I am best at being a visionary. I point the way. My goal is to find talented leaders who love the vision, the cause, and the end purpose. Once on board, I let them establish a successful plan and allow and encourage them to achieve it."

He learned decades ago that it's best to give people space to perform—he doesn't micromanage. "Set the vision and empower others to carry it out," Alan says. "Be a great delegator."

Giving all the time he can

When it comes to being a force for good in the world, Alan sees himself as a dynamo of energy, here to help others grow and succeed. "My days on earth are numbered. I might live until I am ninety-eight years old like my father, or maybe not," Alan says, "But I'm going to give it all I've got while I am still alive and able."

Alan's example shows the abundant life is not about what is gained, but by what is given away. "We should always be willing to share our time, talents, and resources with everyone," he says.

Alan hopes to have many more years to do his work on the earth. In his patriarchal blessing, Alan is promised he will stand at the head of the Church and be a great teacher. He's done so as a bishop and stake president, mentor, speaker, author, leader, and adjunct professor, but it's the next phrase in his blessing that really interests him. The blessing states that Alan has a "great work to do," and when it is completed, God will call him home.

"Why do you think I'm always working on ten big projects?" Alan says. "Someday an angel will show up and say, 'Alan, it's time to go,' and I'll say, 'Oh no, no, I have six important projects on my schedule this week. I've got work to do!' and the angel will reply, 'I don't think so, Joyce's boy. You are done. Please follow me. Your mother has been waiting to see you.'"

Acknowledgements

- I wrote this biography while growing a baby. Both labors of love required a team. Thanks to the folks listed below, we birthed a book!

- Ashlee Swenson, thank you for the many hours you interviewed Alan before this project came my way—your transcripts were instrumental.

- Special thanks to contributing editors, Naomi Clegg and JaNae Francis, for your spot-on proofreading, often under tight deadlines.

- Sincerest appreciation to Elayne Wells Harmer, professional editor and writer, for her extraordinary editing of the final manuscript.

- I am grateful to Ryan Kidman of Design Type Service for your patient and talented design work on many book revisions over the past year.

- Rick Dillman at Artistic Printing, your special talents turned digital documents into a beautiful, heirloom book.

- Thank you, Janis Vause, Brad Mortensen, Alex Lawrence, Richard Christiansen, Steve Tippets, and Fred and Helen Thompson, for sharing quotes and letters about how Alan has influenced you.

- My deepest appreciation to the Renaissance woman who devoted countless hours and sleepless nights to this project. Jeannie Hall, your encouragement and expert editing eye shaped this manuscript. Seeing behind the scenes how you devote yourself to beloved people and causes inspires me beyond words. You and your husband are forever my heroes.

- I owe a deep debt of gratitude to my own good husband, Ryan, who supports my big dreams, like writing books. You help me fly in so many ways.

- Lastly, thank you to my sweet children, Lydia, Bryson, and baby Bridger, who was born during the final editing stage of this book. You give my life story meaning, and I'm excited to see your next chapters.

Further Reading

As I wrote the biography of Alan E. Hall, I took a deep-dive into personal development, business, and mindset books—partly professional research, but more importantly, for personal growth. I wanted to understand more about how great leaders think. You'll find principles in the following books that I believe align with Alan's character, choices he's made, and the lasting legacy he's created. I hope these books are as inspiring to you as they have been to me.

—Crystalee Webb Beck

How to Win Friends and Influence People by Dale Carnegie

The 7 Habits of Highly Effective People by Stephen R. Covey

Your Money or Your Life by Vicki Robin, Joseph R. Dominguez, and Monique Tilford

Mastering the Rockefeller Habits: What You Must Do to Increase the Value of Your Fast-Growth Firm by Verne Harnish

Think and Grow Rich by Napoleon Hill

Outwitting the Devil by Napoleon Hill

The War of Art by Steven Pressfield

The Millionaire Mind by Thomas J. Stanley

The Millionaire Next Door by Thomas J. Stanley and William D. Danko

Millionaire Women Next Door by Thomas J. Stanley

The Science of Being Great by Wallace D. Wattles

Meet Jeannie Hall

———————◦◦◦———————

Paula Jeanne Nowak was born in Houston, Texas, on December 5, 1948, to Henry G. and Betty Adams Nowak. Her father, of Polish descent, was reared in Buffalo, New York, and was a successful chemist who worked in the private aerospace industry. Her mother was from Washington, D.C., and was a skilled educator. During Jeannie's childhood and teenage years, she lived in various cities where her father found employment opportunities to further his career. In time, Jeannie became the older sister to Michelle and Patti. Her parents had high expectations for their talented and beautiful daughters and celebrated their many accomplishments.

In 1966, Jeannie graduated from Skyline High School in Salt Lake City and enrolled at Weber State College as a seventeen-year-old freshman. She was 5'9" with short blonde hair and a radiant smile. With abundant musical talent and a sparkling personality, she quickly began participating in the vocal music and theater departments. She performed in numerous choral and theatrical productions; one of her favorites was the lead in *Finian's Rainbow* alongside Dean Hurst, who became a loving father figure to her throughout her life.

She was a member of Weber State Singers and enjoyed her relationship with the director, Lyneer Smith. Evelyn Harris was her private vocal teacher and a treasured friend. Jeannie was also a scholar, earning a 3.8 grade point average and graduating in three years from college. At twenty years old, she completed her bachelor of arts degree and, as the top student in the psychology department, was selected as "Woman of the Year 1969," in addition to receiving numerous other awards and honors. "Among the faculty and student body, she was considered the brightest and prettiest of all college students," Alan says.

"I remember taking a date to see the Miss Weber State pageant in the spring of 1968. Jeannie was a contestant that evening and it was the first time I had ever seen her in person. She was dazzling and swept me off my feet," Alan recalls. She was crowned that evening as Miss Weber State and that summer competed for Miss Utah in the Miss America Pageant, coming in as first runner-up.

Many male college students were smitten by the lovely Miss Nowak, especially LDS returned missionaries. As a committed Presbyterian, she was happy to date them but reluctant to establish a deep relationship. In her junior year, she became engaged to a talented instrumentalist she had met in the music department. When she met Alan Hall, however, she realized the musician was not the right man for her. By the end of the summer of 1968, she returned the ring and once again began dating others.

She met Alan Hall for the first time in 1968, in a summer psychology class. They sat by each other in class and talked incessantly about their lives and future. Since Jeannie was engaged and Alan was dating a girl at Utah State University, their mutual admiration for one another did not gain traction at that time.

In the fall of 1968, she met Alan again in a psychology senior statistics class. They had their first date on the evening of October 16. Both were still single and unattached. That night after a visit to the university's library and some cookies at Jeannie's parents' home near the campus, Jeannie and Alan fell deeply in love with each other, a love that endures to this day. It's now been over fifty years since that first date and a sweet kiss over the Nowaks' kitchen table.

Jeannie has been Alan's sweetheart and helpmate over the course of their happy marriage. Alan recognizes that Jeannie was given to him by God. "It's clear to me that He brought us together to build a remarkable eternal family," Alan says. Together they have supported one another, been devoted companions, faithful partners, and always caring, no matter the trials or successes.

Jeannie reared their six children and three foster Navajo children with love, affection, and high standards. She taught them to love one another, follow the Savior, and keep His commandments. She taught them the principles of repentance and service. She was always there to encourage them to excel and be great examples of Christlike behavior. She does the same with her twenty grandchildren who all love her deeply. All have been taught to be honest, hardworking, fair, just, grateful, charitable, and loving.

"I know Heavenly Father is proud of this amazing and gifted woman," Alan says. "She's the ultimate mother and grandmother. If you examine the lives of our wonderful children and grandchildren, it is easy to see that Jeannie Hall will be praised forever by her posterity."

Jeannie enjoys hosting dinners at their home on Sundays, being a fairy godmother at birthday parties, attending school events and church programs, and hosting sleepovers and family trips. She always keeps candy in the pantry so grandkids have tasty treats, and she's a shoulder to cry on when needed.

She received her first graduate degree in psychology from BYU in 1972, while Alan earned his MBA. Once most of their children were in school, Jeannie obtained certification equivalent to a second master's degree in school counseling from the University of Utah.

She worked part time for nearly twenty years in the Ogden School District as a high school counselor, first at Washington Alternative High School, then at Ogden High. She was a devoted friend to all students, especially to youth who faced great personal and academic challenges. She often called students before school started in the morning to encourage them to get out of bed and on their way to class. She practiced Spanish so she could converse with Hispanic parents about their children. She helped guide students who needed scholarships to college, and worked tirelessly to find them funds to continue their education.

When not at home, Jeannie is serving at church and in the community. Since she was baptized a member of The Church of Jesus Christ of Latter-day Saints, she has served in a variety of church callings. She's been a leader in the Primary, Relief Society, and Young Women at the ward and stake levels. She's taught Sunday School, been the ward librarian, and is a missionary in her daily life. "No one goes hungry or lonely on her watch," Alan says. "She's fearless in proclaiming the gospel of Jesus Christ."

When she was fifty-four, she nervously decided to audition for the Mormon Tabernacle Choir. She submitted CDs of her singing, took musical exams, and sang before the choir's directors. While lying in a hospital bed after replacement surgery on both knees, she learned she had passed the first part of the evaluation process. Overwhelmed with joy, she wept. She went on to complete the audition process, and on Halloween 2003, opened the letter announcing her acceptance into the Chorale School and then the Mormon Tabernacle Choir, now known as The Tabernacle Choir on Temple Square. She sang in the choir as a second alto for six years and loved every moment of the experience.

Over the next seventy-eight months, before she reached the mandatory retirement age from the choir, she traveled on multiple tours across the United States and Canada, participated in numerous recordings, sang at many special occasions, practiced every Thursday night, and performed every Sunday on *Music and the Spoken Word,* broadcast on national television and radio. She and her fellow singers practiced, recorded, and performed more than 200 days a year.

She grew close to the directors, Craig Jessop and Mack Wilberg, and loved Mac Christensen, the choir president. She enjoyed her fellow choir members who traveled together from Roy, Utah, to Salt Lake City in a carpool on a weekly basis. A highlight for her was when her father joined the choir as a guest singer on two Thursday night practice sessions. Henry Nowak sang with the basses to practice songs for the Sunday morning broadcasts. He never forgot those experiences. He also looked for Jeannie every Sunday morning, hoping the camera would find her singing, usually on the back row. She truly believes the Lord allowed her to be a member of the choir so she could be a missionary of the gospel of Jesus Christ to her extended family.

She loves the community where she lives and reaches out to serve those in need. As the president of the Hall Foundation, she works with Alan to fund charitable organizations that provide resources to the poor.

She serves on various nonprofit boards, where she provides leadership and financial support. She has spent countless hours over many years with the Boys & Girls Clubs of Weber-Davis, Your Community Connection, and Weber State's Center for Community Engaged Learning (CCEL). She served six years with the St. Benedict's Foundation, eleven years on the Weber County RAMP (Recreation, Arts, and Museum Projects) board, and six years on the Utah Commission on Service and Volunteerism (UServeUtah). She has worked with the Utah Nonprofits Association and continues to volunteer with the Joyce Hansen Hall Food Bank, United Way of Northern Utah, and many other charities. She's a popular speaker and enjoys talking to youth groups and adults.

Most of all, Jeannie finds joy in her family. "I am blessed to be the mother of our wonderful children and their equally beloved spouses, and grandmother to our twenty precious grandchildren," she says.

Selected Remarks

———————⊸o⊱⟋⟍⊰o⊷———————

Alan has spoken in public literally thousands of times. Whether he's speaking in a boardroom to a group of executives, teaching from the pulpit as stake president, instructing in classrooms as an adjunct professor, or hosting a distinguished event, Alan prefers to speak straight from his own experience without written notes. He connects to his audience through humor and personal stories, which he uses to teach principles.

For certain official occasions, Alan prepares written remarks. The following includes two of his favorite addresses: the Weber State University commencement speech he delivered for thousands of college graduates at the Dee Events Center in December 2016, and a talk he gave in March 2013 at a stake women's conference, hosted by the Roy Utah North Stake Relief Society presidency, titled "Greater Inner Peace."

The third speech comes from Jeannie's remarks at Utah Nonprofits Association's Utah Philanthropy Day luncheon on November 15, 2018, after Alan and Jeannie were honored with the distinguished Philanthropic Leadership Award. She said she felt inspired about what she wrote, and prayed for guidance to honor the good people of Northern Utah.

Weber State University's Commencement Speech
By Chairman Alan E. Hall
December 16, 2016

Good afternoon, Wildcats! Hello Graduates!

What a grand sight to see all of you here today in this beautiful venue. Please know how very delighted and deeply honored I am to be with you on this very, very special occasion.

You, my fellow graduates, have attended a world-class university. I know this campus and its people well. The president, provost, deans, department chairs, faculty, and staff are all extraordinary leaders. They wake up every morning focused on your well being and success.

You've received a superior education from top-notch, knowledgeable, and dedicated professors at a remarkably low cost. In short, your education has been first class, where your dreams of a college education have come true.

Today, we are here to honor you and to celebrate this wonderful occasion with you and your family. I congratulate each of you for reaching this important and valuable milestone in your life. You've worked very hard to be here and this afternoon, in grand fashion, we will recognize your achievement.

I am here, standing before you to deliver a commencement speech—what might be considered the very last lecture out of thousands you've heard from professors while a student at Weber State.

You're thinking to yourself, it better be a good message. It better be short. We want to get out of here as soon as we can. We want our diplomas, a picture in our cap and gown, followed by a celebration dinner at Red Lobster paid for by our parents.

Please be assured I get that. So, let me see what I can do to meet your high expectations. Because we have little time, let's get right to the point.

For many years, each week, I'm contacted by someone who wants to know the keys to success, the secret formula. They tell me, Mr. Hall, you know what it takes. Please help me to do the same. Being a generous man, I will meet for an hour or so with them and give my best advice.

We generally have a focused discussion, filled with many questions and answers. At the end of the conversation, I always hope my counsel has been worthwhile.

Today, it's your turn to learn about the key principles of success. I hope fifty years from now you will look back at your life and say, I followed what Mr. Hall said in 2016 at graduation and it worked. He was right. I have been successful.

So here we go. I have been successful in every area of my life when I have put people first in everything I have ever done. My focus has been to meet the needs of others and to make sure they are happy and that they know I love them. Whether in my home, at work, or in the community, as I have cared about the welfare of others, I too have been happy, fulfilled, and prosperous.

Think about what I just said: Success is driven by taking care of others first. It has worked for me in business as we have surprised and delighted our customers; as we have taken care of employees, vendors, and investors. It's amazing to me to see how closely company revenues are tied to the level of happiness of all stakeholders.

The same principle has worked in my home, as Jeannie and I have put our loved ones first. We've learned that a happy family is the result of parents who love and support each other and encourage their children to do the same. Our six married children, their spouses, and our 18 grandchildren are wonderful people who are carrying on the tradition of ministering to others.

Lastly, I have found success or joy in being charitable toward people in our community. Knowing that a needy child has new gloves and warm coat, food to eat, medical care, and a safe place to play after school brings me peace of mind and contentment. I trust the Hall scholarships you have received have also been of value to you as well?

As you can tell, success for me is not measured in the accumulation of wealth, power over people and things or fame. I find that they are temporary rewards at best, and never completely fulfilling.

Instead, I measure success by the positive impact I can have in the lives of others; such has everlasting importance and is never forgotten.

Why, you might ask, do I focus on others first?

The answer to your question is found in scripture.

I know and have learned that God blesses us with prosperity if we keep His commandments and demonstrate love towards one another. Moreover, I note that we are to use our prosperity to bless the needy.

Lastly, I have found that when we are generous with our time, talents, and resources, that we actually become more prosperous and successful.

It's a formula that has worked for me over and over again.

Conversely, the moment we become greedy, selfish, and proud, the gift of prosperity ends swiftly.

In sum, I believe there is a God of the universe, the Creator of this earth. I see myself as one of His many children created in His image, and believe that we are all brothers and sisters.

I thank Him for life itself and the opportunity to live upon this magnificent planet to experience mortality. I look forward to returning back to God's presence one day with a bright hope that life is eternal and that family ties and friendships continue on forever and don't end with death.

Based upon splendid spiritual experiences that have reinforced my convictions, I have developed a love for a Heavenly Father akin to the affection I have for my own earthly father. Just as my dad has encouraged me to be a good boy and to help others in need with my talents and resources, I find myself serving God's children in like manner as well.

As I do so, my own heart is warmed as I help to lift the burdens of others whose hearts and minds are heavy laden. In short, my hope, my commitments, and my faith in God are the basis of a solid foundation for how I think, feel, and act about the people in my life.

My beloved parents are the perfect example of putting others first. I love my noble dad and sweet mother. They gave me life, directions, rules, unconditional love, and affection. I truly hope to be like them one day by honoring the powerful tradition of constantly looking out for the welfare of others.

Nearly forty years ago, my father taught me a non-spoken lesson that unconditional love and the sharing of our gifts with others brings joy to our hearts.

One summer day as I was building a wooden fence around our yard, my seven-year-old son, Aaron, eagerly pleaded with me to help with the project. I am embarrassed to tell you that I felt he would somehow ruin my perfect work, and I told him in a very brusque voice to leave and to not bother me anymore. With a pierced heart, he ran away crying with deeply hurt feelings.

My patient dad, who had watched the scene with high interest, followed Aaron to his hiding place. He took with him a hammer, a few nails, two discarded fence slats, and a comforting hug. I watched nearby with a contrite spirit as grandpa and grandson happily nailed two boards together in pure delight. No words were spoken, no counsel was given, no condemnation was expressed by my dad. It wasn't needed. I was taught by my loving father to be selfless in my thoughts and actions and to always remember the special needs and tender feelings of others. It was a powerful lesson, one I will never forget.

My sweetheart, Jeannie, is my best friend, greatest fan, and devoted companion. She is the love of my life and the source of my greatest joy. We have learned together, through trial and error, how to achieve marital bliss as a couple.

Key lessons for us have been to be always supportive, to ask for forgiveness and be forgiving, and to be faithful and fully committed to helping one another be the best we can. She has always put me first in her life.

MarketStar would not exist today were it not for her willingness to use our home as security for a business loan nearly twenty-eight years ago. Had the business failed, Jeannie and I and our six kids would have been living in a van, down by the river, eating government cheese. Thankfully, she has taught me, through her tireless support, how to love unconditionally.

We love our six wonderful children, their amazing spouses, and our eighteen beloved grandchildren with all our hearts. Words cannot express the joy and pleasure Jeannie and I have in being associated with these remarkable people.

Our thoughts and desires for their well being are always on the top of our minds. We'd do anything to help them be happy and successful in life. They know we love them and we know they love us. Putting them first in our lives is a joy.

Jeannie and I are pleased to have our expanded family living within a few miles of our home. We see them often for family dinners, vacations, birthdays, ball games, recitals, and school programs. These special times together build sweet memories and tighten the bonds among us that will last forever.

Some memories are sweet and funny. Once while driving down the freeway at high speed, my ten-year old-grandson, Corbin, wisely asked the following question;

> Grandpa, how fast are we going?
> Seventy-five miles an hour, I said.
> What's the speed limit? he asked.
> Sixty-five, I responded.
> Go sixty-five, Grandpa!

We rally together for good and bad times. Whether it's to celebrate a major accomplishment or to mourn the loss of a loved one, we are all united in love for one another.

Several weeks ago on a Saturday night, I sat next to my grieving son, Christian Hall, at the hospital to help him give a name to his tiny little baby son who had died prematurely. Grandpa Coleman and I along with Christian held in our trembling hands a handsome little fellow who was seven inches long and weighed about four ounces. With great tears flowing and broken hearts, we gave Emily and Christian's son the name of Nixon Coleman Hall.

Never will we forget the profound love and affection we felt for Nixon and for one another on that saddest and most sacred of occasions. As we pondered that sweet moment, we recognized so clearly that there is nothing—no, nothing—more precious, more valuable, or important than family.

Lastly, my heart soars when I see or hear of thoughtful people who bless the lives of others in memorable ways. Such kindness always lifts my spirit and inspires me to do likewise.

This past October I watched a grandson, Cole West, participate in a 5th grade little league football playoff game between his Roy team and a squad from Rose Park.

Unbeknown to family and fans, near the end of the tensely fought game with a few minutes to go, with Roy ahead by several touchdowns, Zach Colohan, the Roy coach, knowing about a special young man on the other team, called time out.

He quickly approached the refs, his players, and the Rose Park coach to suggest that the Rose Park water boy, a physically disabled fifth grader who was unable to play football, be given the opportunity to carry the football on the last play of the game. With gratitude and deep appreciation, the Rose Park coach said yes and invited the young man, in jeans, tennis shoes, and a T-shirt to put a spare helmet on his head and to join the huddle of his teammates on the field of play.

To everyone's surprise, we watched the Rose Park quarterback hand the ball to one very happy little boy.

Cheering wildly, with tears running down our cheeks, we saw both teams carefully escorting an ecstatic ten-year-old, who slowly and awkwardly moved from the 50-yard line to the end zone. As he scored the final touchdown of the game, a feeling of deep love swept over players, coaches, and fans.

After the celebration and victory cheers had ceased, the two teams shook hands and parted as friends. The Roy coach gathered his team around him. "My boys," he said, "today we won a tough game against a terrific team. You played your best to beat a tough foe. But your best moment, your very best moment, was when you joined with your competitors to bring immeasurable happiness to a little brother. What you did today will surpass any victory, on any field of play, for the rest of your lives. Today you became great and noble young men."

Now please give a warm Weber State welcome to that Roy 5th grade football team and its noble coach who are here with us today in section 14.

In closing, my hope for you, for all of us, is that we will awaken each day thinking of whom we might lift, inspire, and encourage, and to then act upon it when the moment arises. Please remember a pat on the back, a kind word, sometimes even a hug, might be what someone needs when they're having a challenging day.

My expectation for the class of 2016 is that each of you will do everything in your power to make our world a better place, and that you too will strive to love and serve others, in your homes, at work, and in your communities. I promise you, as you do good things continually, even in a world of chaos, your life will be filled with immeasurable success, enduring peace, and long-lasting happiness.

Thank you, ladies and gentlemen, and go Wildcats!

Greater Inner Peace
By President Alan E. Hall
March 2013

Dear sisters, I am very grateful and honored to be with you. I consider you to be among the noblest women on this earth. Because of this, I have tender feelings for you and see you as my eternal sisters. Please know that I love you and cherish you. I do so knowing that we are all part of God's family, brothers and sisters, beloved children of our Heavenly Father—a celestial being who knows us well, who loves us and who has a plan for us to return to His presence one day.

I wish to focus my remarks tonight on how we might find and secure greater inner peace in our lives. To accomplish this important goal, I suggest we follow these three steps: 1) ask God to change our hearts and remove our destructive habits, 2) invite Him to take our heavy burdens and heal our pierced hearts, and 3) ask Him to help us fight the evil that surrounds us. As we follow these guidelines, the Lord will bless our lives and we will feel greater peace and strength in an ever-darkening world.

As an introduction, I want you to know that I view you all as nearly perfect saints, beloved women endowed with a divine nature. However, I also recognize, as you do, too, that each of us might have weaknesses and shortcomings that need our personal attention. After all, we are all mortal beings striving to improve ourselves in every way.

Speaking of shortcomings, I would like to share with you a short story that illustrates this point perfectly. Many years ago, as a young man, I became the president and general manager of Ballet West, a well-known professional dance company located in Salt Lake City. As you can imagine, I was not hired by the trustees because I could dance (which I clearly cannot do), but to successfully manage the business side of the enterprise. As to my knowledge of ballet, I was completely clueless. I couldn't tell you the difference between a pirouette and an arabesque if I'd tried! Moreover, I had only seen one ballet prior to this most unusual assignment, so I was not deeply grounded in this magnificent art form. Thankfully, I did have an appreciation for ballet and its fantastic entertainment value. As a small boy, my mother had taken me to see a holiday performance of the famous *Nutcracker* ballet. I was enthralled with what I saw and heard. Oh, how I loved Tchaikovsky's symphonic music, especially "The Waltz of the Flowers" with its beautiful crescendo. I would play that piece over and over again on my record player, deeply enjoying each note for many years thereafter.

Unfortunately, my appreciation for this singular ballet did not help me in my new position. Following my first day on the job, I immediately recognized my lack of knowledge and noted that I must quickly learn everything I could about this art form, its history, and its people if I were to succeed as the president of this company. I am grateful that Priscilla Stevens saw my need and took me under her professional wing. This knowledgeable ballet aficionado was on the Board of Trustees of Ballet West and also on the Board of Trustees of American Ballet Theater, the most famous ballet company in the country, headquartered in New York City.

One day, Priscilla said to me, "Alan, you really should come to New York to see America's finest ballet company firsthand for yourself. It will help you to understand and appreciate what it takes to run a world-class organization. I will be your hostess and introduce you to the manager and dancers of this fabulous company." So with stars in our eyes, my wife Jeannie and I flew to New York City in the spring of 1980 for an experience of a lifetime. Priscilla kept her word and was a gracious hostess, arranging for us to stay in a penthouse apartment directly across the street from the Metropolitan Opera House where we would see America Ballet Theater perform *Swan Lake*. With two tickets in hand and dressed in our finest suit and gown, we entered the most magnificent auditorium I had ever seen to witness the opening night performance of ballet's most famous production. As the curtain rose on the first scene, there on the stage stood ballet's most renowned artist, none other than Mikhail Baryshnikov. As he appeared, the crowd roared its approval and the electricity in the air was palpable. Jeannie and I sat on the edge of our seats, enjoying every precious moment. Never in my life had I experienced such beauty and majesty. Every musical note, every magnificent costume, every set change, and every dance step was delicious sensory candy.

As if the performance wasn't enough of a treat, our hostess invited us backstage afterwards to personally meet Mr. Baryshnikov. We were thrilled to think we could meet this world-famous Russian ballet star. So once the performance ended, we approached the backstage door where a large burly guard stood sentinel, only allowing those with the proper pass to enter. As we waited for our chance to meet the legendary dancer, we noticed an elegantly dressed patron standing near the backstage door who also desired to meet Mr. Baryshnikov, but lacked the pass to do so. However, this refined lady wasn't just any woman. At the time, she was the most famous woman on earth.

Noting her dilemma, Priscilla suggested to Jacqueline Kennedy Onassis that she could join our party backstage using our passes. "That would be fine," she replied. So there we were, standing next to the most famous, perfect woman on earth! She was absolutely gorgeous with her beautiful black chiffon dress, perfect makeup, and coiffured hair. In time, the door opened and the guard let us enter the backstage area where Mr. Baryshnikov waited to meet us. As we walked along, Jackie moved quickly, moving a few steps ahead of us. I suddenly felt a nudge on my shoulder and heard Jeannie quietly say, "Look at her leg!"

"What?" I whispered.

"Look at her right leg," she whispered back. "She has a run in her nylons!"

Sure enough, there in plain sight was a long run in her sheer black nylons. Oh my goodness, there stood the most perfect, beautiful woman on earth with a run in her nylons. What do you know? She, like the rest of us, must be mortal after all.

So you see my beloved sisters, even the very best among us have tiny flaws. We are just like she is: nearly perfect, but from time to time with a run in our nylons.

With that being said, how do we as spiritual beings, having an imperfect mortal experience filled with trials and challenges, secure peace in a troubled world? If I may, I have another story to share with you that will shed some light on this subject. It's the story of the flower garden.

As I said earlier, I was a young executive when I began running Ballet West. I remember clearly that every day was a great challenge for me; I have never felt so much pressure and stress in my life. (Even now, after being in business for more than forty years, I recognize that running Ballet West was perhaps the toughest assignment I have ever had.) During this same time, I was also a new bishop with responsibilities over several hundred single adult college students. They too were in need of my time and counsel with many personal trials of their own. Add to this that Jeannie and I were the parents of four small, active children with two more joining us during my career at the Ballet, and you might guess just how difficult this time was. Needless to say, there were many moments during this period of my life when I felt completely overwhelmed and stressed beyond measure.

Fortunately, Elder James E. Faust of the Quorum of the Twelve Apostles was on the Board of Trustees for Ballet West during this same time. Even with his busy church assignment, he found time to become better acquainted with Jeannie and me. In fact, I can vividly remember an evening when he and his wife, Ruth, hosted us for dinner before a ballet performance in Ogden. They were so kind. Based on this warm reception, I knew Elder Faust would be willing to help me during this difficult time in my life. So I contacted him to see if he would visit with me about how I might better manage my many multiple assignments in life. He graciously agreed and invited me to his office for a personal chat one beautiful spring afternoon.

During our conversation, we talked about the difficulties I was facing and I asked what advice he might have for me. He sat there very kindly and attentively, making some suggestions but not giving me complete answers; he wisely thought that I should come up with my own solutions.

At one point, he asked me to walk with him to the window on the west side of his office. He opened the curtains and we both stood there looking out his large window at the scene below. After a few minutes, he asked, "Alan, what do you see?" I didn't know what exactly I was supposed to find, so I continued gazing out the window with him. Eventually, he put his arm around my shoulder, prodding me along. "I can see the Hotel Utah," I replied. "Look lower on the ground," he suggested. I looked and said, "I see a garden. I see gardeners and gorgeous flowers." "Look even more intently," he said. To which I replied, "I see row after row of beautiful flowers, all arranged perfectly with amazing and dazzling colors."

Elder Faust then paused and said, "Alan, I want you to remember what I am about to tell you for the rest of your life. What you see down there is exactly what I want you to become, a garden of beautiful flowers. I want you to be amazing, I want you to be splendid, and I want your life to reflect the glory and orderliness of that flowerbed. Your ability to achieve this quintessential way of life is highly possible if you will base your thoughts and behavior upon time-tested eternal principles. In short, all your decisions and actions, Alan, should focus on following the Savior's gospel. If you do so, you will experience inner peace, joy, and heartfelt happiness all the days of your life."

What a glorious lesson I learned from Elder Faust that day. It has been many years since this conversation transpired and yet his message of comparing our lives to a flower garden has remained ever present in my life. In like manner, may I suggest an additional thought? So, if you will, imagine that in our flowerbeds there is a very special gardener who is carefully weeding, watering, fertilizing, and pruning each tender plant. Now envision that our gracious Heavenly Father is the gardener of our own personal flowerbeds, constantly and lovingly watching over us night and day. Please know this is the case. For, without a doubt, He does care for us and is always willing to nourish and provide us with His light and power so that like beautiful flowers, we too may flourish and become magnificent.

With this story in mind, and a flower garden as a metaphor for all of our lives, how then might we beautify our own flowerbeds? As an answer to this vital question, I would like to share with you the three steps I mentioned earlier that with God's help we can implement in our lives. As we do so, He will bless us immensely and provide us with an increased measure of personal peace, joy, and happiness.

First, it is vital that we take a step back and examine carefully and honestly our own personal flowerbeds. What do we see? Are we weed free or are there weeds in our garden that need pulling? Have harmful insects been removed or are there multitudes of voracious bugs eating everything in sight? Is our garden receiving sufficient sunlight or is it constantly in the shadows? Is it full of amazing life or is it dying? Are we happy with what we find or is there work to be done? A thoughtful review of our lives will provide the answers we seek.

As I interview people in my calling as stake president, I often find that their gardens need immediate attention. I note that unrepented sin easily kills personal progress and joy. Guilt and shame tend to stifle growth like nothing else. Harboring ill will towards others is debilitating and consumes enormous amounts of time and energy when we won't forgive and forget. Are there other flaws holding us back from growing a lovely garden? Perhaps we punish one another, reproving harshly those who might step out of line. Or it could be that we are proud, arrogant, and condescending, seeing ourselves as superior to others. Maybe our garden is filled with rebellion, envy, jealousy, and stubbornness—an unwillingness to bend or compromise. Perhaps we lack focus, discipline, and order. The list of vices and imperfections seems to be limitless.

Please know, my dear sisters, that at the very moment we remove from the garden of our lives even one unhealthy habit, joy, peace, and happiness will be ours once again. When we deliberately push from our minds and our hearts grievous misdeeds, we are freed to receive the full joy that God can place in our hearts. So I invite you now to take the time to honestly examine your gardens and seriously inspect yourselves, asking, "What am I doing to my garden that is keeping me from growing to my true potential? What is holding me back from completely experiencing all the happiness that God has in store for me?" I know it may seem daunting and maybe even a bit frightening, but please know that an all-powerful God will rescue us if we ask Him to do so. Please know He *will* help us.

I can testify of this because I have pleaded with Him to change my heart on several occasions. Now I will not go into detail on any one of my struggles, but I have had several over the course of my life that have been difficult to shake. I have made errors and committed transgressions, albeit nothing serious. But still, I struggled and knew I could not overcome these trials by myself. During these times, I would pray to my Heavenly Father saying, "Please take this out of my heart. Remove it from my nature. Change me so this is no longer who I am. I don't want to be this way." And as I prayed with sincerity and genuineness, He took those wicked habits from me. I stand here today with a firm conviction and knowledge of this fact. I testify to you that God will remove every bad thing from our hearts if we will ask. He will remove the shackles; He will take off the ball and chains that currently hold us down from enjoying all the great blessings He wishes to grant us. And as a result, we will feel greater inner peace.

My second point concerning our personal gardens is that on occasion, metaphorically speaking, severe personal storms may destroy them. It might be heavy and wet snow, destructive hail, or a fierce windstorm that kills and uproots our tender plants. Perhaps vicious underground insects are to blame for a withered garden, or malicious feet that trample unprotected flowers.

I know many of us can relate to these unfortunate circumstances on a personal level. It could be that we have been betrayed by a loved one. Perhaps we have children or other relatives who have harmed or disappointed us. We may have been abused emotionally, sexually, mentally, or physically. Some of us may have lost loved ones, lost children, or lost the Spirit. We may feel depressed or hopeless. Perhaps our minds are troubled with worrisome doubts and paralyzing fear. Some of us might feel unloved and unappreciated by those closest to us. All of these hardships (and many others unmentioned) are wounds that pierce an aching heart. In addition to the pain and anguish they cause, these struggles also hold us back from growing into the beautiful creation we were meant to be.

What then can we do to remove or lessen the pain these maladies bring into our lives? The answer once again is to call upon God, asking Him to eliminate our burdens and pain. As a loving, all-powerful God, He can lighten our heavy loads, heal our broken hearts, and sweep our minds clear of the terrible things that bring us sorrow and misery in this life.

A beautiful talk by Elder Jeffrey R. Holland summarizes perfectly how the Savior can bring us peace. His remarks focus on the Savior and how He can heal us:

> Brothers and sisters, my Easter-season message today is intended for everyone, but it is directed in a special way to those who are alone or feel alone or, worse yet, feel abandoned. These might include those longing to be married, those who have lost a spouse, and those who have lost—or have never been blessed with—children. Our empathy embraces wives forsaken by their husbands... or [parents] out of work, afraid the fear in [their] eyes will be visible to [their children]...
>
> To all such, I speak of the loneliest journey ever made and the unending blessings it brought to all in the human family. I speak of the Savior's solitary task of shouldering alone the burden of our salvation....
>
> Now I speak very carefully... I speak of those final moments for which Jesus must have been prepared intellectually and physically but which He may not have fully anticipated emotionally and spiritually—that concluding descent into the paralyzing despair of divine withdrawal when He cries in *ultimate* loneliness, "My God, my God, why hast *thou* forsaken me?"...
>
> With all the conviction of my soul I testify that He *did* please His Father perfectly and that a perfect Father did *not* forsake His Son in that hour. Indeed, it is my personal belief that in all of Christ's mortal ministry the Father may never have been closer to His Son than in these agonizing final moments

of suffering. Nevertheless, that the supreme sacrifice of His Son might be as complete as it was voluntary and solitary, the Father briefly withdrew from Jesus the comfort of His Spirit, the support of His personal presence. It was required, indeed it was central to the significance of the Atonement, that this perfect Son who had never spoken ill nor done wrong nor touched an unclean thing had to know how the rest of humankind—us, all of us—would feel when we did commit such sins....

One of the great consolations of this Easter season is that because Jesus walked such a long, lonely path utterly alone, *we* do not have to do so.... Trumpeted from the summit of Calvary is the truth that we will never be left alone nor unaided, even if sometimes we may feel that we are. Truly the Redeemer of us all said: "I will not leave you comfortless: [My Father and] I will come to you [and abide with you]."[1]

As I've considered this wonderful talk on the Savior, the words from the hymn "Where Can I Turn for Peace?" come to my mind. The lyrics are beautiful and convey exactly the point I am trying to make.

> Where can I turn for peace?
> Where is my solace
> When other sources cease to make me whole?
> When with a wounded heart, anger, or malice,
> I draw myself apart,
> Searching my soul?
>
> Where, when my aching grows,
> Where, when I languish,
> Where, in my need to know, where can I run?
> Where is the quiet hand to calm my anguish?
> Who, who can understand?
> He, only One.
>
> He answers privately,
> Reaches my reaching

In my Gethsemane, Savior and Friend.
Gentle the peace he finds for my beseeching
Constant He is and kind,
Love without end.[2]

Our Savior is there for us, my dear sisters. He is always ready to give us the peace and strength we need, even through the worst of personal storms.

The last point I would make regarding our gardens is that oftentimes, they are bombarded by dangerous elements: pollutants, harmful chemicals, or even dangerous toxins within the soil which destroy life. As humans, we too face powerful destructive elements that kill the soul. I speak of Lucifer and his desire to destroy all of God's children. In fact, he is our greatest enemy. His satanic goal is to convince us to break God's commandments and thereby disqualify ourselves from the presence of God. After centuries of hard work, he knows his business well and has a time-tested strategy to bring us down step by step. He has crafted numerous enticements that appeal to our mortal minds and heart. His wickedness is often subtle with half-truths followed by counterfeits of goodness.

As children of a loving God who wants us to return safely to His presence, we need to fight Lucifer will all our power and might. We cannot ignore him, stand idly by, or believe he is not real. He is the ultimate terrorist and must be stopped.

To illustrate this point, I would like to share with you one final story. Nearly twelve years ago when I was still very involved in the corporate world, I oversaw company offices in Oxford, England, and Paris, France. Wishing to visit my employees there and enjoy a brief vacation, I flew to Europe with Jeannie and our daughter Megan. Our first stop was England—a meeting at the office and a tour of London. A few days later on what seemed like any ordinary day, September 11, 2001, we traveled to Paris by train via the "Chunnel." We arrived safely at the Paris train station and then took a cab to our hotel located near the Louvre Museum. As we unpacked our bags, we watched CNN for the latest news. We stopped everything as we learned that a plane had crashed into one of the World Trade Center buildings in New York City.

At first, it appeared to be a small plane that had inadvertently veered off course. Then a few minutes later, we watched in horror as another plane crashed into an adjoining tower.

Our hearts skipped a beat. "What's going on?" we questioned. "Something terrible is happening in the United States. Are we under attack? Has the land of the free become a war zone?" The hotel staff immediately informed all guests that we were not to leave the building for any reason, so we watched from our window as the streets of Paris filled with troops. We wondered if there would there be more attacks in the United States, or possibly even in Paris.

Fear gripped our minds. We were a long way from home and petrified. We worried about our own safety and even more so for our five children who were in Utah. Later that evening, my very distressed wife cried her heart out as she called every one of our family members to tell them we were okay and ask about their safety. We were reassured that all was well.

Unable to stay caged in our room for much longer, we eventually slipped out of the hotel into the darkness of the night to see empty streets everywhere. We walked past the American Embassy, surrounded by armed troops and tanks. We walked past the Eiffel Tower, also surrounded by guards with machine guns. As we hurried back to the hotel and the safety of our room that night, we sadly noted that the world had changed.

A few days later, we were finally able to fly back home. However, it required that we catch a plane in Rome, Italy. No planes were leaving the Paris Charles de Gaulle Airport in the near future. At the Rome airport, heavily armored guards were everywhere. Lines were long and security was very tight. We learned we would be traveling on Delta's first plane headed into New York City since the attack. As we sat in our seats, huddled together, we wondered if we would make it there alive. Would our flight fall victim to the same terrifying circumstances that unfolded just days earlier? Would there be a bomb on our plane?

As the plane began to taxi down the runway, the pilot spoke reassuringly to the passengers and crew: "This is Delta flight [such and such number] and we are heading back to America. I want you to know that I will get you there without incident. *Nothing* will bring this plane down." And so began a long, nerve-wracking flight. When we finally approached the JFK Airport, the pilot flew the plane over the fire and smoke of the destroyed Twin Towers. The horrific scene of destruction was indescribable. We held hands as we began our descent to the runway and offered a sincere prayer that our plane would land safely.

As the plane touched down, loud ear-deafening cheers of joy from 300 grateful passengers filled the large cabin. The captain came over the intercom exclaiming, "Welcome back to America, the land of the free!" I will never forget the joy we felt at being back in the United States. Tears ran down our cheeks in gratitude as we experienced that defining moment. Yet that feeling was mixed with the sad realization that there is evil among us: terrorists who would kill us, who hate our way of life and would take away our liberties and freedoms in an instant.

Since that day, now many years ago, the United States government and local government agencies have wisely increased their efforts to safeguard and protect the American people from additional attacks and terrorism. Even today, we all must remain on guard and vigilant. Evil has not gone away. It will always be with us.

In like manner, the battle over our souls is daily and unceasing. For our own protection and personal safety, we too must safeguard and protect ourselves, as well as those we love. Because the fight is real and very dangerous, we should do everything in our power to defend our gardens with all our might and strength. We cannot compromise on this matter. We cannot back away in any fashion. We must fight evil head on with great courage and faith. Therefore, we must be constantly aware, vigilant, alert, and watchful of what negative influences are in our homes and personal lives, and then stop them before they destroy our souls. This effort begins with each one of us living righteously and keeping the covenants we have made.

Please know God will not leave us alone to battle evil. On the contrary, He will aid us in many ways. First, He will let us know in a very clear way what influences are good and from Him, compared to what influences are wicked and from Satan. Then, as we choose to follow Christ and keep His commandments, He will give us full and complete access to His divine power that crushes Lucifer's evil ways. Lastly, He provides us with strength in numbers. The stakes of Zion have been established by the Lord to serve as a defense for His sons and daughters with the teaching of value-based principles, inspired leadership, and saving ordinances.

In closing, I pray that we will all actively pursue the three steps I have outlined, for I know they will help us find and secure greater peace in our lives. As we ask God to change our hearts and remove our destructive habits, invite Him to take our heavy burdens and heal our broken hearts, and request His help in fighting the evil that surrounds us, our lives will be richly blessed.

As I conclude my remarks, I wish to invite our Heavenly Father to bless you with His loving power. In the name of Jesus Christ and by virtue of the Melchizedek priesthood that I possess, I call upon Him to bless you with an increased desire for righteousness, as well as the ability to more intensely feel His love for you. May He bless you with greater faith, hope, and courage to do what is right. May He also bless you with increased joy and happiness, even in the simple and mundane moments of life—whether it is shopping for groceries, driving the kids to soccer, vacuuming the floor, washing the dishes, preparing supper, or doing the laundry. I pray that through these daily tasks, He can bless you with a sense of fulfillment and satisfaction. Lastly, I invite Him to bless you in your sacred role as women, that you will have an increased love for those under your watchful care, and that your service to others will fill your hearts with contentment and peace beyond measure.

I love you very much, my beloved sisters. I pray for you daily, always asking God to watch over and protect you and your loved ones. Please know I am here for you and will help you in any way that I can. Remember that you are loved and cherished, and that God is with you. He will help you, aid you, and protect you as you grow your own personal beautiful gardens.

For these marvelous blessings I pray, in the name of the Lord, Jesus Christ, amen.

Utah Philanthropy Day 2018
By Jeannie Hall
November 15, 2018

Ladies and gentlemen, it is with joy and gratitude that we stand here today. We are grateful for the organizations that have made this day of appreciation possible: UNA, UServeUtah, AFP, and other sponsors. We are thankful for their leadership and their desire to help all of us who live in the world of serving others. Most of all, we are grateful for you!

In a time of challenges, violence and fear, where sometimes we lose our way, you are here to counsel, to bring peace and understanding. You are the noble who protect those who have been abused or hurt by the actions of others. You are here to lift the burdens of the most needy among us. Ladies and gentlemen, Alan and I truly believe that each of us are brothers and sisters, equal in the sight of God. None of us are the same—we are each different and unique—but all of us are loved by a divine Creator who placed us here with the intent that we would grow and learn to bless the lives of one another.

You have and continue to truly minister unto the least of these, His children, who are hungry, unclothed, lonely, homeless, imprisoned by walls or by their own demons, or wherever we may be along the spectrum of human life and its frailties. The professions you have chosen, the organizations where you work, and the volunteering that you do is not for earthly gain or the praise of others, but is because of the goodness in your hearts and your desire to lift and care for those around you.

I have a powerful memory of January 19, 2018. I was outside in a large arena. The temperature was in the mid-30s; it was lightly raining. We were surrounded by huge dumpsters loaded with green chairs, and standing in slippery puddles of mud. Over the course of two days, hundreds of volunteers were there for a project for Ogden City and the Ogden Pioneer Days Rodeo. Gail Miller and the Jazz organization had graciously donated 7,500 chairs from the remodel of the Vivint Arena. These famous green seats were to be repurposed and make possible safe seating for the thousands of people who come to the rodeo each

summer. Each individual chair needed to be hand sorted by size before
they could be transported to the Wadman Company that would make
this miraculous change in the grandstands possible. Alan and I worked
alongside volunteer rodeo board members, teenagers from after-school
programs in Weber County, and numerous full-time LDS missionaries.
We served next to men in orange jumpsuits, released for that day from
the Weber County Jail. There were people from every walk of life:
businessmen and women, nonprofit leaders, mothers, grandmothers, a
retired major general who had been the commanding officer at Hill Air
Force Base. There was laughter, kindness, and patience as we all worked
together for a common purpose.

As the end of the day approached, it grew darker, the temperature
dropped and the rain fell harder, but the task was completed. I looked
around at the group. We were all muddy, cold, and tired, but we had come
to know and care for one another in our truest sense. We shook hands
and hugged one another. We were able to express our gratitude to fellow
workers, regardless of our backgrounds or current circumstances. Each
of us felt the love and satisfaction of serving together and accomplishing
a meaningful task.

All of us can give and serve one another. But often we need the
guidance and the direction that you afford us with your many agencies
and organizations that seek to bless the lives of others. Each of you
give of yourselves on a daily basis, lifting and caring for those in your
communities. You are there from the moment of birth, and even before
a child is born, to care for a young mother who may be alone or without
any support. You are there to offer help, education, and a chance for a
full life to those who are born or live with challenges, whether physical,
emotional, mental, or spiritual. You are there to bless the lives of families
with food, clothing, shelter, and the necessities of life. You are the heroes
who educate and encourage children and give them the opportunity to
be in a safe place, a nurturing environment where they can learn and
grow and reach their full potential.

You are there to bring the arts, to share the joy of creativity and
expression so that we may not only live in this world but rejoice in
the talents and beauties which surround us. Alan and I are especially

thrilled to be here today to give honor and praise to dear friends and associates from Northern Utah, with whom we are privileged to work and serve.

I would ask them to please stand and remain standing.

In applauding them, we cheer for each of you and express our most profound gratitude. These men and women are shining stars in our lives. It is not often that they receive the praise or the honor that is due them. They, as all of you, have sacrificed greatly to help others. I express my deepest love and admiration for my beloved husband of nearly fifty years, who has made possible so many opportunities and blessings for me. I express our tenderest love for our children and grandchildren, who teach us on a daily basis and bring us joy! They are truly our greatest treasure on earth. And we give thanks to our great God who loves us, sacrificed for us, and has knit our hearts together in love.

Selected *Forbes* Articles

For nearly eighteen months, from 2012–2013, Alan wrote weekly articles as a *Forbes* contributor. In one hundred columns, he shared key principles of business success. The following selections are two of his favorites: "The 7 C's: How to Find and Hire Great Employees"[1] and "Kiss Your Boss Goodbye. It's Time to Be an Entrepreneur."[2] Combined, these two articles have had more than half a million online views.

The 7 C's: How to Find and Hire Great Employees

A founder can't grow a winning enterprise singlehandedly. Some may try, but it is nearly impossible to do so. Every famous entrepreneur has built a flourishing company with great employees by his or her side.

Hiring the best employees is more important than ever.

An entrepreneur can invent and even commercialize an idea as an enterprise of one. In time, however, the tasks of running a business become too great for the entrepreneur to manage alone. At this point, a savvy leader must find and hire the best workers to help achieve the entrepreneurial dream.

In today's economy, hiring the best people is more critical than ever. Entrepreneurs can't afford to lose time, money and results from a bad hiring choice (a recent *Forbes* article by David K. Williams pegs the cost of a single bad hire at anywhere from $25–50,000). The cost of finding, interviewing, engaging and training new employees is high. Employees also require desks, computers, phones and related equipment, let alone the largest costs of being an employer—salaries, benefits and taxes.

Leaders view new employees as an investment and anticipate an excellent financial return over time.

Over the course of my career, I've hired hundreds of people. Some were exceptional employees who were major contributors to our success. Others didn't work out. In most cases, when an employee left or was terminated, I was the problem. Those dismissed were good people. I just did not know how to properly hire new employees.

Historically, and sadly, the only criteria I had used were to find the candidate with the best skills, experiences and ability to match a job description.

I have since identified seven categories—I call them the "7 C's"—that you should consider to find the best new employees, as follows:

1. **Competent**: This is still the first factor to consider. Does the potential employee have the necessary skills, experiences and education to successfully complete the tasks you need performed?

2. **Capable**: Will this person complete not only the easy tasks but will he or she also find ways to deliver on the functions that require more effort and creativity? For me, being capable means the employee has potential for growth and the ability and willingness to take on more responsibility.

3. **Compatible**: Can this person get along with colleagues, and more importantly, can he or she get along with existing and potential clients and partners? A critical component to also remember is the person's willingness and ability to be harmonious with you, his or her boss. If the new employee can't, there will be problems.

4. **Commitment**: Is the candidate serious about working for the long term? Or is he or she just passing through, always looking

for something better? A history of past jobs and time spent at each provides clear insight on the matter.

5. **Character**: Does the person have values that align with yours? Are they honest; do they tell the truth and keep promises? Are they above reproach? Are they selfless and a team player?

6. **Culture**: Every business has a culture or a way that people behave and interact with each other. Culture is based on certain values, expectations, policies and procedures that influence the behavior of a leader and employees. Workers who don't reflect a company's culture tend to be disruptive and difficult.

7. **Compensation**: As the employer, be sure the person hired agrees to a market-based compensation package and is satisfied with what is offered. If not, an employee may feel unappreciated and thereby under perform. Be careful about granting stock in the company; if not handled well, it will create future challenges.

Job applicants will give you their answers to the seven categories. They may be modestly presented or exaggerated. You are searching for the truth. To obtain a clearer picture of potential workers, I recommend you talk to former employment associates. The references a job candidate provides will nearly always provide a biased report. Instead, ask the candidate for the names of former bosses, peers and subordinates.

I'm here to tell you that good references will share the truth and not mince words. With these names in hand, call former co-workers and ask them if the job applicant fits my seven characteristics. This will give you a full and accurate view, good and bad, that will leave you much better equipped to select the best candidate.

For more detailed information about hiring employees I have written an e-book on the *7 C's of Hiring* that is available from Amazon or from my personal website at www.AlanEHall.com.

Kiss Your Boss Goodbye—
It's Time to Be an Entrepreneur.

I recently read a reliable report on the attitude of the American workforce. To my surprise I learned more than half of all employees are not engaged at work. In other words, most workers are not happy, not satisfied, not productive, not loyal, not inspired and will jump ship if another opportunity arises. In fact, most are looking to leave now and have polished their résumés. If this is the case, I would also assume that the managers who supervise these disillusioned employees are probably jerks, or are carrying out the mandates of thoughtless upper management.

If you're a company leader who doesn't focus on keeping employees engaged, make note; your days are numbered. I suggest you change now, with sincere intent to take care of your people, or suffer the disastrous consequences of *your own* unemployment.

I have more to say on this topic to company management. Who do you think does all the work in your business? Who do you think makes your products, sells them, provides support, collects receipts and pays workers? It's not you, my friend. Have you forgotten that you hired these people as a resource to help you build a highly profitable business? Have you forgotten they are a precious asset to be valued and protected? How long do you think you can mistreat quality workers until they bolt? In a word, it's not very long. Do you get the picture? Am I making sense? In sum, your financial success, your promotions, your glory, all depend on how well you treat those subordinates who have placed their trust and confidence in you.

Now a word to les misérables. If you are going to quit, for heaven's sake, don't go to work for another pathetic firm. Do something wild: Kiss your boss goodbye and launch your own business. If you have had enough, become your own king. The money you have made for others now shifts to yourself. Take that idea that's been in your mind for months and turn it into a profitable company. If you are an engineer, a programmer, a salesman, a teacher, an accountant, a whatever, start today planning your escape from corporate prison.

I am sure you are similar to the entrepreneurs I spend time with everyday. As a principal investor, I put money into emerging companies that have all been founded by someone who, for the most part, previously worked for a clueless company. They left seeking their own destiny and fulfillment, hoping life would be much better on their own. I know their employment history, their state of mind and the decision process they followed as they took a leap of faith to follow their dreams.

Over the last few months, I have spent several evenings giving advice to a gentleman who is a full-time employee of a large company. He possesses a great business idea. He is anxious to understand the steps he needs to follow to properly organize his own company.

Today, I am pleased to share with you the same information he is learning. So, if you are ready to soar, please make note of the following initial guidelines:

1. **Keep your day job until the time is right to leave.** Keep in mind; you really have two options to consider:

   A) You can leave tomorrow if you have the resources in hand to sustain your efforts long enough to reach profitability. Give yourself at least one year to succeed. If you can't reach your goal in that time frame, look for other ways to survive and prosper, or,

   B) You can ponder, prepare, organize, and execute your plan over time, at night and on weekends until everything is ready to go.

2. **If you have signed a non-compete with your current employer, honor it.** Wait until you can legally pursue your opportunity. Find some form of income to sustain your personal life in the interim.

3. **Determine your purpose, your vision, your strategy.** Why are you in business? What do you hope to accomplish? What must you do to be successful? Are your answers sound and realistic?

4. **Test your assumptions.** Determine who your perfect customers are. Know everything about them. Talk to them, listen and respond

accordingly. Know how many total potential customers there are. Learn if potential customers will want to buy your product or service. Learn about their needs, pain and current solutions. Determine the right price and where buyers expect to make a purchase. Understand what they watch, hear and read. Know how to promote your offering. Understand the competition. Know their value proposition and why people buy their products.

5. **Evaluate a product's viability.** Consider the design, development and manufacturing of the perfect solution at the best possible cost. Understand why your solution will be chosen by customers.

6. **Evaluate and test a plan to sell your product and collect revenues.** Will you sell directly to customers using the internet, your own sales team or independent reps; will you sell your products to distributors; will you sell to retailers or resellers; will you sell to the government?

7. **Determine if you can make a profit.** Know your costs, expenses, revenues, and margins. Know how much working capital you will need to sustain the business and grow it. Know where you can find money beyond your own resources. Determine if financial resources will be available and committed. Establish a financial system to provide accurate and timely reports to manage the operation.

With positive answers to these initial points, I suggest the following next steps.

- Determine your business location; street, city, and state.

- Name your company. Decide what your firm will be called by clients, vendors, employees and all other entities. Reserve this name for your legal documents and for your Internet website. You do this by contacting the Secretary of State, Business Division, to learn if your chosen name is available. At the same time, search the Internet domain names to learn if the name is also available for your use. If available, proceed to register and pay the related fees to secure your ownership of your company name.

- Secure a business license and any necessary permits from your local city business office.

- Obtain a Federal tax ID number, form SS4, from the IRS. With this information, you will be able to establish an account with a local bank for checking, savings, merchant account and other services.

- Meet with an attorney to establish a legal entity. The attorney will give you several options to consider, such as whether you should operate as a sole proprietor, a general partnership, an LLC, an S corporation or a C corporation. He or she will explain to you the risks, responsibilities, costs, liabilities, taxes, duties, and reports that are associated with each entity. I also recommend you spend time understanding these various formats via the Internet which covers in depth what you will need to know. The law office will also prepare articles of incorporation, by laws, contracts, patents, stock/shares of ownership and provide guidance on company board agendas and minutes, key transactions and state annual reports. In addition, you will be given advice on various labor laws—work hours, safety, breaks, immigrants plus any other legal service you might need.

- Meet with an accountant. He or she will help you understand what responsibilities you will have with the IRS; namely, taxes related to the company, yourself, and employees. This vendor can also assist with state and federal tax filings. An accountant will also help you with financial reporting and various accounting software options.

Now that you are ready, meaning you have legions of customers who will buy your superior product for the right price yielding good profits, it's time to act. Yes, act, moving fast, with faith and a determination to overcome every obstacle on your way to greatness. Don't look back. Keep your eyes on the bright horizon. It's your time to shine. It's your future to enjoy. You're now the boss. Be a great one! Good luck.

Notes

Chapter 1

1. *Ogden City Directory* (Ogden, Utah: R. L. Polk & Company, 1920).

2. *Utah Educational Review* (October/November 1937), quoted in "Ogden High School: History," on the website of Preservation Utah, accessed February 16, 2019, https://preservationutah.org/see-our-impact/our-advocacy/item/40-ogden-high-school.

3. "Ogden Arsenal," Hill Air Force Base website, May 15, 2007, https://www.hill.af.mil/About-Us/Fact-Sheets/Display/Article/397413/ogden-arsenal/

4. "Polio Elimination in the United States," Centers for Disease Control and Prevention website, https://www.cdc.gov/polio/us/index.html.

Chapter 2

1. Valerie Huber, "A Historical Analysis of Public School Sex Education in America Since 1900" (master's thesis, Cedarville University, 2009), 34–35, https://digitalcommons.cedarville.edu/cgi/viewcontent.cgi?article=1020&context=education_theses.

2. Brown v. Board of Education of Topeka, 347 U.S. 483 (1954).

Chapter 3

1. Ida-Rose Langford Hall, "The 1963 Scout Accident," H. Tracy Hall Foundation website, http://www.htracyhall.org/pdf/HTH-Archives/Tracy%20Hall%20Project%20Consolidation/Document%20Library/Ida-Rose%27s%20Stories/1963_Scout%20Accident.pdf. Many of the details in this chapter are taken from Ida-Rose's account.

2. "Brakes Are Blamed for Scout Tragedy," *Chicago Tribune*, June 12, 1963.

3. "Canyonlands Station, June 10, 1963," Weather Underground website, https://www.wunderground.com/history/airport/KCNY/1963/6/10/DailyHistory.html?req_city=Moab&req_state=UT&reqdb.zip=84532&reqdb.magic=1&reqdb.wmo=99999.

4. See "Driving the Hole-in-the-Rock Road," National Park Service website, https://www.nps.gov/glca/planyourvisit/driving-the-hole-in-the-rock-road. htm.

5. Dennis Romboy, "Monument to Lost Friends," *Deseret News*, June 6, 1993.

6. Ibid.

7. Ray and Elayne Schwartz, "Herald Staffers Bring Eyewitness Accounts of Explorer Scout Tragedy," *The (Provo) Daily Herald*, June 11, 1963, https:// newspaperarchive.com/provo-daily-herald-jun-11-1963-p-1/.

8. Louise Englestead and Reed Madsen, "12 Die, 26 Hurt as Truck Rolls on Remote Southern Utah Road," *Deseret News*, June 11, 1963.

9. Garth Sundem, "Man of the Year: John F. Kennedy, A Way with the People," *Time*, January 5, 1962.

10. Kurt Kragthorpe, "50 Years Later, Wayne Estes' Utah State Legacy Lives On," *Salt Lake Tribune*, February 7, 2015, http://archive.sltrib.com/article. php?id=2150373&itype=CMSID.

Chapter 4

1. "Today in Earthquake History," USGS Earthquake Hazards Program, https:// earthquake.usgs.gov/learn/today/index.php?month=5&day=3&submit=Vie w+Date.

2. Robert Muggah, "It's official: San Salvador is the Murder Capital of the World," *Los Angeles Times*, March 2, 2016, https://www.latimes.com/ opinion/op-ed/la-oe-0302-muggah-el-salvador-crime-20160302-story.html.

3. Milton R. Hunter, "Indians of Guatemala," *The Relief Society Magazine*, September 1969, 644–53, http://larryrichman.org/mission/images/indians-guatemal-rs-magazine.pdf.

4. David B. Galbraith, "Orson Hyde's 1841 Mission to the Holy Land," *Ensign*, October 1991, https://www.lds.org/ensign/1991/10/orson-hydes-1841-mission-to-the-holy-land?lang=eng.

5. Terrence L. Hansen, "The Church in Central America," *Ensign*, September 1972, https://www.lds.org/ensign/1972/09/the-church-in-central-america?lang=eng.

Chapter 5

1. Tom Valentine, "Vietnam War Draft," The Vietnam War, July 25, 2013, https://thevietnamwar.info/vietnam-war-draft/.

2. "Peace Corps," John F. Kennedy Presidential Library and Museum website, https://www.jfklibrary.org/learn/about-jfk/jfk-in-history/peace-corps.

3. "William P. Miller," Weber State University website, http://www.weber. edu/ PresidentsOffice/Miller.html.

Chapter 6

1. James Melik, "Solutions Sought to End Use of Kerosene Lamps," BBC News, September 27, 2012, https://www.bbc.com/news/business-18262217.

2. "Schistosomiasis (Bilharzia)," World Health Organization website, https:// www.afro.who.int/health-topics/schistosomiasis-bilharzia.

3. "What's Your Number? The Vietnam War Selective Service Lottery," HistoryNet, November 25, 2009, https://www.historynet.com/whats-your-number.htm.

Chapter 7

1. Gordon Daines, "Marriott Center," BYU Harold B. Lee Library website, December 11, 2008, https://sites.lib.byu.edu/special-collections/2008/12/11/ marriott-center/.

2. "Utah Valley Hospital History," Intermountain Healthcare website, https:// intermountainhealthcare.org/locations/utah-valley-hospital/hospital-information/history/.

Chapter 8

1. "Weber State University Dee Events Center," Waymarking.com, http://www. waymarking.com/waymarks/WMATP1_Weber_State_University_Dee_Events_Center.

2. Ron Pierce, "Orpheum Theatre," Cinema Treasures, http://cinematreasures. org/theaters/26376.

3. "Capitol Theatre—Salt Lake City," Broadway.com, https://saltlakecity. broadway.com/venues/theaters/capitol-theatre/.

4. Anna Kisselgoff, "Ballet West Revives Bournonville's 1855 'Abdallah,'" *The New York Times*, May 3, 1985, https://www.nytimes.com/1985/05/03/arts/ dance-ballet-west-revives-bournonville-s-1855-abdallah.html.

5. Eric Pace, "Nizar Hamdoon, 59, Former Iraqi Diplomat Under Hussein," *The New York Times*, August 10, 2003, https://www.nytimes.com/2003/08/10/ world/nizar-hamdoon-59-former-iraqi-diplomat-under-hussein.html.

6. Kisselgoff, "Ballet West."

7. Ibid.

8. "Bruce Marks," Youth America Grand Prix website, https://yagp.org/bruce-marks/.

9. "Glenn Walker Wallace Dies, Longtime Crusader for Arts," *Deseret News*, December 31, 1988, https://www.deseretnews.com/article/28978/glenn-walker-wallace-dies-longtime-crusader-for-arts.html.

10. Leonard J. Arrington, "Banking and Finance," Utah History Encyclopedia, https://www.uen.org/utah_history_encyclopedia/b/BANKING.shtml.

Chapter 9

1. Joshua Saul, "Barnacles Destroy Boats, But Getting Rid of Them Destroys the Sea—Until Now," *Popular Science*, July 21, 2011, https://www.popsci.com/science/article/2011-06/barnacles-destroy-boats-getting-rid-them-destroys-sea—until-now.

2. John C. Downen, "Utah's Urban Farmers: Agricultural Activity on the Wasatch Front," *Utah Economic and Business Review* 69, no. 3 (2009): 1–15, https://gardner.utah.edu/wp-content/uploads/2015/09/UEBR2009no3.pdf.

3. "Semen Division & Collection," Reproduction Enterprises, Inc. website, https://reproductionenterprises.com/semen-division-collection/.

4. Carrie Antlfinger/Associated Press, "Market for Dairy Bull Semen is Booming," *Wisconsin State Journal*, July 20, 2006, https://www.newspapers.com/image/407154353/.

Chapter 10

1. "Angina (Chest Pain)," American Heart Association website, accessed February 21, 2019, https://www.heart.org/en/health-topics/heart-attack/angina-chest-pain.

Chapter 11

1. "Executive Focus: Alan E. Hall, Founder and Chief Executive Officer, Technology Advancement Corp," *Deseret News*, October 30, 1994, https://www.deseretnews.com/article/384212/executive-focus--alan-e-hall-founder-and-chief-executive-officer-technology-advancement-corp.html.

2. Roger Pusey, "11 Utahns Are Recognized with Entrepreneur of the Year Awards," *Deseret News*, June 11, 1997, https://www.deseretnews.com/article/565747/11-Utahns-are-recognized-with-Entrepreneur-of-the-Year-awards.html.

3. "Bloomberg Billionaires Index," Bloomberg website, March 4, 2019, https://www.bloomberg.com/billionaires/profiles/jeffrey-p-bezos/.

4. Lauren Feiner, "Amazon is the Most Valuable Public Company in the World After Passing Microsoft," CNBC website, January 7, 2019, https://www.cnbc.com/2019/01/07/amazon-passes-microsoft-market-value-becomes-largest.html.

5. "Experience Outsource Sales and Marketing," MarketStar blog, accessed February 23, 2019, https://www.marketstar.com/outsourcing-sales.

Chapter 12

1. "What We Do," Utah Technology Council website, http://utahtech.org/what-we-do/.

2. "UTC Announces A. Scott Anderson, Alan Hall and Kirk M. Ririe as 2014 Hall of Fame Inductees," *Business Wire*, August 7, 2014, https://www.businesswire.com/news/home/20140807006039/en/UTC-Announces-A.-Scott-Anderson-Alan-Hall.

3. "Our Mission," World Trade Center Utah website, https://wtcutah.com/about/.

4. "About," Plus 550 website, http://www.plus550.com/about/.

Chapter 13

1. Thomas J. Stanley and William D. Danko, *The Millionaire Next Door* (Atlanta: Longstreet Press, 1996).

2. Luke 12:48 (KJV)

3. Moses 7:18, *The Pearl of Great Price* (Salt Lake City: The Church of Jesus Christ of Latter-day Saints, 1979).

4. Amy K. Stewart, "Millions Must Be Raised for Ogden High Historic Restoration," *Deseret News*, September 19, 2009, https://www.deseretnews.com/article/705331094/Millions-must-be-raised-for-Ogden-High-historic-restoration.html.

5. Nancy Van Valkenburg, "Ogden High Honored with National Preservation Award," Ogden *Standard-Examiner*, October 28, 2013, https://www.standard.net/news/local/ogden-high-honored-with-national-preservation-award/article_0d559a12-bcb4-51a5-b299-10653000f500.html.

6. JaNae Francis, "Utah Gov. Herbert visits Roy High, Lauds Improved Graduation Rates," Ogden *Standard-Examiner*, June 7, 2016, https://www.standard.net/news/education/utah-gov-herbert-visits-roy-high-lauds-improved-graduation-rates/article_183bcf24-ef30-5485-80a5-191b3a12b0c6.html.

7. Anna Burleson, "Weber State Exceeds Fundraising Goal by $39 Million," Ogden *Standard-Examiner*, September 20, 2016, https://www.standard.net/news/education/weber-state-exceeds-fundraising-goal-by-million/article_eb10d3be-d480-549e-a437-216fd0dc63f3.html.

8. "Tracy Hall Science Center," Weber State University website, https://www.weber.edu/cos/TracyHall.html.

9. "Hall Global Entrepreneurship Center," Weber State University website, https://www.weber.edu/entrepreneurship.

10. "USHE Enrollment Projections," Utah System of Higher Education website, https://ushe.edu/43000-additional-students-expected-at-utahs-public-colleges-and-universities-over-the-next-ten-years/.

11. "About Us," Midtown Community Health Center website, https://www.midtownchc.org/about-us/.

12. Cathy McKitrick, "Medicaid Expansion Would Help Midtown Clinics," Ogden *Standard-Examiner*, September 15, 2014, https://www.standard.net/news/medicaid-expansion-would-help-midtown-clinics/article_a87c489a-77ab-58a2-924d-47ee948e18b0.html.

13. "Joyce Hansen Hall Food Bank," Catholic Community Services of Northern Utah website, https://www.ccsnorthernutah.org/programs/joyce-hansen-hall-food-bank.

14. Mark Saal, " 'Jazzy' New Seating at Ogden Pioneer Stadium Ready for Pioneer Day," Ogden *Standard-Examiner*, July 12, 2018, https://www.standard.net/sports/jazzy-new-seating-at-ogden-pioneer-stadium-ready-for-pioneer/article_620f03ec-3ad1-5bdb-8eef-eb047daf3d9c.html.

15. Cathy McKitrick, "Ogden Pioneer Days Rodeo Ranked in Top Five Nationwide," Ogden *Standard-Examiner*, January 22, 2015, https://www.standard.net/news/ogden-pioneer-days-rodeo-ranked-in-top-five-nationwide/article_707aed9c-2675-58f4-8f56-a0e1cbc5e6c3.html.

16. "New Hall of Fame Inductees Enshrined," Wrangler Network, August 5, 2017, http://wranglernetwork.com/news/new-hall-of-fame-inductees-enshrined/.

17. Katie Mecham, "Hometown 'Horseman' featured in new 'Meet the Mormons' film," Morgan County News, August 11, 2016, https://morgannews.com/2016/08/11/hometown-horseman-featured-in-new-meet-the-mormons-film/.

18. "Philanthropy Day Announces 2018 Honorees," *Deseret News*, August 22, 2018, https://www.deseretnews.com/article/900029067/philanthropy-day-announces-2018-honorees.html.

Chapter 14

1. Alysa Landry, "How Mormons Assimilated Native Children," *Indian Country Today*, October 7, 2017, https://newsmaven.io/indiancountrytoday/archive/ how-mormons-assimilated-native-children-Cc6f97ZsA0mL7eCMcnQG6g/.

Chapter 16

1. *Fires of Faith: The Coming Forth of the King James Bible*, directed by Lee Groberg (Bountiful, Utah: Groberg Films, 2012).

2. *First Freedom: The Fight for Religious Liberty*, directed by Lee Groberg (Bountiful, Utah: Groberg Films, 2012).

Chapter 17

1. Colin Eatock, "50 Years After 'Sound of Music,' Summer in Salzburg Set to Sizzle," *Houston Chronicle*, April 15, 2015, https://www.houstonchronicle. com/life/travel/destinations/article/50-years-after-Sound-of-Music- summer-in-6201489.php.

Appendix II

1. Jeffrey R. Holland, "None Were with Him," *Ensign*, May 2009, 86-88.

2. Emma Lou Thayne and Joleen G. Meredith, "Where Can I Turn For Peace?," *Hymns* (Salt Lake City: The Church of Jesus Christ of Latter-day Saints, 1985), No. 129.

Appendix III

1. Alan Hall, "The 7 C's: How to Find and Hire Great Employees," *Forbes*, June 19, 2012, https://www.forbes.com/sites/alanhall/2012/06/19/the-7-cs-how- to-find-and-hire-great-employees/#3e88585053c8.

2. Alan Hall, "Kiss Your Boss Goodbye. It's Time to Be an Entrepreneur," *Forbes*, July 15, 2012, https://www.forbes.com/sites/alanhall/2012/07/15/ kiss-your-boss-goodbye-its-time-to-be-an-entrepreneur/#1058e2617fb8.

About the Author

Crystalee Beck, MPC, is a writer, speaker, and mamapreneur who celebrates words and people. Her award-winning research on managerial gratitude in the workplace was published in an international corporate communication journal.

She met the Halls when she worked at MarketStar, where she wrote marketing copy for global tech brands, edited the company magazine, and helped plan the company's twenty-fifth anniversary celebration.

After MarketStar, she set sail on entrepreneurial waters with her own marketing company. Then she cofounded The Mama Ladder® to empower women to "create their own ladder" at the intersection of motherhood and entrepreneurship. See more at *www.themamaladder.com.*

Crystalee holds a master's degree in professional communication from Weber State University, where she was named the Outstanding Graduate and taught for two years as an adjunct communication instructor. As the university's chairman at the time, Alan Hall signed her degree.

She lives with her husband and three children in Ogden, Utah, and gets her best ideas on mountain trails. Meet her at *www.crystaleebeck.com.*

Made in the USA
Las Vegas, NV
20 November 2020